For

CW01084042

Shikoku

with all my

admiration.

David Tepfer

Clink
Street

London | New York

Published by Clink Street Publishing 2021

First edition.

ISBNs: 978-1-913136-09-3 Paperback
978-1-913136-10-9 Ebook

for Becky

The first light was colorless, grayish, fragile, clear. Returning life? Desire? So many shadows to fill. He glanced into the darkness of the past six years. Redeem a loss, pass over uncomfortable visions and voices? Dare to hope, with all the risks?

Prospect Park was frozen in a winter dawn with patches of snow reflecting a brackish sky. Bare branches fused into volumes of pure black. Something even darker rushed across this vision; then the expanding light displaced confusion and regret. Dawn rolled out across the trees and meadows.

It's a day for cleaning up and throwing out, the last week of 36 years in my job; so many illusions to trash. Keep your eyes on the pavement. Don't look back. One more turn of the pedals. Look down and believe.

Today he will teach his last class. In a few days, he will be ex-professor of French.

Who would believe this blurred slow motion? Forget those classes, meetings and commutes to work. All those eyes half listening, while you drone on about French literature. Thirty-six years gone, evaporated. Tough climb. Look down just beyond the front wheel.

He left the window with the light flowing clear and certain over the trees and grass of the park, his beloved park, their salvation from the city. Time for the morning routine: eating and drinking, brushing and flushing. Same old stuff. The ride was his wake-up call, starting with the gentle park — then busy streets and intersections, the bridge and the chaos of Lower Manhattan. He liked the exercise, and looked forward to it twice a day. New York adrenalin was his daily drug. This morning he felt toasty crossing the

1

park. He froze on the bridge, and his gloved hands were numb when the building appeared. He warmed up climbing the six flights of stairs. His faithful office was always welcoming: warm in winter, cool in summer. It would be missed. Now to give the last lecture, brave the retirement party and finally confront his office with the harsh news of their imminent separation.

The last class was a review. Easy gig. There were the usual girls, showing their legs, and a few males, hiding in the back. No legs — just a backdrop of dark sweaters. The girl sweaters were better, with a pointed or rounded patch of enlarging skin leading up. It reminded him of climbing from a deep mountain gorge into an expanding sky. Trying hard, these college girls. Too hard. He didn't trust them. They left comments on his teacher evaluations about him being distant and aloof.

What did they want? Physical contact?

The current fashion of showing cleavage had made the job harder.

Distracted? Aloof?

He had to defend himself. They should do their part, too. Learning was not a guided bus tour with stops to take pictures. He wanted evidence of personal adventure — of discovery and original thought. The challenge was rarely met. But maybe that was his fault.

"In this last class we'll review what we have tried to understand. The 17th century in France was a period of turmoil, transition and artistic accomplishment. Accomplishment unusual in its intensity and…"

A girl in the front row uncrossed and crossed her legs, flashing a nice piece of thigh, a lure in dark water.

"… grandeur. Accomplishment anchored in a desire for order… for structure, above all. For rigor, rules and beauty. But beauty according to new conventions in philosophy, literature, architecture and…"

The large windows caught the clearing sky as a net catches a butterfly — gently without breaking it. Fluttering winter sunlight warmed the classroom.

"Did this flowering have socioeconomic roots? If so, what were they? Did they drive the cultural changes that…"

A cell phone rang.

He stopped and walked to the window, closed his eyes and looked into the sun, feeling the winter light focus warmth on his retinas. It calmed his budding anger. He was not on good terms with cell phones, but there was no choice. Several students were recording him with their phones. If his anger exploded in fittingly foul language, he would be viral on Facebook and YouTube within the hour. He would be attacked by journalists, lawyers and irate parents. He would be incarcerated in the Brooklyn Zoo, raped by the bonobos, left to die and finally chopped up for turtle food.

So he continued with his review.

"Who were the major playwrights of the century? Why do we read them today?"

He was playing to their obvious interest in exam questions. Normally they would be whispering and stealing glances at their phones with bluish phone light reflected on their faces.

We used to worry that machines were becoming human, but it's the opposite. Humans are becoming machines.

Several of the girls stayed after the class — probably to fish for exam hints. They were in charm mode, as only twenty-ish coeds can be, making compliments about how much they enjoyed his lectures. He saw eyes rimmed in mascara, plucked eyebrows, cool lipstick and that cleavage reflecting the southern window winter light. But there was no great beauty showing through the charm. No celestial beam of warm sun on this freezing day. He kept his scholarly composure, according to professorial tradition. Everyone played their role in the university community. It was predictable stuff about love and survival — the quest for immortality. Time to move on.

"See you at the exam. Good luck." And so ended his last class, after thirty-six years of coping with distraught students and nasty colleagues.

He sat at his desk and contemplated the piles of papers, shelves of books, mementos and the half-hidden scholarly volumes that had won him tenure and promotions.

It should be something to be proud of, but who really cares about my personal struggle? A few jealous colleagues and desperate graduate students?

His life's work was out of print, safely catalogued and stowed away in a few libraries. His lecture notes filled a filing cabinet. He would trash them with no regrets.

Travel light and fast. Ride a road only once. Take another — one way, no return. Forget without regret and move on.

The day was ending colder than it had begun. The sky had closed its winter cloak. The next chore was the department farewell party, with the usual speech by the department head, a retirement gift, and a few words said by him. All was organized by the department secretary, another charmer, intent on being attractive to a retiring widower.

The drinks, coffee and donuts were ready. Somebody had made a cake. All it needed was candles to be a birthday party. A few people had arrived.

Such a predictable event — this ritual booting me out of the house of romance languages.

People straggled in, and at fifteen minutes past the hour, a glass was tapped with a spoon, and the department head began his speech, according to formula, saying how happy they were for him (to be getting out of their hair), and how they wished him a long and joyous life after work (just so long as he stayed away from the university)… He had made similar speeches many times in his own department head days. But now the coin had flipped. His time had passed. The smile on his face was a mask for another smile, riddled with irony and disbelief.

Never drop the mask — that was the trick. Play the social role. It's still your job, but in a few days — your job no more. Wear the mask no more. Don't look back. Climb to the light.

His retirement present was a surprisingly generous gift certificate for a nearby bike shop. He made a short speech, hardly listening to what he was saying, rambling about the past and future tense and how it defines lives and careers. It felt easy, and there was applause and approving nods. There were lots of students, including people he had not seen in years.

In the post-speech stand, eat, drink and be merry session he learned that the farewell party had been announced in the alumni magazine, on the department website and to the alumni email list. Several students asked him to autograph his books, which was the second time that day the sun had plowed a path through the damp, gray cloud cover. There was a girl he hadn't seen in years, but he recalled her name. She was as he remembered her, a fine specimen, a just-emerged butterfly still drying her wings before flight.

He talked with another student, who had shown keen interest in the Symbolist poets. He was now in graduate school at Columbia, working on Mallarmé. They started speaking French, and they were joined by the butterfly girl, who listened, but said nothing. The boy left, and she continued in French, with a slight Québécois accent. He had no recollection that she could speak native French, but he had not seen her in years.

Another student approached to have a book signed. They switched to English. He was feeling good about the whole event, better than he had felt about anything in ages. Maybe he would miss the contact with young people, after all. Maybe his university job hadn't been so bad, after all.

The crowd was thinning, so he approached the butterfly girl before she left. He was curious to know about her French.

"So where does your native French come from? I don't remember you speaking French in my class."

"Oh, I've always spoken French. We spoke French at home. My mother was Québécoise, and my father was bilingual. It was my first language. I didn't speak it in your class, because I didn't want to discourage the real French majors, learning the language the hard way."

"So you were taking my class just for the fun of it?"

"Yes, it was a relief from my other studies. I was a pre-med, and the P-Chem was hard. Your class was pure pleasure."

"That's what I always wanted for my students. Thank you for the compliment. Now I understand why you never took notes, but you were the top student in the class. Have you been to France?"

"I cycled in the Pyrenees and the Alps last summer."

Flash of recognition. He started to say he loved to bike those mountains… but he was interrupted by the department head dragging him away to talk to the dean, who had appeared for the end of the party. He looked back at the butterfly girl, making a telephone receiver gesture with his hand and mouthing words of calling.

The dean was as sincere as a dean can be, doing his job like everybody else, except maybe the butterfly girl, who was there for the pleasure, not the job. She reappeared wearing her coat, returning the telephone hand sign as she brushed by.

The next three days were cathartic. Trashing a life of work was liberating, exhilarating, terrifying and fun. He piled books by his door for colleagues to take. They vanished almost as quickly as he could put them out. He happily dumped his university records, files of letters and drafts for his books and articles. The lecture notes were different, meriting a polite goodbye. It was time to close and forget.

Toward the end of the third day, when he could see his way to finishing the job, he decided to go home early, but he couldn't find his keys. He had used them to open the exam question file drawer. He had tossed the exam files into one of the many cardboard boxes he was filling with trash. Did the keys go into the box? *Sans* keys there was no bike, no home. Condemned to sleep in his office?

Don't panic. Try to reconstruct. Pockets?

Relief. They were in the pocket of his jacket, but so was a business card announcing one Sara Jansen, M.D. The butterfly girl had slipped her card into his pocket while he was talking with the dean.

He turned on his computer and sent her a message. "Just

found your card in my pocket. How were the Pyrenees? Did you climb the Col d'Aubisque?"

He could see it clearly, the legendary mountain pass in the Pyrenees. The road racer's delight and killer climb. He knew it from two occasions. The first in cold fog, the second in hot sun. It was tough, but worth every turn of the pedals for the effort, the conquest and the views on those lucky, good weather days.

She answered instantly, "Great! How did you know?"

He replied, "You look like the type…"

"Merci! I am the type! You've climbed it?"

"Twice, but slowly. No racing, just savoring the climb and the scenery. Tell me more in person?"

"Please call. I don't have your number."

They met for coffee in Manhattan the next morning, which evolved into lunch and a walk in Central Park. She had been through medical school and two years of internship in a New York emergency room. She had gone to the Pyrenees to celebrate her release from ER work and to think about the future. She had dumped her boyfriend on the Col d'Aubisque.

"My ex-boyfriend is a total bike nut. He shaves his legs; races on the weekends. It's the weekend warrior syndrome. I'm a cyclist more than a racer. I prefer exercise and adventure to competition, but I did train for racing to be part of his world. We met on the loop in Central Park. I was fixing a flat; he stopped. I was doing fine by myself, but I let him help. We met a few days later in the park, and one thing led to another. A sort of relationship evolved. We were working a lot.

"One day he tells me he's planning to ride across the Pyrenees from the Atlantic to the Mediterranean, so I ask if I can come, but it's clear he's not enthusiastic. He'll be riding with two buddies. I say he won't have to wait for me. We can each go at our own pace. I speak French, which could help. He finally lets me at least start with them.

"I arrange to keep my bike at the hospital, so I can train in Central Park when I have a few minutes to spare. I ride about an hour a day for the two months, before leaving for France. I start riding in the peloton. Then I join the club, and learn more about road racing. I like the psychology of it. I really get into it. As training progresses, I discover I can easily keep up, but I'm not really a racer. I don't care about winning.

"I'm supposed to meet him in Saint Jean de Luz, so I order a really good racing bike for pickup in Paris. I take the plane wearing a light dress, sweater and sandals. In a rack trunk, I have toilet stuff, swimsuit, sunglasses, tights, arm warmers, a rain cape, a wind jacket — the absolute minimum. No phone, no makeup.

"The bike is hanging in the window of the bike shop. They take it down. It's all Dura-Ace and carbon fiber. While a mechanic makes a last check of the bike, I buy a helmet, shoes, shorts, a jersey, an extra tube, patch kit, pump, a minimalist cable lock, a multitool, gloves and a seat post rack for the rack trunk. In a dressing room, I put the shorts and jersey on, and they carefully adjust my position on the bike. I ride out into the Paris traffic. I stop to buy detailed road maps for the Pyrenees at the Vieux Campeur. At the Montparnasse station I take the fast TGV train to Saint Jean de Luz, with the bike in its reserved spot alongside me. I sleep the whole way. I arrive, take a swim and have dinner with my boyfriend and his buddies, but he insists I take my own room. He says he needs to rest and concentrate. I keep my new bike in my room. I'm falling in love with the bike. I wonder if I care more for the bike than the boyfriend?

"We leave early the next morning. His friends treat me

like one of them. The bike is dynamite. I can easily keep up, even on the climbs, and there are some steep ones. I'm happy. We do 150 km, spending the night in a cute hotel in Laruns, at the base of the Col d'Aubisque. At dinner, they talk about the famous Tour de France racers and their exploits on the Aubisque. They coach me on managing the 18 km climb, keeping energy for the last three kilometers, but this is their first time in France. It's all book learning. Anyway, the distance is short, even if the effort is heroic.

"As we leave the next morning, I say they should go ahead at their own speed. They take off fast, but I continue at a moderate pace. It's early on a beautiful Sunday morning, and there are climbers going up, with few cars. I'm feeling good. I start to warm up. I pass a couple of older guys. The grade is constant, but not too steep. I hit a hard patch, but I try to keep my rhythm and stay aerobic. I pass another older guy. I'm starting to feel the altitude, but I know my cardio-vascular quirks, so I go into really deep breathing mode and keep spinning. It gets steeper, and I'm passing more men. I go around a man and woman on touring bikes with camping gear, and then I ride through Eaux Bonnes and get into the really steep stuff, which seems to go on forever... so I gear down and start breathing hard. Next thing I know, I'm coming up behind my boyfriend. I feel great. I stand on the pedals and gear up a notch. The bike responds like a magic carpet. I pass him! I pass him!

"Something clicks. I'm standing, breathing as hard as I can and accelerating. It hurts, but I'm a woman. Pain is my game. I go around my boyfriend's buddies, and I pass quite a few more young guys in terminal agony. I drop the pace to recover before the final switchbacks, and then I can see the pass. I accelerate, and I sprint for the top. There are patches of snow. My lungs scream. I'm in the max zone, but feeling I can do it. I pass a week's worth of air through my lungs in the last 500 meters. I do it. I arrive at the top and lean the bike against a wall.

"I had no idea I could do such a thing. I'm so pleased with myself, dripping sweat, breathing desperately hard, barely able to stand up, leaning against the wall and laughing. A guy comes over eating a sandwich. He admires the bike; hardly looks at me.

"The boyfriend arrives about fifteen minutes later. I'm talking to more admirers of my bicycle. He's looking his usual cool, but breathing very hard. He tells me he decided to take it easy, because he had a headache from the altitude. I say the new bike was like a rocket. He says he noticed. We have lunch in the cafe, and descend the other side. It's my first big mountain descent. It's cool and fast. I'm glued to the corners. The bike is awesome. That evening he says he's checked his email, and his office wants him back in New York. I say OK, but I'll finish the ride to the Mediterranean. That's the last I saw of him.

"The rest is a dream. It rains on me only once. I've got my altitude resistance. There are three more big passes, including the Tourmalet, and a lot of scenery, rivers, cafes, cute hotels, good restaurants and plenty of people on bikes. But I just keep going around them. I find I can max out my heart rate and stay there for long periods. I get to Perpignan in four days from Saint-Jean-de-Luz. Nothing to do there, so after a swim I take a train north, get off in Orange, and the next morning I do the Mont Ventoux from the west side. It's tough in hot weather, but immensely rewarding. I descend to Sault, ride through fields of lavender to the north, and then through hilly country to take a train at Montélimar to Lyon and into the Alps, where I eat, sleep and attack the Col de la Madeleine. Wow. A killer! I'm feeling great, so I continue with the Glandon (very steep) and its big brother, the Croix de Fer, ending up with a fast descent into

Saint-Jean-de-Maurienne in time to take the late train to Paris. What a day! The next day, the shop packs the bike, after cleaning it and replacing the brake shoes, and I fly back to New York. There was nothing from the boyfriend. I decide to let sleeping dogs lie."

He responds to all of this with smiles, laughs and exclamations.

"It's better than watching the Tour de France! The poor guy didn't have a chance. You've got the power to weight ratio. He's probably too big and muscular to be a climber. How was recovery? You must have a heart of steel. No, I don't mean that in a bad sense. You're tough. I couldn't begin to keep up with you. You should be a pro racer. What were you taking? No, I didn't mean that either… doctors, you know…"

She is laughing.

The next day, he finished up at the university and rode home for the last time. He looked out from their windows on Prospect Park, in the dark — winter dark.

Don't want to eat or sleep. I'm lost in the maze of forty-two years past. My wife is dead, and so is our life. The office was easy. Home's too hard, too steep to climb. Don't look back. Keep eyes down, just ahead. Climb to the light.

He thought about the Pyrenees and his youthful traverse. Sara's story had revived fragments from a sequence, a landscape with people flowing through it. Then he imagined the second traverse, with his wife, but he couldn't bear it and peeled off, back into the darkness.

He took his touring bike out of the storage room in the basement, where it hung beside his wife's, among numerous bicycles and tools. It took him a week to rebuild it. He called Sara to invite her to spend a day in the Catskills.

"If you'll be gentle," he said. "I'm not your boyfriend."

He planned a ride in rolling hill country, a short train trip from the city. When she appeared at the train station, she had a well-worn racing bike. He was pleased to see she had kept her old bike. She was bundled in winter tights and over pants, but the butterfly was in there — spring butterfly, newly emerged, still drying her wings.

In the train, he asked how she had decided where to go after Perpignan. (She had heard about the Mont Ventoux. The Madeleine and the Croix de Fer were picked on the map, because of good train access.) He asked about the weather. (There were often thunderstorms in the afternoons, so she had to be down from high altitude before they hit.) She also talked about being an emergency-room doctor. (She wanted freedom to work anywhere — work when she wanted. She liked the intellectual challenge, the quick decisions. The constant contact with frightened and suffering people was a burden, but there were many joys, when she could help them.)

They started the ride with her leading, and he could see she was solid and natural. It was a winter day with patches of snow in the woods, but well above freezing, even in the shade. The sunny spots were reservoirs of warmth. She seemed to know where he was, without looking back. There was little traffic, so they often rode side by side or exchanged taking the lead. She was not surprised to find him strong and consistent.

> *He's the real thing. Nothing flashy. Just fine-tuned, supportive, relaxed. Respects the etiquette. Not condescending. Strong, punctual. No panting. It's an easy ride for him. Feels cozy to ride with him. Hope for more.*

They rode fifty miles to catch a return train as the winter darkness fell. They talked in the train; he offered to rebuild her bike. She protested, but he could see she was pleased. He insisted.

"What color do you want the frame painted?"

He left his bike with her, and took hers home on the subway. The rebuild stretched out over the next two weeks. He replaced the wheels, bottom bracket, cranks, brake levers, saddle, cables… and he had the frame repainted.

She was writing her second article about sleep. The first was published in a medical journal, as a review of the effects of sleep deprivation on emergency room doctors. The second was more general and for a lay audience. She hoped to publish it in a large circulation magazine. For the moment, she was living on savings. Sleep was a new subject for her, and the complexities were frustrating. Generalization from published research was hampered by small sample sizes, flawed experimental designs and lack of follow-up — the usual pitfalls. She worked at home, a long way from the physical engagement of the emergency room. The weather did not invite biking or anything outdoors, but her mind wandered to the past summer in France, when she went to bed shortly after dinner and got up before the sun, feeling recovered and ready for a new climb. Now images of graphs, tables of figures and statistics troubled her sleep.

In the mornings, she wrote for a few hours and then ran on the High Line, above the street noise and grime. Running seemed so simple, and it kept her warm in the coldest weather. She sometimes went out in the evening, invited for dinner or a concert. An acquaintance from medical school moved to town to do a second internship. She let herself fall into a love relationship. The physical attraction was there, but as usual, the deeper feelings were missing.

She received an email inviting her to exchange bicycles and try her restored bike on the Prospect Park loop. It was a dry day, well below freezing. She wore her ski clothes. They met at a cafe.

"I don't believe it. It's so perfect. Where did you find the decals? The Reynolds 531 was nearly scratched off, and now it's perfect!"

She goes over the whole bike, noticing every detail. It looks like it wants to fly.

They ride the Prospect Park loop. The bike is like new, but with the familiar old comfort. She is fast, but always within reach, carefully pacing him. There are few other riders, and many know him. After an hour, the cold starts to penetrate, and despite the physical effort, his hands and feet start to freeze. She invites him to an early dinner in Park Slope. The restaurant is nearly empty. The food is upscale Italian.

"I'm surprised so many riders know you. You must come here often."

"I live across the street, so it's an addiction. I've also helped kids in the neighborhood fix up racing bikes and learn to ride. They're adults now, so I have friends in fast places, but I can't keep up with them anymore. It's been a good contact with the neighborhood, which was mostly Haitian, when we moved here, and French speaking. Between French and bicycles, we were accepted almost from the beginning."

"So what do you do when you aren't restoring racing bikes?"

"That's a good question. Now that I've freedom to choose, the choice is daunting. I don't have to work. I don't have to play, but I need to think, to daydream — to fantasize. I need to clean up my accumulation of mementos. I'm drowning in objects. I want to travel light. I feel drawn to light. Maybe I should become a photographer?"

"Do you write poetry? You teach it so well, and it's a minimalist art form."

"I do. I do, but I don't. It was my original interest, but I needed a job, so I started teaching it more and writing it less. People don't seem to care about poetry, unless it's their own. Today's poets are songwriters, ad writers and rappers. Poetry of the sort I taught is an academic commodity. But I've never stopped writing. A lot of it's in my head."

There is a darkening. Something is not being said.

"Please show me some poems."

"They're not very interesting. Mostly word games to disguise emotions…"

Again words are forming, but still hidden.

"Maybe occasional expressions of love, hidden in words and… I'm alone, you see. I have no children. My wife is dead."

For an instant, the mask slips and almost falls. A smile falters, an angel dances on the head of a pin.

"Give me your hand. Please."

She takes his hand.

"Please show me a poem."

"Tell me every detail about the Col d'Aubisque."

Laughter. "You're too wily for me! You could be a pro, a professor…"

"An old professor goat, freshly put out to pasture?"

"I like goats. They can climb anything, eat anything."

"OK, how about dessert?"

Eating dessert through masks is complicated, but they try, aided by questions and answers, neutral subjects, mutual interests…

She asks him about his student days.

"Centuries ago, so long ago and faded. I was a chemistry major. My parents were first generation molecular biologists. Jim Watson of DNA structure fame was a buddy of my Dad's. The French was secondary. It became important as I learned the poetry, and I met my wife. I liked the chemistry. It only lacked — hard to say what exactly. I guess my muse was French.

She sees again that look of surprise —with something dark and rushing across, a deep river vanishing.

"Your wife was French?"

Now the dark rushing water briefly obscures his face and drifts aside.

"You get an A for awareness and an F for Freudianism."

"Thank you, professor. I'm a professional now. I don't care about grades, but I expect to be paid — in the form of a poem."

He sees himself on the Col d'Aubisque, pushing hard, yet saving for the switchbacks at the top. A young woman flashes by, ponytail flying.

"Oh dear! Now I've done it! Please forgive me! I'm so embarrassed — I didn't want to intrude, really I didn't. I swear, I'll make it up to you!"

A few days later a poem arrives in her mailbox.

An unmade call

I put the phone in its cradle,
But it cries inconsolably.
I pick it up and
Rock it back to sleep.
But back in its cradle,
It starts to whimper,
Then cries and cries.
So I repeat my attempts,
But to no avail.
Where is my courage?

She responded by sending a reprint of her paper about sleep deprivation in emergency room doctors, with a note,

"So pleased to read you. Here is a tiny token — long-winded and awkward in comparison to your beautiful, restrained and passionate poem."

It took him hours to read her paper. The statistical analysis was daunting.

He stands, eyes closed, before the windows overlooking the park, limp under a blanket of cold mist. He feels a tinge of light from the heavy-lidded morning sky.

Salvation in photons. Hope and resurrection in photons. Be patient. Climb to the light. Accept the present, this gift of living.

He leans into the corner, inside pedal up, hands on the break hoods. He switches on the next turn — back and forth, loose, timely, minimal. The air smells green, flowing over his shoulders, around his neck and through the open jersey. Cool, not cold. Ears singing. Wandering thoughts.

So amusing these twists and turns. Focus, bring it back, rock with the road. Beware of memories — treacherous sirens. Focus on the curves and straights, now and forever.

He turns toward the room, eyes still closed. He pictures the general space, concentrates on sections of it — randomly at first, then methodically. A mental catalogue builds; it overwhelms memory and collapses under the weight of objects. Eyes open, he tries to recapture the things forgotten; images blur. He moves a chair and sits, back to the window, inspecting the room, until he sees everything. He closes his eyes and reconstructs a catalogue. Again, the weight of the room's contents brings down this flimsy structure.

"How much can my memory hold?" he asks out loud. How long can I keep the list within grasp?"

Answers come from resonating walls.

"Forget to remember, remember to forget."

They bought the apartment when real estate was cheap and owners desperate, when the neighborhood was in a death agony — worthless. They both had jobs, and they were lucky to get a loan, so they did the crazy thing: they bought the building. The one next door had been gutted by fire. On the other side was a squat, inhabited by armed drug dealers. He and his young French wife set up camp on the sixth floor, cooking with a camping stove and sleeping in a tent. For months there was no heat and no electricity. They sank a large hunk of their lives into salvaging the building — because it was theirs, because they needed a place to live and because it was a shared adventure. They managed to restore basic functions, and nights, weekends, vacations — even early mornings — they slowly replaced and repaired five floors plus a basement with help when they could afford it. The neighborhood improved; they rented the other apartments. She knew instinctively when to sell the lower part. They suddenly found themselves well off with no idea of what to do with their fortune. It was invested for retirement, and she managed it at her leisure. They added a penthouse studio with an interior stairway. Their exterior signs of wealth were kept muted. When friends came for dinner, the door leading to the studio was locked, and nobody knew about his bicycle repair shop in the basement and the rooms on the floor below. They had no car. They also owned an apartment in Paris that she had inherited from her parents, where they spent vacations, and where two bicycles were stored. Their lodgings were their private gardens, shielded from the world at large.

She painted in the rooftop studio. They had offices on the floor below. Their life flourished, bound up in walls, furniture, mementos — even in the pots and pans in the kitchen. She was a cook of the French school. He made Japanese food. They had dinner parties for friends and colleagues from their professional worlds. They had missed rearing children by twists of fate and bad timing, so there was room in their lives for other endeavors and pleasures.

They were addicted to the park for walks, jogs and bike rides in all seasons. Their home entertainment was restricted to books and music, and they went to restaurants, concerts, movies, plays and exhibits. There was no television in their lives. They were baby boomer yuppies — well-heeled intellectuals.

Now what to do with these riches? All he really needed now was a bicycle. Maybe he should become a bicycle gypsy, alighting in the world's most beautiful places?

But I can't ride forever. Now to accept consequences, to come into the present and arrive at the top of the climb, to discover the other side.

His thoughts bounced off walls, sailed through closed windows, ebbed in past and future oceans. He listened from afar, trying to not be involved. Helpless drifting was not the solution. The future had to be. Sleep was coming on little cat feet, soft kitten feet with fur and claws. He let himself roll off the chair and sink to the carpet. He pulled over a pillow and blanket. His sleep was full of flying scenes, toplit underwater scenes, mountain cloud scenes, the music of a garden fountain, the wind in leaves and an island volcano above a clearing storm. Truth in sleep, the only refuge. Golden sleep, finally and with no regrets.

The morning light landed softly through padded sky. The room took it for a ride, bouncing it gently over paintings, white walls and wooden floors.

Yes, the answer had to be in photons — in their light and warmth. Follow the light to the origin of life and start again.

He stood up and contemplated the dark outline of the park. There was spring hiding there. He remembered a tea ceremony in Japan on a cold, but sunny, early spring morning in a traditional house near the Seto Sea. The hostess had asked each of the guests to write a poem before the ceremony. He had written a haiku with an extra line. Now he took a scrap of paper and a pen and let this poem come back.

Seto

Winter smiles at spring.
She her coat removes,
First blush reveals in blossoms
Yellow, pink and white.

Sara received the poem in the mail. They had not communicated in more than a week. She was immersed in her writing. Her article was going through another expansion, and she wondered if it was turning into a book about sleep. The thought had kept her awake. She was becoming obsessive, so the arrival of a poem about a Japanese spring was warmly welcomed. It brought back memories of the three months she had spent in Hiroshima as a high school exchange student, when she saw the first signs of spring and the cherry blossoms.

Japanese spring. Longingly, womanly, Japanese restraint. How could he know how much I need to go there? Do I dare? Yes.

She drew a cartoon of a volcano, something like a Mount Fuji from a wood block print, sitting on a sea of clouds. This she copied and sent by email. She got a quick reply in the form of a cartoon of a hand miming a telephone receiver. She called.

"I loved the Japanese poem. I didn't know you were a Japan fan. I am too, but I was only there for three months. Please tell me more about Japan — maybe at my favorite sushi bar?"

They met in Forest Hills, which seemed to him an unlikely place for Japanese food, but the chefs were from Osaka. Sitting at the bar, they ordered miso soup, hot sake and sashimi. As they drank the soup, they watched their chef construct a sashimi masterpiece from carefully chosen pieces of fish in the refrigerated case before them. The dish was decorated with fresh *shiso* leaves, a few radish sprouts and small green cups, conjured from a cucumber and filled with salmon eggs. The fish was gleamingly fresh — most unusual for the USA were the raw shrimp and scallops. The fish was propped up against a tuft of shredded daikon that was prepared by peeling a veneer from a cylinder of the radish. It had unrolled magically under the Japanese knife. This thin sheet was folded and thinly sliced.

"You know, Sara, I've tried to do that, and I just can't make it work. He makes it look so simple. In my next life, I think I'll be a Japanese cook."

"Why not now?"

"It would take years and a mountain of work, and even then, I think you need to be Japanese. I'm resigned to being an imitator, so I use a shredder to prepare the daikon."

They ordered more hot sake, and talked about Japan.

He had been in Kyoto with his wife. She was doing research on Japanese bank failures, and he was on sabbatical leave. They lived near the hills on the eastern edge, with a view over the city. Bamboos, trees and wild camellias covered the mountains behind them. The Philosopher's Walk and the Silver Pavilion were close by. He was supposed to be writing his second book, but much time was spent shopping for ingredients and attempting to make the Japanese dishes they discovered in restaurants. There seemed to be no end to the inventiveness of the cooks. They used similar starting materials, which changed with the seasons, but each created personal concoctions. They stayed six months, seeing fall with the maple leaf colors evolve through winter into spring with the sakura cherry blossoms.

"Did you learn Japanese?"

"Very little, but the sound of the language became familiar, and the few words I learned were sufficient. We met Japanese academics who spoke English. People were open and friendly. It was easy. We got to know local artists. The vendors at the market and the cooks in our neighborhood restaurants were our teachers. Often there was no common language, but it didn't seem to worry anybody."

"Please tell me about the tea ceremony and the poem."

"We spent a night and were treated to a tea ceremony at the house of a potter, in a village near the Seto Sea, south of Kyoto. It's an inland sea protected from the Pacific by the island of Shikoku, across from Hiroshima and Okayama. The house was traditional and unheated. Minimal electricity was the only concession to progress. It was late February and very cold at night, but the afternoon sun had warmed the south-facing tearoom, which was open to a dormant traditional garden. The potter's cups, bowls and tea utensils were laid out on the tatami mats. Water was simmering on the charcoal brazier. We were asked to compose a poem before the ceremony — a haiku, but I added an extra five-syllable line. The poem was to be written with a calligraphy brush. The ceremony, the tea and the sun were the turning point, when I first realized the depth of the Japanese aesthetic… How about your experiences in Japan?"

"I was an exchange student for three months at the end my senior year in high school. I was already accepted to college. I went to Japan in the early spring, just after my eighteenth birthday. I became very attached to my Japanese host family. We still communicate ten years later by phone and email. I learned a little Japanese, but the time was too short to become fluent, and the little I learned has mostly evaporated. The son of my host family is getting married this spring. I've received an invitation."

"Are you going?"

A look of wonder and longing passed over her face, "It's something I'm considering, but… but I hesitate…"

They are interrupted by the chef who inquires about the next part of the meal. He suggests a yosenabe, and indicates they should move to a table near the window. The thick seafood and vegetable soup is prepared in an iron kettle before them. While it cooks, they drink more sake and talk about Japan, and the things they saw and liked.

The hot yosenabe is a world apart from the cool sashimi, as different as summer and winter. Japanese rice is served in a lacquer bowl, with a bamboo paddle. Maybe it's the sake or maybe the chefs speaking Japanese in the background or the impression that the whole meal had been prepared just for them, but they begin to bob on friendly sea waves, catching glimpses of each other, sometimes up, sometimes down. Conversation brings them closer to synchrony, but words become distant formalities or just musical accents. The restaurant recedes around them, leaving them on a sandy island.

She takes a pen from her purse, and on a paper napkin she draws a cartoon mountain with a snowy top and a cyclist riding up one side. He takes the napkin and draws a second cyclist, beneath the first one, with drops of sweat falling and a bubble that says, "I'm having trouble with the altitude!" She draws a bubble for the first cyclist, "Your pace is my pace."

And so they decide to bicycle in Japan. But there are details to settle and many questions to answer. The next day they exchange rapid emails.

"What will people say when we show up together — an old guy with a young woman?"

"We'll tell the truth. You're my mentor and escort."

"But what will your family think?"

"Nothing."

"Nothing?"

"Please meet me tomorrow for lunch at Grand Central Terminal, in the cafe on the mezzanine in the Main Concourse."

He thinks of the main concourse as an acoustical black hole, capturing voices and footsteps in its volume. But before words are tamed, they bounce across the room, off the ceiling signs of the zodiac, and they roll down the stairs to pick themselves up and mix with the footsteps of people intent on important things. Words are diluted and lost in a lake of ambient sound. It's a place to be anonymous — so public it's private.

She waves when he looks up at the cafe at the far end of the main concourse. How did she see him in the hundreds of people swirling in all directions?

"I've never sat here before. What a sight! All those people! I'm not sure I've even noticed this cafe. I guess I was always going or coming. Where do we start, Sara?"

"With the menu."

The ordering over, they talk in earnest about a trip together.

"Are your feelings the same this morning? Be honest, Sara, please. I know the tricks of sake and cozy surroundings. You have no obligations. Second thoughts are fine. You can change your mind at any time. Would you honestly consider cycling in Japan with me? Maybe you need more time to think about it?"

She is thoughtful, but not hesitant.

"No, it's better to go on instinct, and all my instincts say do it. I've made my decision. I truly want to go back to Japan, and I want to go with you. What are your true feelings?"

"My instincts tell me to jump at the chance, but a voice asks if I can keep up with you. Not just on the bicycle, but also in the way we live and general vigor. We come from different generations, different worlds. I don't even have a cell phone. Maybe I would bore you."

"Not for an instant. I can't imagine being bored by you. Your pace is my pace. Anyway, what do we have to lose?"

"We have everything to gain and everything to lose. Travel can bring people together — or drive them apart. I'm a spontaneous traveler, but so are you, so that shouldn't be a problem. But maybe, maybe… despite the differences… maybe…"

"We'll fall in love?"

He laughs. "I didn't dare say it."

There is a pause. She looks into the distance; then at him.

"But there are so many kinds of love. Make no promises. Have no expectations. Just be open and true in the moment. Let it happen. People come and go. Look at them down there. Paths cross. Sometimes they tangle."

"But if one path is straight and strong, and the other wobbles and shakes…"

"You're in good shape, and I'm not racing."

"And professionally?"

"You're right. That's important, and I've thought about it. Spring for the sakura cherry blossoms would be good timing, because by then I'll need a break from writing. I'm in the first phases of a book about sleep. I need to experiment with sleeping in different places on different surfaces. Why not on a futon on a tatami mat? If there's a familiar person in the room, that would be a comfort. If there's a day on a bicycle behind me, that would also be a good thing. It's only imagined, but it feels right. Isn't the sakura about renewal?"

"Yes, but it's also about the fragility of life, the momentary glory of youth. And you're so young. Spending precious time with an aging samurai? Is that right for you now?"

"It feels right."

"And how about your parents? I know nothing about your private life. Do you have a boyfriend? Are there conflicts?

"Sure. I have a boyfriend. We see each other every couple of weeks. He's doing a second residency in internal medicine. He often works all night. We knew each other distantly in medical school, and now it's a real relationship. I'll admit to that, but it stays on a superficial plane, in one dimension. It hasn't deepened with time. We have no long-range attachment. It's convenient because it fulfills our physical needs. I doubt that it could go beyond that."

"And your parents?"

Her eyes fall. Her brightness dims, and she looks straight at him.

"I wish it were not true, but my parents died ten years ago, when I was eighteen. I have no siblings. Aside from an uncle in Texas, I have no family. My family is just me and my memories."

There is silence in the Great Hall. The paths of people

crossing and the sounds of their steps mixing; the stars of the zodiac shimmering through the fog of lost sounds; the trains leaving; the people wanting and waiting — it all stops and listens.

"I'm also a family of one."

He takes her hand. With the other, he pulls a sheet of paper from his jacket pocket and reads to her and beyond — into the zodiac.

Who art thou?

O Muse, do I scare you?
Am I too loud or too happy?
Should I underplay my part?
Maybe I don't listen?

Too enthusiastic?
I could hide in shadows
And try to follow from
Afar, the keen admirer,

But I would rather ride
Bucking waves to glory,
Than sink below surface
And breathe filtered light.

You can keep your secrets,
Your mask of beauty and
Golden smiles so open,
So rich in seductive thrill.

This is no attack,
Just a progression in time

Unorchestrated, natural,
A call to travel lightly.

Fear not, for Art thou art,
And I, a fervent fan,
Connoisseur of fine things
And lover of beauty.

Just let me bid on
Future's lonely gamble.
I'll buy my ticket
With kisses and champagne.

If I lose — no tears,
Not even a message,
Never answered. Just a
Faint echo in your ears.

Shadows when you walk
Years hence, lives hence
When all is settled dust
And our time has passed.

The general logistics were simple. An early April flight to spend a few days in Kyoto for the wedding, then transportation south to wherever the cherries were blooming. Perhaps to Shikoku? The details were complex: maps, bikes and their transportation, clothing, tools, cameras… guide book? So many blanks to fill in. It was his turn to lead. Sara concentrated on her book, determined to produce an outline and a sample chapter before they left.

Bags for the bikes? A phrase book? Train travel with bikes? Ferries? The internet was helpful and confusing. Sites in Japanese were hopeless, but he discovered one in English suggesting that foreign cyclists use the *Touring Mapple* road maps for motorcyclists. They show the small roads, hotels and landmarks as symbols on the map, even if the names and notes are in Japanese. The essentials are there in book form, region by region.

He read rave reviews from cyclists who had ridden the Shimanami Kaido, an island-hopping cycle route between Honshu and Shikoku. He was drawn to Shikoku, the smallest of the four main Japanese islands, for its 88 Temple Pilgrimage, made on foot, bicycle, train or bus, and for the proximity of ocean and mountains. There were reports of traditional architecture and food. It seemed right — not far from Kyoto and connected to Honshu — not only by the Shimanami Kaido, but also by ferries between other strings of islands. It would take at least a month to begin to do it justice, even with help from local trains.

They rode several times a week on the bicycle loop in Prospect or Central Park, often including a lunch or dinner in a nearby restaurant. He put in extra time, spending several hours on the bike each day. The benefits came slowly at first, but he soon felt his body finding new strength and his mind new peace.

Training was his refuge. Endorphins worked their magic. He was free to revisit past events of senseless consequence, and to relive unresolved puzzles and struggles. The movement of his legs was music to his body and brain; the past became diffuse and distant. Pieces of his scholarly writing came back — sometimes in repeating patterns, like fragments from his article on the French fairy tale about the beauty and the beast: *La Belle et la Bête*. He was breathing hard when he heard her voice say, "*La Belle et la Bête*" in her Parisian French. He heard it again. He stopped, stood holding his bike and strained to hear her ghost once more. Nothing. Just his breathing and a breeze on dry leaves. Back on the bike, it came again. His French bride was playing tricks on him; this time it sounded clearly like "*La belle est la bête*." He wanted to go home, but the way was blocked, so he rode on through darkness.

The air tickets were purchased, so the trip had a beginning and an end. The trick was to fill the space in between with ideas and hopes, while keeping it free of commitments.

He bought a new bike. They had opted for traveling light, and he wanted to sample her world of carbon fiber. As winter loosened its grip, they did several full day rides in the Catskills. He bought an indoor trainer, and used his old bike on it daily. His horizon was opening. New sensations of speed and power were building. He longed to shed winter and feel sun and wind on his skin.

Sara was deep into the subject of sleep. She thrived on deadlines, and the outline and sample chapter had to be submitted before their departure.

> *What's essential and interesting to a lay audience? What's reliable in the medical literature? How to present the uncertainties? What's sleep? Is it necessary? Memory? Sleep in other organisms? Benefits of naps? Sleep for training body and mind? Why these rest periods? What happens biochemically? Genetically? Dreams: another subject for a book.*

She needed to focus, but starting from a broad perspective, taking a long view. The bike rides helped, but did not cure her obsessions. She moved into warrior mode. She submitted the outline and sample chapter the day before they left.

On the day of departure, they put an "out of office" automatic reply on their email accounts. They had packed the ultra minimum, and she left her mobile phone behind with no regrets. They flew to Kansai airport, not far from Kyoto. The bikes were safely boxed, with their wheels removed and lashed to the frame. Everything was carefully padded with clothes and bubble wrap. They had rack trunks and small handlebar bags. The rack trunks were taken on the plane. The seat post racks were packed with the bikes. They wore mostly bike clothes. What they would wear for the wedding was a mystery to be solved. They had booked two rooms in the hotel suggested for the out-of-town wedding guests, and they had insisted on not needing a pickup at the airport. She had described him to her Japanese friends as a mentor who had lived in Kyoto and was serving as her escort.

At the airport they consigned the bikes to a luggage transporter with instructions to keep them until notified in a few days. Shortly after their arrival at the hotel, the groom appeared to pay his respects. He and Sara greeted each other with low bows, followed by handshaking, Western style, more deep bows and a big Western style hug. It was a warm, formal and at the same time informal reunion. He and the groom bowed and shook hands.

They were given a schedule in English, announcing a dinner that night, the wedding the next afternoon and then a banquet. A tea ceremony was planned for the last day. They were included in the intimate family circle for all the events. They would be met by one of the family at every stage and taken to the venues, which were nearby. All had been planned according to Japanese protocol, and they were honored guests.

They had adjacent rooms. After resting and showering they found themselves on their respective balconies, admiring the view over Kyoto.

"Hello over there. How do you feel? Did you take a nap? I can see the place we lived, over there against the mountain."

"My first view of Kyoto, and in the early spring. Beautiful, stunning. How I would love to go out on a bike ride! My kimono fitting is in half an hour. What are you going to do?"

"Walk and breathe. Sit and listen. Try to stay awake. Maybe go to a karaoke bar…"

He did none of the above; instead he bought a Japanese suit, white shirt, tie and some fancy shoes in a nearby department store.

The dinner was in a traditional Japanese room with tatami mats, shoji screens and an alcove with a scroll and an ike-bana floral arrangement. Seating was on the floor on cushions with backrests at a long, low table. It seemed that the women were going to arrive after the men, and the bride and groom would not attend. Drinks were served. He asked for carbonated water, but whisky was added, and it tasted good. The men introduced themselves and exchanged name cards, which he had fortunately remembered to bring. They were left over from his previous Kyoto sojourn, with his name and professional address printed on one side in English and on the other side in Japanese. He was happy to have purchased the suit. Everybody was wearing one. After standing and talking, the men sat cross-legged in their designated places, leaving conspicuous gaps for the women.

They arrived with noises in the hallway, high voices and then sounds of feet brushing tatami mats. Screens at the end of the room slid open, and the women made their entrance. Grand and dazzling, they were all dressed up. Some wore Western clothes, and some were in kimonos. He didn't see Sara at first, but there she was, arm in arm with two Japanese ladies dressed in kimonos. She was beaming. The butterfly had taken flight. Flying high with long, strong strokes of her yellow wings. He blinked, confused for a moment; then he saw the intricate woven patterns in yellow with muted reds and browns and bright, circular highlights. It really was a butterfly motif, a fitting tribute to a beautiful young woman.

He tried to imagine how she had managed this transformation. Not just the dress, but also the makeup, and her hair was done-up and decorated. She was smiling at everybody and bowing with each introduction. When it came to him, they bowed, and he realized how perfectly Japanese she had become. She was seated across from him with her legs folded under her, Japanese style, flanked by the same ladies in kimonos.

The other women were elegantly dressed and coiffed. They were beauties, both young and old. But all eyes were on Sara. This was clearly not going to be an ordinary event, but if only it were real… it had to be a scene from a Japanese movie, a jetlag-confused dream sequence that would soon slip away, beyond his grasp.

He was seated next to an English-speaking man his age, who offered to be his translator for the evening. There were questions: polite and sincere questions about where he lived and what he did. Drinks were again served, and he managed to avoid the whisky. The dishes started to come, slowly and modestly at first. Small delights in elegant settings. Miniature works of art were delicately grasped with chopsticks to disappear forever. He had forgotten the sophistication of it all. The tastes came rolling back with surprises from behind, unexpected outbreaks of passion — just enough and in balance with the rest. He thought about the metaphor of food, covering all of the emotions, even love and music. Past lives faded and returned transformed. Voices swirled, but only their music was discernible, with the meanings blurred. A word here and there… then he was asked about his work.

"Do many people study French in America?"

"Yes, foreign language study is encouraged, but not just the language. I teach the poetry and theater. It's more meaningful in the original language."

There ensued a lively discussion about poetry and the influence of Japanese art in Western countries, particularly in France in the latter part of the nineteenth century. He discovered that the man at his side was an academic and translator, fluent in French and English. He saw Sara whispering behind her hand with her two lady escorts. They were glancing at him. People were whispering among themselves and looking at him. The man at the end of the table stood, bowed in his direction and asked him to recite a poem for them.

He looked at Sara. She mouthed the word "please," and he stood up and recited the poem for the tea ceremony near the Seto Sea. There was warm applause, and he was handed paper and pen and asked to write it down. The multilingual academic next to him stood and gave a Japanese translation. He was asked to repeat the poem in English. There were exclamations of understanding and thanks. The party had started. A barrier had snapped with the poetry. He was part of the family.

A new series of dishes is served, with more of those Japanese taste surprises that jump out and astonish. There are more drinks, including sake, which he can never resist. Somewhere in his brain it feels like language functions have faded into irrelevancy. He hears words without understanding them. Language is more vibrant than ever, but it has lost its meaning and entered linguistic Nirvana. Even the elegant food ceases to exist in the usual way. It's somehow plugged into something more basic. The primitive brain is contacted. It responds at levels he had never imagined. Yes, he is high, but in a new way, in spite of the alcohol.

A man at the end of the table stands to make a speech. The speech is simultaneously translated for him by his neighbor. It's about youth, beauty, passing of years and the explosive, fragile beauty of the sakura. Silence, nods of approval and then applause — applause of leaves rustled by the cool, breezy wisdom of age. Eloquent and touching, he thinks; then he realizes the room is silent, and all eyes are on the woman on Sara's right.

She pulls an embroidered handkerchief from her obi. Her eyes are full of tears, and the tears are contagious. He sees Sara's eyes filling and those of the woman on her left. Napkins are grasped around the table. A misty silence of tears inundates the room, and he feels his eyes filling.

The woman starts to speak. His translator is silent. It's not the stand-up speech of speeches, but something unprepared and deeply moving. She is strong and composed, and the touching of the handkerchief to her eyes accents the rhythm of her words. She talks to every person, one by one, and then into the distance. She loses herself, searches for words, finds none; hangs… suspended. There is no applause, just the silent flowing of tears.

Then Sara is singing in a rich, resonant voice: "Autumn Leaves" in French; now she sings it in Japanese, and others sing with her.

Sara singing 'Autumn Leaves' in Japanese? What a surprise!

A man stands up and starts a lively Japanese folk song; people clap in rhythm and sing along. The party segues slowly into happy mode, but the woman to Sara's right is only half present, trying to come back from a distant place. Sara holds her hand tightly, and they cry together.

There is much singing, more food, more drink. He realizes he is running on reserve power. The party ends at midnight. Sara shows no signs of fatigue. He makes it back to his room and barely into bed before falling into a sleep drugged by jetlag, alcohol, fatigue and total pleasure.

Hours later he is fully awake. He has slept in the robe he found folded on the bed. As he rises, he reties this cotton *yukata* and remembers the dream he was having a moment before. He sits again on the bed to concentrate on recalling it fully, but it fades too fast. Yet he remembers a fragment. A woman — maybe a Shinto deity — appears from a dark cave and leads him away. He can't make out where. It's so close, so pleasurable, but not quite there… just the faint imprint of a young woman in a flowing white robe. Her beautiful face blurs, and she turns and walks away from him into the sun, through a misty fog. He follows, pulled by quantum forces, but she disappears into a foggy wave of light. He struggles back, awake.

He slides open the glass door and steps out onto the balcony. The first hint of dawn over Kyoto. What a miracle to be back. So many years since they watched the dawn flow over this city. The trees on the hillside form a descending black diagonal, and the outlines of buildings are forming below. The light catches low clouds on the horizon. They burst into flame. The day promises to come, but at its own pace.

"Patience, I'll be here soon," it says, "but not yet. Savor this moment."

Yes, savor it. Cling to the peace before the dawn. Cling to this vestige of self-control. But how long before I crash and burn? At least they don't know me here. Here, I'm free to play the fool, falling off my toy bicycle. So you laugh that contagious giggle — your siren song. Yes, mock me, for I am poor, lost and unraveling, madly in love with a young woman, and you laugh from your high perch in the past — at me, the clown, swerving and falling off my bike.

He hears a door sliding; it's on the adjacent balcony. He feels her presence, but doesn't turn, riveted on the dawn. Finally, he says,

"Dawn viewing over Kyoto. Moving light. Return to reality? But which reality? I've had the strangest dream. I was possessed by a Shinto goddess, who led me toward a beacon of blinding light. I think she was a kami. Maybe Amaterasu, the spirit of the sun."

"What did she look like?"

"I've lost most of the image. She was young and beautiful, but she was somehow distant."

He turns toward her. She is wearing a *yukata* with the haori jacket. She looks perfectly rested and awake.

"Would you like some tea?" she says.

Inside her room, he sits cross-legged by the glass door. She kneels on the tatami floor, Japanese style.

"Sara, you're transformed. I expected a mundane dinner last night, but instead I got a revelation. I've never had so many surprises in one evening. I can't assimilate them all. I had no idea you were so close to these people. How did this happen? How did you conjure up that stunning dress? I heard you sing like a pro. How come you know 'Autumn Leaves' in Japanese? Who was the woman next to you who made us cry? What was she saying? It was so unexpected. I'm seeing a new being in you."

"The party was given by my host family from Hiroshima. The woman who was on my right is my Japanese mother. I call her Mama-san, but her name is Chieko. We were reunited yesterday afternoon, after you went out. It was very moving. We had not seen each other in ten years.

"Her son, whom you met when we arrived, is my Japanese brother. He's getting married today to a girl from Kyoto, the daughter of the woman who was on my left. The man who gave the speech is the bride's father. I think the man translating for you is the bride's uncle.

"The kimono fitting included a visit to a fashion designer. The dress I was wearing was a gift from my Mama-san. It was created just for me. Only minor adjustments were necessary, since she knew me so well, and she had a recent photo and a dress I had left in Hiroshima. The finished dress was delivered well in time for the dinner party. My hair was done by a stylist who came to the hotel, and the makeup was by my Japanese mother. All of this was a total surprise to me. I had no idea what I was going to wear before yesterday afternoon.

"Mama-san was very moving. She's a profound and mysterious power in my life. She's strong and gentle at the same time. Last night she spoke about her husband, my Japanese father, who died just three years ago. I wish I had understood what she said. He was a brilliant, loving and fascinating man. We were deeply attached to each other.

"The song came rushing back to me in Japanese. I had learned it in Hiroshima from Mama-san. I just sang it spontaneously. I was surprised other people knew it."

"What a beautiful story, Sara. I'm so relieved there's a logical explanation for last night. The dream about following that radiant kami goddess — it felt so good! I was under the spell of last night's magic and illusions, but I had to struggle back to the world of reason. Your explanations have helped."

"But you shouldn't worry. Look at the dawn now! It's a perfect day for a wedding!"

They were silent as a wave of light rushed in, and another and another. Oceans of light filled the room with the solar breeze, photons purified of lethal particles by the Earth's magnetic field. The sun was just clearing the horizon… and the sky slipped headlong into their midst.

There was a long silence while they absorbed the changing light flowing around them, and Sara continued, "You're right. There was magic last night. Everybody was part of it, and you contributed your beautiful Japanese poem."

She made tea for them with the tea set found in every Japanese hotel room. Japanese green tea. A welcome taste.

The way of tea. I'm back on the path to harmony, respect, purity and tranquility.

They were the first to enter the breakfast room, wearing their *yukatas* and haori jackets. A table was set with their names on it. The breakfast was voluptuous, and it brought back the many he had enjoyed, with clear soup, smoked fish, lettuce, squares of nori seaweed for picking up the rice with chopsticks, eggs… and the salty plums, pickles and many breakfast treats he had never been able to identify. Everything was served in elegant bowls and dishes. Most exotic of all was the slimy natto, the fermented soybeans, a favorite of his, but generally shunned by Westerners.

Since it was early, and they had no commitments until late in the morning, he suggested taking the nearby philosopher's walk, to check on the sakura.

The blossoms were swollen in their buds, but only showing hints of white. As they walked along the path that followed the stream, he asked if she wanted to tell him about her stay in Hiroshima.

"Yes, I'll talk. I'm ready now. I was eighteen, at the end of my high school studies, and I wanted to experience something different. I won a scholarship for a three-month exchange with a Japanese student, who came to my high school. My host family in Hiroshima was perfect for me. Their son introduced me to his friends. His parents made me feel at home. I had already studied a little Japanese, so the cultural shock never happened. I just slipped into a warm sea and swam in it."

They walk through the budding, but not quite opening, sakura blossoms. All that is needed is another week of warm weather. They sit on a bench overlooking the stream. She is thoughtful and composed… she says she can tell him the rest of the story, but she needs to hold his hand, tightly.

The grade is steep. Confront. Years lost. Breathe. Calm. Resonate. Be true. Gently, now, here I go…

"One month after arriving in Hiroshima, there is a gigantic explosion in my life. It starts with a phone call. The American consulate is calling my Japanese father. Minutes later the doorbell rangs, and somebody I don't see is let in. I'm taken to the sitting room to meet this person, not daring to imagine why, but aware that my Papa-san is extremely disturbed.

"The doors close, and I'm alone with an American man who takes my hands in his, and he doesn't let go. He guides me to sit in an armchair. He sits down before me, looks me in the eyes and says my parents were killed in a car accident. Mama-san rushes into the room and picks me up. She clutches me tight, rocking back and forth, running her hand over my hair. The room empties, and we stand there crying gently at first and then more and more violently and desperately. I struggle like a child, but she holds me tight until I'm exhausted.

"Mama-san guided me in my first steps through grief. We saw nobody for days. She slept on a futon next to mine, holding my hand. We just cried and cried. There was nothing to say. Papa-san finally came to tell me I was needed in New York. He wanted to go with me. I insisted on having a single round trip ticket, and I flew home alone.

"My parents were killed by a suicidal drunk, driving at night the wrong way on the freeway with his lights off. There were legal matters, family matters, estate questions, a funeral and a memorial. I had to make decisions very fast. I had a time limit. I absolutely had to return to Japan, and I did. I was back in Hiroshima one week after arriving in New York.

"My Japanese family was waiting at the airport. I was escorted through the next two months by these people, by their friends and by students and teachers from school — the neighbors and the local shopkeepers were with me. Mama-san slept in my room every night.

"My childhood thus came to an abrupt and violent end. This family saved me. I can't imagine what I would have done without them. They asked me to stay in Japan. They offered to adopt me, but I decided to face the music at home. I had to go back. The separation was heartbreaking for all of us, especially for Mama-san and me.

"I went straight from Hiroshima to the university as a pre-med. The course work was heavy, and that helped. My French poetry class from you was heaven. I went to medical school, and I did two years of internship and residency. It was a strange and numbing time. Ten years evaporated. I wore my youthful smiles and pretty clothes, but I was running away, and it never stopped hurting.

"I stayed in contact with my Japanese family, through letters, phone calls and emails, but the distance diluted our intimacy over the years. Then Papa-san died, and I wanted to return to Hiroshima to be with Mama-san, but she knew I was in the last year of medical school. She refused to let me come. She said she wanted me to wait for a happier time.

"Now you know why I desperately wanted to come to this wedding, but I needed your support and calming presence. Now I'm here and reunited with Mama-san and the family, and all is well. This was meant to be. I'm so thankful to you. This is the first time I've told anybody the truth about Hiroshima."

"Maybe you should spend more time with Mama-san. We can shorten the bike trip."

"She'll have nothing of it. She's worried about me. She wrote me a letter in Japanese that had been translated into English. She fears I've been in a tunnel for ten years, out of contact with the world of human affections and commitments. She knows my emotions are still bruised. She says I need a profound love relationship. She wants me to look my best at this wedding. She keeps saying I have to learn to love again. I suspect she has lined up suitors. We'll see what happens at the reception tonight."

They walk into the garden of the Silver Pavilion, past the formal sand sculptures, along the paths on the hill and down the rock-paved steps. A stream pauses to collect coins in a pool of pure light. A young couple in kimonos strolls on a path strewn with red camellias.

"I started singing and playing the piano when I was very young. My mother was a singer and my father a pianist. Music was essential to them. There were frequent jazz and classical sessions in our house, and I sang in them from an early age. I grew up with the American and French songbooks in my ears. I studied vocal technique and piano with private teachers. I sang with the high school jazz band, but my parents were my primary musical resource. I learned opera roles from my mother. I played jazz with my father. He built me a miniature opera theater with puppets, and I invented opera stagings. They loved it when I sang for them.

"I didn't sing after my parents died. Something had broken in me. Mama-san is right. I went into emotional hibernation. I started to come out of it on the Col d'Aubisque. I was truly happy there for the first time since my parents were killed. I found energy that I hadn't imagined in me. I felt free to live, after ten years of struggle and self-doubt. The Aubisque got me started on a new path. I learned how to climb — to climb out of the past.

"After the bike trip in France, I returned to New York and worked for three months in the emergency room. I quit to write the first paper about sleep. That's when I received an email from the Romance Language Student Association, inviting me to your retirement party.

"And now I'm reunited here with Mama-san. Last night was the first time I've sung for an audience in ten years. This is more than a wedding celebration. I'm home again, alive again, and the future excites me: a bicycle adventure with you!"

They have tea in the cafe at the Pavilion entrance, sitting outdoors under a giant red parasol.

"I also have something to celebrate. Last night was the first time I've read a poem in public in many years, and the bride's uncle (who translated for me) also asked me to read at the reception, so when we get back to the hotel, I'll write out a couple of poems I know from memory. He offered to translate them. Will you be singing?"

"Yes, I had a similar request from him, and I'll also write out the words for him. It looks like we have a busy time ahead of us, and I'll be wearing a real kimono at the ceremony. That will take a lot of preparation. But I feel confident. I have Mama-san."

The wedding ceremony took place at a Shinto shrine in the eastern part of Kyoto. The afternoon sky was clear and deep blue. Close to twenty family members and friends waited in a reception hall adjacent to the shrine; then they moved slowly through the double doors. A procession came toward them, down a stone-paved path, led by two priests and two shrine maidens. All were sumptuously dressed in traditional clothes. Behind them were the bride and groom, walking under a grand red parasol. The bride held her mother's hand, with the bride's father, Mama-san and Sara behind. Family and friends merged and climbed the steps, led by the immediate family.

The bride was in white embroidered silk, with layers of under and over garments and tassels. She wore a large, white hood that framed her face in a halo. The groom was dressed in a rich white kimono jacket, with tassels, and pinstriped *hakama* trousers. They walked slowly across the temple courtyard and up the wooden steps and into a hallway leading into the shrine. The ceremony included a purification, vows, statements of commitment and the drinking of sake. Symbolic offerings were made to the Shinto gods.

Mama-san and Sara were linked arm in arm as mother and daughter. Not a word passed between them. Both were dressed in traditional kimonos. Mama-san wore light beige with a subtle print of tiny dots and an embroidered obi. Sara was dressed in a silk, *furisode* kimono, worn by unmarried women for special occasions, with a unified sakura design traversing the entire garment on a deep pink background. The wide obi was decorated with a crane motif, embroidered in silver and gold. The sleeves nearly touched the floor, giving the impression she was about to take off and fly when she walked. Sara was wearing makeup, and her hair was styled and ornamented in tiny orchids. She was the perfect young Japanese woman.

He stayed in the background with the friends of the family. He imagined a huge mirror that let him see the entire wedding party from afar and from close up. He was the only Westerner in this objective image. Sara was Japanese, and she looked so perfectly the part that she could have stepped out of a nineteenth century wood block print. Was it the makeup? The way she walked and stood? It was easy to see how the bond between her and Mama-san had formed and persisted. Perhaps the lack of a common language was part of their closeness? Perhaps they were free to communicate simply and directly, without the complications of language?

The afternoon was waning when they left the shrine. The drive back to the hotel took them along streets and gardens where signs of spring were accumulating — in the vegetation, in the way people dressed, in their smiles and in the warmth that lingered in the air. But the cherry trees were holding their own, refusing to bloom until they were sure the time was right.

How could they know? What were the signals that flipped them into reproductive mode?

Nothing was scheduled until the reception, and Sara was busy with Mama-san, so he wandered in the neighborhood until he found a luggage store that he had remembered from the first visit. He bought a suitcase, thinking they would need it for their clothing acquisitions. He reviewed the poems he had picked from his mental store. Were they appropriate for a wedding reception? What would Sara think?

The air is cooling and the light starting to dim. He goes out on his balcony to view the city and contemplate the events of the day.

Who is she, this Sara with me now for three days? Yes, a cultural chameleon, but how did she overcome her family tragedy? Does her strength come from this?

He tries to imagine himself at eighteen confronting such a challenge.

She seems so adaptable — or is it a veneer? This lovely young woman really seems willing to travel with me. How lucky I am. How crazy and lucky I am to be here.

He hears the sound of the sliding glass door on the next balcony and her voice: "A penny for your thoughts?"

He answers without turning.

"I was just recapping the day and admiring how you've coped with your tragedy. I was also thinking about the wedding ceremony — its simplicity and beauty — and I was thinking how lucky I am to be here, with you, thanks to you, to witness this celebration and your transformation into a Japanese woman. I was also thinking about your stunning kimono, and your mastery of the Japanese look, and…"

He turns toward her, and stops in mid-sentence as she comes into view. "Sara, I'm dazzled. Where did you get that gown? You're gorgeous, stunning, over the top beautiful. Wow. Can I come over for a cup of tea?"

She hums "Tea for Two." He leaves the balcony and makes his way to her room. She is serving tea. The gown is pure gossamer. She is Cinderella, but in contemporary mode. Her hair is up and glowing. Her makeup is just right, almost invisible. She beams golden light.

"Mama-san did it again," she says. "And here are the shoes." She holds up a pair of high heels. He sees Dior printed on the inside. "And these are for dancing." She shows him a pair of tango shoes.

He sits. "Breathtaking. Pardon me if I stare. So impolite of me, but I'm transfixed. Gone to heaven. You're the most beautiful thing on Earth."

The wedding venue is a large hotel in the center of Kyoto. Drinks are served in a lounge; then the double doors open and the party moves into a Western style banquet hall with a stage at one end, where a trio is playing a jazz version of the wedding march from *Lohengrin*. The guests are placed at round tables, each with a different floral arrangement.

They are seated with their translator and his wife from the night before. She also speaks English. It turns out to be a table of Japanese who speak English, chosen to help them feel at ease. There is a mix of generations. Two of the young women are from Sara's high school class, and there is animated talk about friends, teachers and Hiroshima. The dinner is sophisticated Chinese, recreated from the culinary writings of Imperial chefs, and the wine is French. The dinner is a journey through a Chinese landscape of often unfamiliar tastes with many visual surprises.

There are pauses between courses for speeches and entertainment. Each speaker is given a microphone. The lights dim, and a follow spot comes up on them. The first speakers are the bride and groom at the head table. They begin by reading from prepared texts, welcoming and thanking all of the participants. They then talk spontaneously about their meeting, their decision to marry and the love and commitment they feel for each other. Each speaker introduces the next speaker. The bride's father begins, followed by the uncle, who serves as translator for the Western guests. Mama-san is introduced. This time her comments are joyous: about love, prosperity and long, fulfilled lives. She says that love and trust are the keys to overcoming the obstacles in life.

He is handed a microphone, and the light is on him, alone with his two poems. He sees that everybody has a paper with the Japanese translations. The first poem takes the voice of the bride, and the second that of the groom.

The greening Earth

In the low land, jumping wild,
Bluish dots on green.
On the high slopes,
White and yellow trumpets
Herald the change in season.

Life turns inside out,
Released from winter prisons.
Leaves explode with crazy thoughts,
And fancy reigns over reason.

Song springs with love's pursuits
Heedless of hunting poets,
Voyeurs and consequences.
Music everywhere. Sleep abandoned.

Now we welcome, without regret,
This new life, this golden,
Sun-basked opening of the new,
This glory of ageless springs.

Let us drink the fertile potion,
Relinquish care and dance,
Drunk and naked, along
The arching hillsides, summits,
Crests and hollows of the greening Earth.

Am I a rock?

Am I a rock, with river flowing over?
Do I lie low, snuggling and round?
Or am I of ragged species,
The unseen maker of ripples and whorls?
Surely I am not the giant kind,
Blocking the course and making waves.

I would rather be a grain of sand,
Calm in summer, swirling in high water,
A wearer of rocks, but nearly microscopic.
I welcome you, a fleck of gold,
And we will stay as long as
There is sun and water and changing seasons,
And rough rock to polish into sculpture.

And we will stay until the last drop
Of river changes course,
Leaving our last atoms to the sediments.

He finishes to applause and smiles. Sara beams at him. He is handed a note, "Please introduce Sara." He does his best, telling about her becoming an emergency-room doctor and a sportswoman. (His words are echoed in translation.) He then talks about her connections with Japan and the support from her Japanese family in her most desperate hour, and how happy she is to know that her Japanese brother is married to a generous and beautiful woman.

The spot shifts to Sara, and she stands and walks to the bandstand. She moves slowly through the dark room, glowing gossamer under the light. The band starts to play before she reaches the stage; then she is up and onto the stage. She takes the mike just as the band finishes the intro to "If I Were a Bell." She is exuberant, fast and audacious. After the theme, she scats and the pianist takes a solo. She comes back in, and they finish flying high and joyful. There is a blackout; the band continues to play; then we see her dimly in blue; then in bright golden highlights as she begins "Body and Soul." She takes a slow tempo and delivers the music straight with no movement. There are no solos. It is pure and sincere. The light slowly encircles her as the song ends. Her face is immobilized, hanging in the darkness. Blackout, and then the light comes up on the band. They have begun "La Vie en Rose." Her back is to the audience during the intro. She turns downstage to come in, as the follow spot catches her in brilliant white in a rose-colored wash. She is Edith Piaf reincarnated, passionate and free, singing in French, and then in Japanese. She moves with the music. The rose color catches her gown. As she sings, the follow spot on her fades slowly, until she disappears into a sea of rose glow.

The last song begins in blue and red light. She is turned toward the band. She scats with the pianist. They tease the audience, withholding the melody. She at last turns and sings "Somewhere Over the Rainbow" in bright blue with red highlights on her hair. Then they modulate up and into a syncopated double time. The song takes flight. The base player takes a solo; then the drummer and the pianist. She comes back with a wild and exuberant improvisation, full of syncopations and inventions. The song ends on a high floating note, as the light goes blue, leaving her face suspended in white on a blue sky. Blackout.

There has been no time for applause between the songs. Now there is stunned silence in the darkness; then the stage is fully lit, and she and the band are bowing. The audience stands, applauding and cheering. The show ends, and she disappears. The band starts a waltz, and the light shifts to the dance floor.

His short sojourn in heaven is interrupted by the realization that the seat next to him is empty. The Sara he knew has vanished, metamorphosed into a jazz diva. He fears he will never see her again.

The party shifts into dance mode, with the bride and groom doing a slow waltz. Other guests join in. There is a hand on his shoulder. It's Sara. She has changed into a short light dress, and she wears the tango shoes. They waltz, and he feels her hand slip something into his jacket pocket. At the end of their waltz a young man appears to dance with her. The music morphs into a rock beat. (The musicians were seamlessly replaced while playing.) He watches as Sara dances with him, and then another appears. They are politely taking turns. She never stops. There is no hint of fatigue — just smiles, bows and words exchanged with each partner. What language are they speaking?

He reads her note. It says she is in Mama-san land — not to worry about her, but to please get her up at eight.

He wakes up several times during the night, and sleeping again is difficult. His attempts are interrupted by the sound of footsteps in the corridor, which seems odd. Everybody should be wearing soft slippers in the hotel. The sounds stop in front of his door, pause and move on, diminishing in the distance. Later, he hears steps again; they slow, but don't stop at his door. The third time they stop, and then turn back on themselves. He feels abused by this strange and tantalizing occurrence, so close and real, but so unreal. Somebody is trying to reach him, somebody foreign to the hotel, wearing shoes inside — heeled shoes. He hears them again, and rushes to open the door. The hallway is empty.

The new day started the way it had ended — with echoes of music. He tried to untangle the events of the wedding, but musical memories distracted his attention. Echoes of songs washed in and out, leaving notes and sequences of notes high and dry, to wash away and be replaced by other fragments.

"If I were a bell…" The morning light was diffuse through high clouds. "…birds do fly." A change in the weather? And today is a travel day. "…birds do fly." But they haven't decided where to go!

> *That pretty well sums it up. How could anything be more beautiful? So she morphed again! Butterfly girl to Japanese print creature, to jazz diva. But not a diva at all. No diva gestures. Nothing extra, nothing missing. At perfect ease and natural. Totally in the music from the music for the music. The stage persona emerged on a fountain of music, and the words were there, clear and convincing. It was sound and light, pure and simple, body and soul.*

He knocked on her door at eight. No answer; he tried the door, which was unlocked, so he opened it and called. There was a moan from the room beyond the corridor. He tried again, "*Ohayou gozaimasu*!"

"OK. Just a quick shower and I'll be ready."

She entered his room in her *yukata*, hair wet, looking happy and ready. They talked about the coming day: tea ceremony at eleven o'clock and travel south to pick up the Shimanami Kaido bicycle route that links the islands of Honshu and Shikoku.

"When we were preparing for the wedding, Mama-san asked me about our plans. I told her about the bikes and the Shimanami Kaido. She said she would arrange our travel, so we have tickets for a five o'clock train to Onomichi, and the bikes will be delivered to the train station by the baggage service at four o'clock. Mama-san is magic."

"Speaking of magic, the word doesn't begin to describe you last night. I have millions of questions, but I'll wait until we're on our own. In the meantime, I'm listening to your echoes."

"I'll tell all. I promise. But now for breakfast and maybe a stroll on the Philosopher's Walk to check on the cherry blossoms? I'll pack everything first. Thank you so much for the suitcase. By the way, did you notice that the tea ceremony dress recommendation is for casual, with walking shoes? It looks like we'll be having our tea in bicycle clothes. We'll be the fashion talk of Kyoto!"

On the Philosopher's Walk, the buds were swollen to the point of showing occasional patches of white, but nothing was open. They tried to untangle the events of the day before. He wanted to know how they had prepared the songs.

"I gave Mama-san a play list with the key for each song. I picked standards I thought the Japanese might know, and a couple of songs I just felt like singing. 'La Vie en Rose' was for Mama-san — it's her favorite song. The lighting was a happy surprise. It really helped me find my cocoon and feel at home on stage. I'm so glad to be singing with a trio again. It's been over ten years, and I was afraid I had forgotten how to do it! But they were top notch — with me and around me, never too strong or intrusive, always supportive and stimulating. We were so busy afterwards that I didn't get a chance to talk to them. I loved the way the jazz combo was replaced by the dance band. The pianist just slid over, and another replaced him without missing a note. The dancing continued to 2 am, and I met quite a few attractive men. I was so happy to dance with Shiro, my Japanese brother. What a night! I was afraid I would turn into a pumpkin at midnight, but I fought it, and it didn't happen. I didn't lose a glass slipper, so I'm still a free woman. Kyoto has been a fast and thrilling ride, and now I'm ready for the real thing — on the bicycle. But first the tea ceremony, I've never been to one before."

"It's simply serving tea to a small number of friends in a special place. You often enter the tearoom through a low door, and once inside there may be a view over a garden. You have tea ceremony sweets to eat, and the tea is made for each guest using special utensils. The water is heated on a brazier in an iron kettle. The tea is matcha, finely ground green tea made from young leaves. It's whisked to produce a foam. The whisk is made from a single piece of bamboo. You'll see what to do by watching your neighbor, but the important elements are the utensils, the gestures, the setting, the tea and, above all, the friendship. The tea ceremony is an expression of love."

They were driven with their baggage to the western side of Kyoto, near the Katsura River. The car stopped in front of a rustic thatched gateway. As they got out of the car, he was hit by a wave of recognition.

"I've been here before! This is the entrance to the gardens of the Katsura Imperial Villa. I don't believe it. This is a gigantic privilege. Visitors are only allowed to enter after applying to a special commission, and when permission is granted, it's just to be guided through the garden. Could we be having tea in one of the Imperial teahouses? It doesn't seem possible!"

The other guests arrived, and they were met by an official from the Imperial Household Agency. They started their stroll along a garden path, with the official explaining in Japanese and English the significance of the garden plan, the choice of plants, the visual aesthetic and the history of the gardens, teahouses and villa.

"The teahouse and gardens were built by prince Toshihito, who was born in 1579. He was fascinated by *The*

Tale of Genji, a novel written by a noblewoman, Murasaki Shikibu, in about 978. It is a primer and chronicle of court life, and sets an artistic standard still revered in our time. Later, the Togukawa Shogunate ensnared the aristocracy using cultural lures, such as calligraphy, poetry and tea. Similar methods were being used by Louis XIV in France to subjugate the aristocracy and consolidate power. Toshihito was probably aware of a reference in *The Tale of Genji* that describes a place called Katsura: 'Far away, in the country village of Katsura, the reflection of the moon upon the water is clear and tranquil.' He acquired Katsura and built a garden and teahouse according to his personal aesthetic, which included an aversion to ostentatious wealth. The teahouse is called Shokin-Tei. It is simple and rustic, with different views to be enjoyed at different seasons. The walk through the gardens spiritually prepares visitors for the tea ceremony. We will walk slowly and not talk. Please enjoy the beauty and tranquility."

They wound their way, climbing gently through a large and complex garden. There were stone steps, streams to cross, hills to climb and ponds with colored carp. The foliage had not yet developed in this early spring, so there were long views through branches and thickets. The Shokin-Tei teahouse appeared across a large pond. There was gravel raked in concentric circles around trained and wild, bonsai-like conifers setting off the teahouse with its thatched roof and rough wooden pillars. The air seemed full of history. They walked around the back and were led, shoes off, into a small room with tatami mats.

"Sara, this is the ultimate privilege. We're having tea on the summit of the tea aesthetic. This place inspired Frank Lloyd Wright, van Gogh, Monet and so many western artists and architects. We're so lucky. I don't believe we're doing this!"

After a while, a low door slid open, and the guests were invited to pass through by crawling on all fours. The tearoom had been opened on three sides, with views of the pond and the gardens. Shiro and Naomi, the newlyweds, were waiting for them, dressed in kimonos. Each guest was given a place to kneel on the tatami mats around a sunken hearth, where an iron kettle was gently steaming on a charcoal-fired brazier. The tea utensils were arranged near the kettle. Naomi kneeled and bowed deeply. She prepared the utensils, using hot water from the kettle, a triangular red cloth to wipe them and slow, stylized gestures that were precise and serene. Shiro served tea sweets and provided each guest with a bamboo knife for cutting them. All eyes were on Naomi, while she made the first cup of tea. Each of Naomi's gestures was deliberate and careful, but not self-conscious. Time flowed slowly and naturally as she measured out the finely ground tea, poured the hot water with the bamboo ladle and whisked the mixture to a foam. The first guest was her uncle. He bowed, hands in front of his knees; then Naomi presented the tea bowl. He admired the bowl, a dark-colored, family heirloom, carefully conserved over many generations. It embodied the way of tea: simplicity, naturalism, restraint, profundity, humility, imperfection and asymmetry. He rotated the bowl a quarter turn before taking his first sip.

Each guest was carefully and lovingly served in sequence. The surroundings blurred as if a dense mist had descended. Sounds were muted, except those of tea being prepared and served. Time slowed and turned inward. New connections were made and old ones renewed among those present, and between them and their exquisite surroundings. Words vanished. The sequence of gestures was the common language — sufficient in itself.

The visit ended with leisurely walk to the entrance gate,

and it was time to say goodbye to all but Mama-san, who was to accompany them to the train station. These were Japanese goodbyes with lingering and waving as they drove off. Suddenly they were back in the real world. How to retain their new serenity? Having seen the way of tea, the challenge to live it was before them.

They were reunited with their bicycles at the prearranged rendezvous adjacent to the Kyoto station, and the baggage service took their suitcase in exchange, leaving them with the clothes they were wearing, a rack trunk and a handlebar bag for each of them.

They unboxed the bikes and slipped them into their lightweight Japanese travel bags. Mama-san gave them their tickets to Onomichi and helped them choose lunch box bentos to eat in the train. Their parting was sweet for the time together and sorrowful for the indefinite looming separation. They tried to thank Mama-san, but she would hear nothing of it. She just asked that they call from time to time during their journey. She wore her brave face, but the ties between Mama-san and Sara were so strong, and they had had so little time together alone… they promised each other to meet again soon. As they walked through the gates, there was much turning back and waving, with moist eyes, anguished smiles and feelings of loss and emptiness.

> *Goodbye claws my soul. Ghost voices slip over the threshold. Afraid to turn back? Yes, but I do. Why fear? Fly me to the moon, going home or leaving home — I am Princess Kaguya.*

In the Shinkansin bullet train they store the bikes behind the last row of seats, and settle in to eat their bento lunches. The train is comfortable, flying through the countryside, inducing sleep with its gentle movements.

Sara slips into a deep nap. She is at her computer. She types two words, return, clicks on the Wikipedia entry "incest taboo." She reads about Lévi-Strauss, anthropology from the 1950s, homozygosity, heterosis, consanguinity… the page dims.

> *The clan survives. Cross out, cross back. Endogamy, exogamy. Who am I to break taboos? But alone we are at last; that counts. Who cares about taboos?*

The train charges on. They are alone in Japan. He tries to replay each day of their visit, starting with the tea ceremony and working back to the pre-wedding party, but his mind will not go beyond the tea ceremony. It doesn't seem possible they were served tea in such an exclusive place. He will long cherish the visit to the Imperial Villa, beginning with the stroll, discovering the teahouse, having tea and ending with the walk. It seems so natural and so magical. Natural, but contrived to not be contrived. It is art.

Now I have a window on her life. I see clearing storms, a young, energetic, turbulent, weather horizon. I'll savor every moment with her — just us together in Shikoku.

Arriving in Onomichi, they stopped in the tourist bureau to pick up maps and pamphlets for their island-hopping traverse to Shikoku, via the Shimanami Kaido. They settled into their hotel, and then walked through the old town and the hill above, taking narrow walkways and stairs. They found a neighborhood restaurant, a shokudo, and decided to have a simple meal. The menu included photos of the dishes, making it easy to order. They had a thick mushroom, oyster and tofu stew, prepared at the table, sea urchin (*uni*) on rice with a raw egg in the middle, decorated with strips of nori sea weed, and they also had slightly caramel-ized sweet potato… or so it seemed. The pattern for future meals was thus established. They recognized some foods; others seemed familiar, but at closer inspection were not, and still others could not be identified at all.

"The *uni* has an amazing taste. Pungent, with a hint of peanut butter. It mixes well with the bland rice, and the egg yolk gives a cool, rich sensation. What part of the sea urchin are we eating, Sara? You're the biologist."

"The gonads. The sex organs. The sea urchin is a complex creature. It's covered with spines that move, so the urchin can crawl and hollow out a cavity in the rock. Between the spines, there are small stalks with a beak on the end that grasps particles of food, which are passed from beak to beak to the mouth on the underside. Tubes with suction cups anchor the urchin to rocks. When you look at an urchin in seawater through a dissecting microscope, you see hundreds of these appendages — all moving in coordination. The first time I saw a living urchin up close, I was so fascinated I was glued to the microscope for hours. We saw urchins release eggs and sperm and watched fertilization, with a cloud of sperm clinging to the outside of each egg, and each sperm wiggling desperately to get his or her DNA into the egg before the others. We watched the eggs divide, and over the next week we saw the embryos develop. I was so excited I couldn't sleep."

"So how can you eat something you admire so much?"

"No problem. I love the taste."

"So taste trumps everything."

"Yes, and eating what you love is an interesting subject. Some of the tribes of Papua New Guinea ate the brains of their loved ones when they died. It was considered a compliment and an expression of love. Unfortunately, their necrophilic cannibalism transmitted kuru, a disease caused by a prion protein. Prions are the agents for scrapie and Creutzfeldt-Jakob diseases. Other examples of food lovers, or lover food, come from spiders. In some of the 'black widow' species the female eats the male after they copulate. So love and food are intimately associated. I hope you're enjoying your meal."

"I want my money back."

"Man the stomach pumps."

"You know, Sara, you're a skillful chameleon. I admit I asked for it, but you just morphed again — this time into a biomedical expert on exotic diseases and sea urchin embryology. A few hours ago you were a jazz diva, and before that you were a perfect courtesan in a nineteenth-century woodblock print. I also vaguely remember an ER physician. How do you do it?"

She laughs. "And you? You used to be a distinguished and aloof heartthrob professor of French — a world-renowned expert on French poetry and theater. From there you became a bicycle mechanic; then you shed half of your years to look and act like the boy next door. I'm serious!"

"Are you happy?"

"I've never been so happy. Here we are, starting a bicycle adventure, carrying next to nothing, free from computers and telephones. Just us and a few hills to climb, a few menus to figure out, a few lodging logistics to solve and a few roads to find."

"You're right. This is it. We're bike gypsies."

They stood up, hugged across the table and ordered another round of hot sake.

He became pensive and slightly mischievous. "I've got a proposal for you. Please say no if you want, but it's important, so here goes… Should we continue to take separate rooms?"

"I've noticed that you tend to ask such questions after several rounds of sake. Do you snore?"

"Never, and I promise to behave myself and keep my *yukata* on."

"I'm only worried about the snoring. What you wear is your business."

"If I snore, you can stuff my *yukata* down my throat."

"That's not such a good idea. I'm a doctor, but performing artificial respiration through a stuffed *yukata* wasn't part of my medical training, and it's not covered by my malpractice insurance."

"So you don't mind sharing a room with me?

She gave him a doubting look, "I'll try it. Now I have a return question for you. We brought visitors' gifts, but I completely forgot about a wedding present!"

"I acted for both of us. After getting advice from the hotel manager, I gave the appropriate amount of cash in a special envelope, in both our names, and I also left a letter offering the newlyweds a stay in New York at their convenience."

"I'm relieved. How generous! You thought of everything, while I was busy playing Japanese princess. I want to split the wedding bill with you."

"Somebody already paid all the local expenses. Our hotel tonight seems to be paid for as well. If it's all right with you, I'll cover the rest of the trip, and we can split the total when we get back."

"Very generous. I accept. I'm looking forward to new experiences. Trying all kinds of food and lodging is important to me. Less is more. I want to eat and sleep in the low and high ends. It would be boring to stay in fancy lodging all the time, but one or two splurges might be nice…"

So the deal was made. All they needed was a good night's sleep, and they could start the ride across the islands of the Shimanami Kaido to Shikoku.

It stormed all night, troubling his sleep. The wind played the building's edges and improvised a symphony of whistles and moans with a chorus of sighs and solo screams. He was semi-awake, listening for meaning, hearing human sounds in glissandos and trills. These voices were devoid of words, yet full of emotion. Sleep brought a strange dream. He was desperate to climb into a train, but encumbered by baggage. As he struggled with the last suitcase, the door closed, stranding him outside with his luggage inside. The train departed.

In the morning the rain had stopped, but the wind was still strong. From their windows they could see the Seto Sea and mountainous islands everywhere. It was a storm sky with fast-moving clouds but signs of clearing.

Over breakfast they read the tourist office information for cyclists:

"The Shimanami Kaido toll road was built in 1999. It connects the main island of Honshu to Shikoku via the small islands of Mukaishima, Innoshima, Ikuchijima, Omishima, Hakatajima and Oshima. Bicycle and footpaths are provided for all but the first bridge to Mukaishima. A marked route guides cyclists across each island with suggestions for visiting local attractions."

"What do you think, Sara? We could ride it in a day, but the tourist map shows many diversions and distractions. Maybe we could climb to get a view and a feeling for the place. The map shows an orchid farm we could visit. It's part way up the highest point, Mount Takami, at 288 meters. The official route follows the flat seacoast. Should we take the straight, marked path or head for the hills?"

"I want to see everything, but it would take days just on Mukaishima to see the thirteen places recommended on the map. I'm a climber — let's go up."

After stocking up on dried fish, peanuts, rice balls and other snacks in the supermarket, they took the little ferry that runs every few minutes across the narrow strait between

Mukaishima and Honshu. There was room for only two cars, and a schoolboy in his uniform was also crossing by bicycle. The wind in the strait was strong, but the ferry captain was skilled, and in a few minutes they were riding onto Mukaishima. They passed through the sleepy town, and climbed at a leisurely pace through bamboo groves, farmland and orchards.

"How is it riding on the left?"

"Great, just so I'm following you."

"When it feels natural, you can take the map and lead. I'll just kick back and relax."

They found the orchid farm by its position on the map and a sign of hand-painted orchid flowers. It was a large establishment on a hill, with views over the valleys. The showroom contained hundreds of orchid plants in prime bloom, and a plethora of varieties, from giant to tiny, in a rainbow of colors.

Orchid flowers, cherry blossoms. At least plants have it figured out. Inventions and invitations.

They continued to climb steeply on a one-lane road through a bamboo grove. They stood on the pedals most of the way to the junction with a two-way road, which they took upward. On a hunch, they took a left to continue up steep switchbacks to an empty parking lot on the crest of the mountain. There they found spotless public toilets, typical of Japan, and a large map in Japanese and English. Hoping for a view to the north, they pushed their bikes along a narrow path beneath a defunct chairlift, covered with rust. They followed this to a modern building that turned out to be an abandoned hotel. The doors were open, and inside they found a dining room. Windows were broken and restaurant equipment lay about. Ghosts were strewn everywhere.

They went out on the terrace, dodging broken floorboards. The view over the inland sea to the north and northeast was pristine Japan, in contrast to the chaos inside the hotel. There were many islands, with Honshu distant, and looking down they saw fishing villages, inlets, ports and farms.

They returned to the parking lot and found another road, which took them to the summit of Mount Takami and a lookout point, where a woman was having a *hanami* picnic with her granddaughter, with homemade bento boxes and drinks under a blooming pink plum tree. The view to the south was cloudless, and the wind had stopped, so they ate their rice balls, dried fish, oranges and peanuts, prepared in the Japanese style with little salt and no oil. Before them stretched islands as far as they could see, and below was a monumental suspension bridge.

"It was a good climb getting here. For somebody writing a book, you're sure in great shape. When my heart was pounding, you weren't even breathing hard."

"Oh, but I was. I'm just too proud to show it."

They descended fast from their high perch to the coastal road to sail along the shoreline and wind in and out with the terrain through villages, farms, forests, sandy beaches and rock outcroppings. They came to a sign showing the bicycle entrance to the suspension bridge, with a box in which to drop a 100 yen coin. It was a dedicated, two-way bicycle road that wound its way gently upward to the lower level of the bridge, reserved for bicycles and pedestrians. The crossing was long and high in the air. No other people were encountered.

"They built this just for us!"

At the end of the bridge, they took the bicycle ramp down to the coastal road of Innoshima.

"I want to see Treasure Island with Peter Pan and Captain Hook!"

"Well, you're right, Sara. According to the visitor's map, this island was a haven for pirates in the fourteenth to sixteenth centuries, and some of their castles can be visited, but all that is at relatively low altitude. If you want to climb again, I see a small road that will take us up to the summit of Mount Shirataki, which is at 227 meters. The map shows statues there."

They climbed to a first ridge, admired the views, and continued down to a fork in the road, decorated with a contemporary steel sculpture. Next they climbed steeply to a parking lot, where they found two cherry trees in partial bloom and others in bud. A miniature monorail wound its way up the mountain. It was a cog railroad with a gasoline-powered engine and one car about 1 meter long. It seemed like an ingenious, way to carry cargo up a mountain.

They parked the bikes and continued on a footpath with stone steps and planted shrubs and shortly encountered a young woman with a young child in tow. She carried a large shoulder bag. The boy was having trouble with the steps. They said, "*Konichiwa!*" She returned the greeting in English, and the boy gave them a big smile and held out his arms. He was rewarded with a piggyback ride to the top. The young mother knew some English, so they exchanged the usual "Where are you from?" She lived close by, at the bottom of the hill. They were coming up for a *hanami* picnic. At the top of the ridge, they passed through a covered gateway and entered the compound of what seemed to be a shrine with a tile roof. No guardian was evident, but they were not alone. Granite statues were everywhere.

To the right and above was a group of monumental religious figures, including Buddha and his disciples. Behind these, they followed a grand avenue to the top of the mountain, walking between lines and through groups of statues. At the top was a final cluster of large figures, an observation platform and a large bronze bell under an ornate tile roof. They sounded it by pulling back a horizontally suspended log and letting go. The deep sound rolled out like gentle thunder over the mountains, valleys and sea. To the north they saw Mount Takami, where they had snacked, and behind that Honshu and Onomichi, the town where they had spent the night. To the west was the gleaming white suspension bridge with its lower level for cyclists. Down a path they found an altar and a strange square stone block, with the sandy soil raked around it in a circle. On the top surface, an orange and black butterfly was soaking up the warm spring sun. To the south and southeast they saw islands floating on the blue-green Seto Sea. Just below were farms, ports and towns, and a large glass structure surrounded by lawns, which were still wearing their yellow-brown winter coats. According to the map, this was the Prefecture Flower Center.

"We couldn't ask for better weather. Perfect for these short climbs. I just realized the places we've biked together have been almost flat, until now. Climbing seems so easy for you."

"You're right. It makes my heart happy to bite into the uphill and fly on the downhill. But you can't go up forever."

They descended the aisle of statues and returned to the shrine, where they were greeted by the guardian, who gave them a bag of oranges and a pamphlet in English. They feasted on the oranges, while reading the pamphlet. "The Goddess of Mercy Hall was built by a pirate clan about 430 years ago. The approximately 700 statues were sculpted 150 years ago by Denroku Kashihara, a native of Innoshima, with the help of two assistants. After each chisel stroke, he bowed three times to inscribe his faith in the granite images."

Beyond the shrine, they explored another outcropping of granite, covered with monumental statues and bas-reliefs. It seemed miraculous that three people using hand tools had carved so many massive and elaborate sculptures in hard granite.

They descended on foot, admiring the red and white camellias and the flowering plum trees. Next came the fast, cool drop on bikes to the coastal plain, where they visited the Flower Center, which was wide open, devoid of guardians and visitors. The vast grounds were in early spring mode, with extensive plantings of flowers, towers and spheres of petunias in colored sectors (sometimes in spirals), ornamental cabbage plants, planted in designs and hyacinths. The greenhouse was a tropical forest with exotic plants on several levels, including cycad ferns, full-size palm trees and a large collection of orchids in bloom. There were places to sit, a pond and a feeling of open coolness. They continued their walk on the grounds and found a series of plum trees in full pink bloom. As they were leaving, they noticed a folding bicycle set up for touring with bags, but no cyclist was apparent. They had seen nobody during the entire visit.

Having spent much of the day exploring, they felt like riding, so they paralleled the coast to hook up with a larger road and climb inland. It took them back over the island to the north coast, which they followed southeast over coastal headlands and high points. At times they were slowed by headwinds. The views were of forest coming down to sandy beaches, but few villages. This was prime road biking: continuous change with tight corners, climbs and drops. Sara was leading at a lively pace. They came to a straight stretch and rode side by side. He was feeling euphoric.

"Why do I feel this intense pleasure? Is it endorphins?"

"Maybe they're part of it. Exercise is addictive. Does your mind wander?"

"It does. I dream. The bike carries me far away sometimes. Sometimes into the past or the future."

"Where have you been today?"

"I was in rural France on the first warm day of spring. And you?"

"I was taking a medical exam, but I didn't know the subject. I was in the wrong room, taking the wrong exam. So I shifted down, and they announced that everybody was in the wrong room, but me. Everybody left, but me, and they handed me the exam paper for the subject I knew. What happened in your bicycle dream?"

"I rode through barren fields and woods with no leaves. The woods were carpeted in delicate, white flowers: snow drops and orchids. I tried to walk through them, but I was crushing them with my feet."

The day was ending; the lodging game was getting close, so they stopped in a gas station and asked, "*Hotelu, minshuku dokodeska?*" The answer was to point down the road and say, "Akasaki," which they surmised was the next town, just before the bridge they saw in the far distance. In Akasaki port, with a little more asking, they were shown a multistory business hotel. It was getting dark, and the air temperature was falling.

They took a traditional Japanese room, with bath. Their bicycles were parked in a storage room. The air had turned cold when they set out in search of food. The old town was nearly deserted, with a few empty bars and clubs. They found the restaurant recommended by the man at the hotel desk. They slid open the door and passed into a small room with a few tables and a sushi bar. There were no other clients, just a man and a woman behind the bar. They sat down to the obvious confusion and embarrassment of their hosts. They had no common language; they were extraterrestrials, just landed, trying to find food. A non-conversation ensued.

Sara said, "*Nihon ryori suki des*," meaning "We like Japanese food." There was a smile from the other side of the bar, but no sign of recognition. She said, "Miso?" and pointed to a large pot on a hotplate. After some hesitation, they were served hot miso soup with a generous portion of large, tasty clams. Next, they tried pointing to various pieces of fish, asking for sashimi and then for sushi. The fish was prepared expertly before them: high-class and beautifully presented. They also ordered rice, and thus they ended up eating a full dinner and having the first of many linguistic adventures in restaurants, where the menu was in Japanese, but with no pictures, and nobody spoke English.

The hotel room was small, with the futons taking up most of the floor space when the low table was pushed to the side. *Yukatas*, haori jackets and towels were laid out on the futons, which were covered with thick down comforters. There was a TV, tea equipment and the standard overhead florescent light fixture controlled by a pull string. It could be set at three intensities, the last being a dim night-light. The bathroom plus toilet was a modular, plastic design. After bathing and washing out their biking clothes, they sat on their futons and tried to reconstruct the events of the day. Sara began.

"Another day in paradise! What a perfect start to our bike trip. There was so much to see, and we hardly saw half of it."

"I'm surprised, too, by how much there was. Elsewhere, the sculptures would be a World Heritage Site, but here they belong to the landscape. No signs, no entry fee, and that's part of their natural serenity. According to the map information, before the sculptures, there was a holy site with a lodge on a mountaintop, strewn with granite boulders. I can't imagine how they were sculpted. Just moving them around would be difficult. The carving is first rate, with both comic and serious characters. All the emotions are there. They're like Edo woodblock prints in black and white stone, and the religious figures are joyous. The sculptors worked with dedication and intensity. I still can't understand how they did so much."

"I agree, but there was more. There was magic. There was the calm of the tea ceremony and the meeting of the land, sea and sky… a special place for the human spirit. And the young mother and her son were so cute together! She's a beauty, with those finely shaped Asian eyes. They brought life to the natural grace of the statues."

"The oranges tasted so good! They were the perfect gift. The guidebook says we're in an orange producing region. Let's hope for more."

"And it's been a flower day. Orchids are prized here. The Flower Center was wide open. Nobody seems to worry about theft."

"There was hardly any traffic, and the few drivers were courteous. The ride along the coast provided lots of ups and downs, with different sights and smells at every turn. We climbed a lot today."

"Did you notice the bird calls coming from the woods?"

"I did, and there were exotic odors from the vegetation, and there were curious bee hives. Tomorrow is another day and more islands… ready for lights out?"

She hesitated; then said, "Just one request…"

"Don't snore?"

"You can snore all you like, but only if you will hold my hand while I fall asleep."

She is asleep in a second. He is too excited to sleep. The room is silent, except for the sound of her breathing. Hand in hand, he feels her warmth — a human connection at long last — the magnetic pull he missed so much. A door opens in his imagination, letting sounds filter forward from the past. He hears the voice, the giggle, the familiar resonance. He responds,

You mock me — you enjoy my predicament! I would rather have a note of sympathy. A note of symphony? You jest. OK, I'll take symphony. Something romantic. Mahler? Forgive me. I'm only human, lying on a futon holding her hand. I need this intimacy desperately. I'll be awake all night, savoring every second, holding her hand, lying here on my back, not daring to breathe. Are you jealous? OK, so she has me by the hand — in tow, tethered. She wore me out today. Tired and tethered, I am. Tarred and feathered you say? So you don't approve of my adventure? Oh, you don't approve of my fatherly decorum? Go for it, you say? If only it were so simple... but she laid out the futons with barely a foot between them. This is my reward for patience. I'll ride this road as far as I can, right into the rainbow or the hailstorm or even the tsunami.

They bought breakfast bentos in a supermarket and sat on a sun-warmed concrete sea wall, eating their rice balls, pickles, eggs and smoked fish, like true bicycle gypsies. Sara needed to call Mama-san, so they stopped in a convenience store to buy a prepaid phone card, and they found a phone booth. She managed to tell Mama-san where they had been, and that all was OK.

They paused on the dedicated bicycle approach to the bridge to Ikuchijima, admiring flowering plum and cherry trees in nearly full bloom. In the bridge's wide bicycle lane, they felt like seagulls, crossing the strait beneath the two triangular towers. Once on Ikuchijima, they decided to follow the official bicycle path, staying on the coastal plain, near the water. The sky was cloudless, with little wind. They stopped for ice cream, and rode to the town of Setoda, where they visited the art museum and admired ancient scrolls, paintings and wooden statues. Much of the coastal road had a separate bike and pedestrian lane, along the water. The beaches were deserted and unspoiled, but equipped for large crowds in high season. They admired a wind-driven sculpture implanted on a rock at the edge of the water. The Tatara Bridge to Omishima Island was visible from a long distance. Its pointed, double towers seemed more like contemporary art, than objects of practical value. The climb to the bridge and the crossing were on a bike lane. On the bridge, they felt pulled along weightlessly by the suspension cables that vanished to a high point on either side of each tower.

The far side brought them to a bike path that gently climbed through farmland over the center of the island. They saw increasing numbers of blooming cherry trees and many ornamental plums. Some were just beginning to lose their petals. The path seemed to be following a railroad grade, and the surface was paved and in good condition. The grade was constant; the rhythmic moving of his legs was a lullaby for daydreams.

I can't keep up with her. She's never out of breath — just out of reach. What does she see in me? The bike, the bike… so I fix her bike. I pump her tires. She's the beauty. I'm the beast. Just one kiss, and I'm her prince in "La Belle et la Bête," the fantasy fairytale. But why me — the éminence grise, the bike mechanic, the stagehand? So I play the clown professor in Der blaue Engel. Sara's the perfect Marlene Dietrich. Before, in New York, I hid behind my professor mask. Now it's fallen, exposing a clown… a happy clown. Could I be Quasimodo, Hugo's hunchback? I'm in love with Sara's Esmeralda. But wait! I could be Erik, the phantom of the Paris Opera. Sara's my Christine, and I'm her angel of music with the rotting face. It's too trite to be true. I'll die so she can love somebody else. Where did Gaston Leroux find his fantôme? Was there a real young woman in Gaston's life? A dancer from the ballet? Only an impossible desire could inspire the romance in the Fantôme de l'Opéra. Desire the impossible. Prolong desire until the sakura fall, tasting the food of love —oh the desiring of it! So I'm the gothic novel, the fallen professor, the hunchback, the phantom — trapped in this romantic plot! Slow down. Snow down sakura petals, Sara petals. I pedal my heart out, chasing her through a gothic novel. She's boundless spring. I stand. I sit. I brake. I lean. Shift up. Shift down. Shift all around the town. But catch her I cannot.

They followed a river on the downgrade to the western coast, where the *Touring Mapple* map showed an *onsen*, which they found by asking for directions; otherwise, there was no way of knowing that the white, modern building just behind the sandy beach was a public bathhouse. They locked up the bikes and entered, exchanging their shoes for slippers. The young woman at the desk spoke no English, but she sold them tickets and small towels, and she indicated the entrance for men (in blue) and for women (in pink). They promised to meet in the lobby at the massage chairs in an hour and a half.

The first room had clothes lockers; keys were worn on a wrist strap. Through sliding glass doors were high ceilings and large windows, looking toward the ocean. Part of the room was taken by rows of washing stations, where bathers clean their bodies before taking the soaking baths. He sat on a low plastic stool. There were shampoos and hair rinses, but no way to know which was which from the Japanese characters. Each station had a standard fixture with a faucet and showerhead on a flexible hose. There were disposable plastic razors. He washed, using the shower. He heard splashing. Another man filled a plastic tub with water and doused himself, sitting on his low stool. He found this sensual hit of hot water more fun than the shower. Other bathers used the small towel as a washcloth, so he did the same, scrubbing everywhere. When he had done his washing time, he tried the first bath, a waist deep pool with hot water flowing through it from a cascade at the far end. Men held their towel discretely in front of their genitals. Once in the bath it was folded and put on the edge of the pool or on their heads. The few children just ran around naked. He soon got hot and decided to see what was behind the door in the wall of steamed-up glass. Outside air was a cold shock, but he quickly got hot again in the stone outdoor bath. He sat up to his chin with his towel on his head with a view of the beach, the sea and the islands. The sun was about to set, and the sky was a calico of black, blue, pink and red.

At the center of this backdrop the sun races downward, toward night; it gathers crimson blankets and sinks into a bed of burning roses; they splash slowly upward. As the sun finally quenches in the ocean mass, a shape appears above the horizon — it's a face, faint but clear in embers and afterglow. It lingers, and as he watches, the dead love of his life vanishes in gray smoke, leaving ashes hanging and then drifting downward in the darkened sky, like fragments of exploded fireworks. Two men are talking at the other end of the outdoor bath. He is frozen in the hot water.

Shaken, he goes back inside. Taking a clue from another bather, he wrings out his towel and returns to the dressing room. The towel serves as a sponge to remove excess water from his skin. An electric fan finishes the drying. There are mirrors and disposable plastic combs. Dried and dressed, he returns to the lobby, where he finds Sara in a massage chair.

"I'm in heaven. Exquisite bath, and this thing gives a mean massage!"

"I'll try it. Did you watch the sunset?"

"Sure did. What a spectacle, and I'm cleaner than I thought possible. There were children and women of all ages. Everybody was happy!"

The woman at the desk managed to explain that the *onsen* did not have lodging, so she called a local *minshuku* for them that did. One of attendants drove ahead while they followed on the bikes. After a short distance they came to a traditional house, bearing no indication from the outside it was a guesthouse. An elderly woman greeted them at the door, and led them through a small garden and into a Japanese home. After putting on slippers, they were taken to their room. They removed their slippers and stepped into a tatami room decorated in carved woodwork, screens, an alcove with an *ikebana* and antiques, including a large doll in a glass case. Their hostess spoke no English, but they managed to understand that dinner would be served in an hour.

They took a walk on the beach. It was dark and starting to rain. The air smelled salty from the wind coming over the water. Back in the house, their hostess opened the room adjacent to theirs, where they found a low table set for two with cushions for sitting or kneeling. A Japanese dinner was waiting, with pickles, miso soup, sashimi, a meat and vegetable dish cooking on the alcohol-fired brazier, various breaded delicacies on skewers and *oden*, the mixture of ingredients simmered in a soy-flavored dashi broth. It included eggs, daikon, fish cakes and a gelatinous cake, called *konnyaku*, according to the guidebook.

"So, how do you feel after a day of biking and then bathing with naked men?"

"Mellow but not marshmellow. More like Japanese gelatinous mellow — after the *onsen* and a sumptuous dinner in this beautiful house with the best of company.

The ride was good — not quite as spectacular as yesterday, but a full day with fine ocean views. On Ikuchijima the bike path avoided hills, so I missed the climbing. The best part of the ride was on Omishima on the railroad grade, riding through the farms and seeing sakura blossoms, nearly at their peak. As usual, the best cycling was off the main path, away from towns. The *onsen* was the highlight of the day for me. Sitting outside in cold air, immersed in hot water, watching the sun go down over the sea and islands — that was a timeless experience, and it transported me someplace else… where I'd been afraid to go."

"But you did go — and you came back. I envy you. I was also transported, but I was afraid of not returning, so I held back. I wanted to let myself go… I liked being naked with women I didn't know and feeling at ease with them. There are so many body types! The staff at the *onsen* were helpful in finding us a place to stay. Our hostess is elegant and beautiful. She must be in her late seventies. People are interested in our welfare and ready to forgive our Western looks, odd behavior and lack of Japanese language. I have the impression they like cyclists."

"Sleepy?"

"Yes, and it's your turn for a request."

"Mine is the same as yours last night: would you hold my hand as I fall asleep?"

"Request granted with pleasure. Can I make another request? Could I hear a bedtime poem?"

Birds at the feeder

Birds at the feeder
Flashes of white, yellow

On black, brown, rust
Heads cocked, tails twitching
Movement too fast to see.

Dive for seeds and suet
Snatch a bite from danger
Retreat to safe branches
And peck open the large
Black and white sunflower seeds.

Violent tapping with toes
Holding the seed, but never
A miss. No friendly fire.
Perfect release of embryo
From the tough integument.

Then return in a swoop
Of flashing wings to raid,
Even less afraid, the feeder
And snatch another bite
Defying the odds of life.

Counting and still counting
The wing strokes, heartbeats
The minutes and seconds
Enabled by a single seed
Justifying the risk.

Is life for you as simple
As a claw grasp in landing?
A finely tuned ascent?
Or a minor conflict over
Access to food and love?

Do you worry, care, regret?
Is the future a mirror of
Past misadventures?
What is the state of
Your fear, your soul?

You answer in movement,
Small chirps and songs
But with all your meaning
The response to my questions
Remains obscured in language.

His sleep was long and intense, thanks to the exercise and the silence, but just before morning he had a dream – like the footsteps and the wind symphony, but shorter. His dream was haunted by distant screams. He was chilled and half awake. Sara seemed deep in sleep. He listened to her breathing, calming himself and trying to forget the lingering screams. Her breathing recalled another existence. He was drawn to but afraid to approach her warmth, and for a second he thought she was someone else.

She lay awake, thinking about anthropology.

Humans group for survival. Cooperation crosses kin boundaries. Conflicts cross too. What switches between peace and war? Genes? Groups cross out to counter inbreeding. Is racism the clan defending its genes? Does the incest taboo drive outbreeding? How to break free of instinct and culture? How to cross the divide when the sakura are in full bloom?

The morning was cloudy with rain on the horizon and a salty wind from the sea. During breakfast, Sara noticed a fleeting distance in his eyes, and she remembered the same look in her father's face.

"What are you thinking about?"

"Just recalling a strange dream. I heard faint sounds, like screaming in the distance."

"A human voice?"

"A high voice — maybe a woman's. Just guessing, though. Maybe it was an animal? A dream has a life of its own. It's so imprecise, but sure of itself. It wasn't really a nightmare. There was no fear, and somehow the voice was familiar. I couldn't quite place it. What have you been thinking, Sara?"

"Anthropology, mostly, and racism and war."

"Sounds like an interesting connection. What's the link?"

"The incest taboo. Human groups, clans, nations… heterosis…"

"Heterosis?"

"Hybrid vigor. Outcrossing counters inbreeding, but it conflicts with group identity. Racism and war defend the group, but even large communities need fresh gene variants. The human species is too homogeneous. Look at Japan, an extreme example: little immigration, falling birth rates. Bad genetics make bad demographics. The incest taboo counters island isolation, but it can't compensate for the drift toward homozygosity. I wonder what turns it off and on. The Earth is a genetic island. Just some stray thoughts. They probably don't mean much…"

"Fascinating, Sara. The incest taboo can break down, for instance in royalty, but love is normally the driver of heterosis. That's the hope for Cuba, where the white/black boundary has blurred into many shades of brown. Got to go there some day…"

The *Touring Mapple* map showed small roads crossing the backbone of the island. They decided to continue along the seashore and turn inland to pick up the coastal road on the opposite side. The ocean had exchanged its blue coat for green, with tufts of white. A village seemed to be in the right spot for the road cutting inland. They followed a narrow lane between the houses, climbing steeply up a valley. Passing through orange groves, the road became too narrow to be the one they wanted. But the sun had come out, and it felt good to climb, so they continued up the valley anyway, passing a few farmhouses and more orange groves. The weather had turned warm and sunny. The road ended at a small Shinto shrine, surrounded by flowering fruit trees. They were pleased with their discovery, and descended back to the main road. The junction they had been looking for was just around the next bend, clearly marked.

The climb over the island was gentle, and then the coastal ride hugged the water line, winding in and out of the topography. There was no traffic — just a few clouds in a blue sky without wind. They stopped in a cove to snack on tiny dried fish and sliced almonds. The bridge to Hakatajima Island was of conventional architecture, but with wide lanes for bicycles. The strait was narrow, and looking down, they saw swift currents.

The tourist map showed cherry blossoms on the north end of Hakatajima, and the *Touring Mapple* map showed a road leading to them. They took this one-lane, steep road through forest, with views over the straits. They stopped to watch the water flowing fast — a powerful and vast river created by the tide. The top was a major effort, but worth it for the sakura cherry blossom viewing festival with hot food served from a small building. There were cherry trees everywhere, with some in nearly full bloom and others on the brink. The trees were hung with red and white-sectored paper lanterns. People were having *hanami* picnics on tablecloths spread in the shade. Spring had kept her promise of return.

They lunched on octopus and *oden*, served on skewers,

and they climbed the observation platform for long, clear views over the islands before and behind them. There was a small shrine, and in the place above the door normally reserved for a carving of a fierce dragon, they noticed a piece of driftwood that looked like the real thing. He stopped.

"Look at that dragon. It fooled me for a moment."

"Yes, it's scarier than a carving. Isn't it interesting how we expect a dragon to be there, so we fill in the image where it's really just a piece of driftwood."

"It says something about art. It's really the observer who creates the art with suggestions from the artist, but what are the limits?"

"Maybe we can go forward and backward in time, just using our imagination!"

"Let's try, Sara. Back is easy, but going forward, I'm not sure. Just looking at these buds about to bloom… can we desire them into full, glorious flowering, and instantly make this entire orchard a riot of white blossoms?"

She closed her eyes.

"Yes, almost, but incompletely. It works better with my eyes closed, but even then the desire isn't satisfied. So there's your answer: keep wanting until you can't stand it; then let the whole mountain explode in pure, white sakura!"

"I'll remember that."

He took another look at the dragon. There were clearly two dragons, and he thought they were making love.

They descended to the east, passing a sign indicating they had been in Hiraki Mountain Flower Park. They were attracted to a path with sculptures and bonsais, leading to a traditional house with an elaborate Japanese garden. It did not seem possible such a perfect garden could belong to a private house. Farther down the road, they discovered a traditional Chinese lantern, but about five meters high, made from massive flat stones, held in place only by their weight. They retraced their steps and got back on the bicycle route leading to the bridge crossing to Oshima Island.

Oshima was forest, orange groves and seacoast, in descending order. The coastal road was tempting, but they stayed on the interior bike route, having decided to make it to Shikoku that evening. As they neared the final bridge leading to Shikoku, they nevertheless left the bike route to climb 200 meters for an evening view. A steep road took them to a lookout with scenery in all directions, including the last set of bridges and the gleaming white city of Imabari.

They watch the sun slip beyond the islands and bridges. A fiery dragon of a sunset, quenching itself in a cold black sea, grasping at black islands — slowly writhing, hanging… extinguishing in a puff of golden steam. The air chills, and he puts on his wind pants, sweater and jacket. Sara is transfixed by the ending of the sunset. He attaches his lights, and she says, "Please start down, I'll catch up in a second."

> *Red fire fading cold black. Time for warm clothes. Night, falling fire, steam. Sensuous black overtakes light. Drunk on fading, fire, going down, gone my youth, drunk on fire on falling black.*

She attaches her lights, but doesn't turn them on, to not disturb the lingering luminous haze that envelopes her and the mountain. She has not changed to warm clothes, and the cold air feels good as she starts down, dropping fast, believing she can catch him before the bottom.

> *Catch him if I can. I can. Fast down. Yes, speed — unlimited. Road clear. Clear. Cold clear wind, last light, gravity… flying fast. Bird diving free, pure, clean free fall.*

*Explosion! Head on! **Monster**! Windshield! Brake! **Skid**! Back right. Missed me. Alive. Alive?*

*Black car fast. My lane! No lights! I'm falling fast, too fast, shaking. Bike shimmy. **Grab top tube**, knees, tube, brake, brake... Clip out. Shaking cold terror. Death so close, too close to be true, there, right in my face.*

Sara is trembling, the top tube pressed between her knees to stabilize the bike, hands on the brake levers. She shakes with fear, frozen. She nearly forgets to clip out of the pedals; then stands in shock at the side of the road; puts down the bike and trembles hard and harder. It doesn't get better. Finally, she sees a dim point of light moving side-to-side, coming from around the bend below. He is climbing up to look for her.

He is just below her when she speaks his name; then he is with her, arms around her, wrapping her in his jacket, rubbing her back and shoulders. He gets out her warm clothes and helps her dress in tights, wind pants, fingered gloves, fleece sweater and jacket. They turn on her lights and descend slowly to the main road and bike path. There is light at the entrance to the bridge. They sit on a bench. He gives her a chocolate bar. She trembles, even with his arm around her shoulders. The sugar kicks in, and the shaking begins to subside.

"I got cold. I guess I went into shock. So stupid of me not to dress before starting down. Maybe I was drugged by the sunset. I'll be OK now. This is the last bridge to Shikoku. I'll be fine in a minute. The sugar helps. Thank you. Thank you for being there for me. Thank you for waiting for me. Thank you for coming for me."

They ride the island hopping, five-towered, monumental suspension bridge with just a hint of light on the horizon. A full moon rises from behind the mountain where they had watched the sunset. The bridge crosses two small islands on its four kilometer and six span traverse to Shikoku. It's a highflying ride, a night bird sailing on the wind.

On the Shikoku side, the bike lane descends on a spiral ramp. They see below a lit building, and thinking they will ask for directions to lodging, they follow the bicycle path to the door of what looks sort of like a hotel. It turns out to be the Sunrise Itoyama, the bicycle hotel for the Shimanami Kaido. They find themselves warm and safe in an elegant hostel. The rooms and dining room look out on the sea and the bridge they have just crossed. They agree to meet in the dining room after their baths.

It's an Italian restaurant. He asks for a bottle of Prosecco and takes a table with a panoramic view of the bridge, lit in bluish white. No sign of Sara. Then he realizes she is there in front of him, in silhouette, but outside the glass windows, standing on the grass with her back toward him. He finds her gazing at the bridge and takes her hand. She seems calm at first, but even in the dim light her face shows trauma.

"I'm being a burden, I know."

"You've had a scare."

"I missed by a few inches. It couldn't have been closer. It lasted less than a second from start to finish, but it's left me terrified to the core."

"And I was waiting for you near the bottom, and a car came up fast. It was black, driven I think by a man, with maybe a woman passenger. I figured they were heading up for the sunset. I thought it strange that their lights were off. I had a sudden feeling of danger, and I started climbing back up."

"For me the car was a massive black monster coming head-on out of nowhere. My right hand was already on the rear brake. I jammed it. It was my rear wheel skidding that turned the bike toward the other lane. I released and the tire gripped. The monster passed, almost touching me. Then I realized what had happened, that I had been so close to death, like the near cadavers brought into the emergency room, hopeless victims of road accidents. I often wondered what it would be like. I even imagined it as a solution."

"A solution? What do you mean, Sara?"

"I mean the death wish I've struggled with since my parents were killed."

"You mean you've just relived the last second in your parents' lives."

"That's right. I confronted their death head-on and swerved in the last second."

"Then, Sara, you should be rejoicing."

"I can't. This is different. My parents were killed by a drunk in the wrong lane."

She walks away from him, into the shadows. He comes up behind her, and he sees her shoulders shaking. She is sobbing. She turns to face him.

"This was different. It was my fault. I was in the wrong lane."

He holds her like Mama-san in Hiroshima, as she fights grief, terror, trauma and guilt.

The waitress opens the bottle of Prosecco, taking care not to let the cork pop. The light-yellow liquid traps bubbles that escape and burst on the surface. There is silence; then he raises his glass.

"Welcome to Shikoku, Sara. You crossed the last bridge. You made your choice, and it was the brave one."

"I can't believe I started out in the wrong lane. Did I think I was in the USA? Was I drunk? No, deep down I knew right away it was my fault, not a mistake, and that started the shaking that made the bike shimmy and almost crash. I've not felt such terror since Hiroshima."

She pauses, looks over his shoulder at the illuminated bridge, and then at him, "I only swerved because I knew you were there, waiting for me."

"I'll always be there for you, Sara. Always and forever."

They forced themselves into normal conversation with him taking the lead. The food was Italian, but in Japanese style. The bridge was before them, with its white towers gleaming through the darkness, framed by panoramic, two story, glass windows. They put on their normality masks, and she began the daily recap, hesitantly at first, and then as if nothing had happened.

"It was really a fine day. I liked taking the wrong road; it was right for seeing the valley with the orange trees and the intimate shrine in such a special place. And I liked the hard climb to the sakura park, with the delicious *oden*, looking out on the young blossoms — teenage virility on the brink of bursting out all over the summit of sakura desire."

"And I was knocked out by the sunset, and the night ride over the bridge, then discovering this cozy place — so unplanned and unexpected. The day worked out, and lucky we are. I wish we had a week to explore each island, but now we're on Shikoku at last. What should we do next, trusted Sara guide? It's so vast, compared to these small islands."

"For contrast, we could go to Matsuyama, the big town of Shikoku. The guidebook says there's a medieval castle there, and the famous Dogo Onsen, one of the oldest in Japan. A cyclist I met in the lobby suggested a guesthouse nearby. A city would be an interesting change, and I think we can ride there via a village that has an *onsen* on the beach and a youth hostel."

"Sounds like a good plan. According to the map, we could cross the interior mountains, ride down the western coast of Shikoku and back over mountains to arrive in

Maysuyama from the interior. Maybe we can lose ourselves — forget time and places. I want to savor the feeling of having a lifetime ahead without commitments, just adventure and beauty."

"It's all there, just down the road. The addictive road where we chase the mirage…"

"And catch it."

There is a long silence

"Sara, I have an idea. I want to see you fly. I feel that riding with me might be clipping your wings."

"Your pace is my pace."

"But you're a natural climber. I've never seen you out of breath. You seem to have unlimited oxygen. So please feel free to go ahead. You can wait for me at the top or even descend and do the hill twice. I'll enjoy watching you defy gravity. It'll be your interval training."

"I'll think about it."

"It will be strange to be in western beds tonight. Will you sing me a lullaby?"

She thinks for a moment, "It's hard to sing after so much emotion, but I'll sing 'Nana' from the seven Spanish songs of Manuel de Falla. It might help. My mother often sang it to soothe me into sleep."

Soon in their room, lying in the dark, her voice is light, pure, ethereal, rich, simple and direct. The Spanish lullaby soothes and smoothes the rumpled air of the room. Lights off, eyes closed, sinking slowly. No bubbles. Gentle sounds of music and healing shore waves.

So Sara has a dark side. Her wounds are fresh after ten years, but today she swerved… missing death, but only in the last microsecond. She's deeply shaken. Was it a moment of jet lag that sent her down the wrong side of the road? What about the black car? Who was driving it?

Were they coming to get her, forcing her to choose? Who's to say where the truth lies? It often does, but I'm sure of one thing. She needs me.

> *It was easy to die with my hand on the brake lever… I was road kill on a car hood. What does he think of me? He saved me with his warmth; drew me away from the precipice. Now to find the sleep and peace I need. Sing me another lullaby please. I desperately miss you, Mama. I miss you so deeply.*

The next morning was pure sun. Saturday in bicycle land, with families renting or unloading bikes for a weekend or a day ride. A group of mostly Polish cyclists had ridden from Beijing, and now they were headed to Tokyo for a flight to Los Angeles and a traverse of the USA. They had a van to carry camping gear. Camping or lodging was found as they went. There was also a group of schoolgirls in identical sports clothes, fixing their hair before putting on their helmets. A couple unloaded racing bikes from a van. It was a party.

They rode through Imabari, and then into the mountains, leaving the main road for a small one that narrowed and recaptured the charm of rural Japan, with the grade increasing abruptly. Sara was riding behind him.

"Hello Sara back there. Please go ahead. I'd like to see you attack this thing."

He felt her go by as a peripheral blur, then a rush of wind. She was standing on the pedals when she rounded the next corner. She reappeared a few minutes later, descending and grinning. In another five minutes she passed in full sprint. This time he could hear her breathing. When he reached the pass she was just catching up to him again, after three intervals to match his single climb. He was completely out of breath, but she was just breathing deeply and laughing. They stopped to snack at the top.

"So now I believe your story about the Col d'Aubisque. You're some kind of metabolic mutant. You've got unbelievable energy. You're a born climber. You're amazing! I can't wait to watch you on the next hill."

So, mutant am I? Extraterrestrial? Careful, go easy. Showing off? Aubisque? Why not? It's just between us. I trust him, and I need a strong body to heal my sick soul. So let it happen, see where it leads. Unravel this puzzle — one CLUH at a time.

At the summit, the one-lane mountain road changed into a standard two-lane, which was convenient for a fast descent to the coast. In the youth hostel in the seaside village of Hojotsuji, they were greeted warmly by the proprietor and his dog. They went directly to the nearby *onsen*, which was like the first one, with the same system of washing stations and indoor and outdoor pools. Some were filled with seawater, perhaps from a seaside hot spring. Outside there was an unobstructed view of the sea. He could hear female voices beyond a bamboo screen. The air temperature dropped with the last piece of sun, but the sky remained inflamed, and then slowly extinguished. There was a light wind, adding to the contrast in sensations between his immersed body and exposed head. The sky filled with golden light and the high-scattered clouds turned scarlet against deepening black. He was joined by other men, who had timed their visit to catch the sunset. He finally returned to the inside bath for a final soak, before drying and dressing, and then he met Sara in the lobby.

"What a scene in the ladies' section, with lots of young children, and outdoors was pure art. The sky never stopped changing. Those last vermillion clouds against the black were so three-dimensional! I wanted to fly through them."

Back in the youth hostel, dinner had been prepared by their warmly eccentric host. They talked about the day and Sara's interval training on the climbs.

"Are you sure you didn't mind my hill climbing antics?"

"I loved seeing your grinning face each time you passed me coming down. I thought I was a strong rider, but I can't imagine climbing that fast. You inspire me. I'll try to be more aggressive, but I could never catch up with you. I'm happy with my role of observer. Please continue, but don't forget to wait at the top!"

There was a massage chair in their room, and thanks to the hot baths, the food, drink and the massage, they melted into sleep. He awoke during the night and lay awake, wondering at his luck.

I'm in Japan with a hill-climbing wonder. How does she do it? Now I've got a challenge. I've got to give more — got to concentrate on breathing and finding new lungs. I need mental power over my muscles. I want to show that I appreciate her tolerance of my pace. Yes, I'm jealous of her youth and vigor. I thought I was a strong rider, but I can't begin to compete with her, and that's an obstacle worth overcoming to gain esteem in her eyes. She would never pressure me, but it's not really the pace. It's the intent. I want to show her I'm trying to gain a foothold in her world — to climb out of my aging body and meet on her turf.

The next morning they rode down the coast, and then over a mountain pass, where Sara again did three climbs for his single. He reveled in seeing her fly by him going both up and down. It was easy for her, and he did increase his pace, making the top with a deep oxygen deficit, aches in his legs and a racing heart. It felt good, and he recovered fast enough to be convinced the extreme exercise was good for him.

At last they dropped into the city of Matsuyama, near the Dogo hot spring and the guesthouse. It was Sunday, and Dogo Park was filled with cherry trees in glorious, explosive climax. Tablecloths were spread under the sakura blossoms, and the park was covered with people having their *hanami* picnic, with food either brought with them or bought from stands lining the paths. Clouds of smoke rose from charcoal braziers, and beer and sake flowed. Many men and women were in kimonos. There was singing and laughter and invitations to share food and drink. They ate squid, octopus, fish and sweets. It was a perfect day. They checked into the guesthouse and took baths in the historical Dogo Onsen, visiting the Imperial apartment afterwards. The guesthouse had a roof terrace, so still warm from the *onsen,* they watched the moon rise over Matsuyama.

"Sara, it was a good idea of yours to be in Matsuyama on a Sunday for the height of the sakura. People are happy, and the weather is perfect. The cherry blossoms are like white puffy clouds clinging to the trees. The density of the flowers was a surprise. I now understand the fascination of the Japanese for this spring moment, made possible by the planting of cherry trees in parks, around temples and shrines and along river banks. The sakura is a celebration of fertile spring, of creative joy."

"The ride over the mountain was fun, and navigating a bike through this city felt friendly and obvious, thanks to the low key driving of the Japanese. The people having their picnic were so relaxed and full of smiles! I was amused by the orderly groups of adults, with their shoes all lined up beside the tablecloths. The younger groups were more chaotic, but more likely to be dressed in kimonos. The children were so cute and devilish — as kids should be. The smells of barbecue were intoxicating."

"I'm glad we did some climbing today. I gave a little more on the climb. It felt good to feel my heart pound. You're an inspiration! You're never short of energy or oxygen. Have you ever tried to explain the joy of climbing hills to a non-cyclist?"

"It's impossible. Most people are terrified of climbs. Why do we like climbing so much?"

"We men think it's a chance to strut our stuff, but women are better suited to climbing, and you're proof of that!"

"We like rewards — like endorphins and the ride down the other side. It's also a taste acquired with self confidence, and the mountainous areas are less populated, so they seem to be built to the scale of a bicycle."

"It's true that the elevation gain is cash in the bank that you can spend descending. And there's the climb from the dark valley to the opening sky. The sky grows, and the more effort you invest, the grander the sky gets. The summit is a powerful metaphor."

"You're right about that. The sky grows. You ride into the light. I love to climb. That's definitely part of it. Another part is the contrast between the hard and the easy. We like contrasts and surprises. That's maybe not for everybody. Maybe it depends on how you were brought up."

"When you were a child, Sara, did your parents show you how to travel freely, to seek the unexpected?"

"They were hikers, and some of our trips were minutely planned, particularly in the Alps in high season, where lodging was reserved in advance. But others were free rolling with just starting and ending points and choices to make along the way. Except in the Alps, we usually camped in wilderness, which required finding a good spot, building a fire, making our dinner and setting up our tent. The weather was often a plan changer. When it snowed at high altitude, we had to descend to below timberline. In the Alps, civilization was never far, but in the North Cascades, we were on our own. Sure, there were challenges, but healthy ones. Our family adventures brought us close together."

"Do those adventures affect the way you live now?"

"I suppose I'm comfortable taking calculated risks and changing plans, but that might be a hard-wired trait. We also traveled in Latin America, usually on local trains and buses. As young children, we copy our parents' every move and word; then as teenagers we try to be different. I never got to the point of embracing the parents in me. I'm not sure how to be like them. It's hard to answer your question, but I do like challenges and being a bit scared. Maybe it's an adrenalin addiction or maybe it's showing off or maybe it's the thrill of the conquest, like on the Col d'Aubisque."

"You're the most fearless person I know."

"Maybe I overcompensate to hide my fears."

"That couldn't get you through your performance at the wedding."

"Oh, that! That's just jazz. Jazz is like climbing hills on a bicycle — not so hard, when you know you can do it."

She is making morning tea in their guesthouse room, guessing at the dose, listening to the water simmer in the kettle, steam forming. Outside the window, the first light appears like falling snow, accumulating and outlining. She remembers Kaguya, a story from Japanese folklore.

> *The childless bamboo cutter finds a tiny infant in a shining stalk of bamboo. He calls her Kaguya, and raises her with his wife. The girl grows into a beautiful young woman, coveted by suitors, whom she rejects. She cries when she sees the moon. Her home is there, and there she has to return, leaving her earthly parents and admirers with broken hearts.*

She carries the tea tray to the futons and pours the light-yellow liquid, vapors rising. He is awake, taking his teacup. She stays with the moonchild. He watches her, and in the dancing steam, shadows appear — shadows of moonlight overwhelmed by dawn. Ghostly shadows rise and evaporate.

They visited the Matsuyama castle on the citadel in the center of the city. Access was on foot or on a chair lift, a healthy cousin of the rusted one by the abandoned hotel. They took the chair lift for a better view of the sakura. The castle was surrounded by cherry trees, and in the courtyard there were many *hanami* picnickers; some wearing kimonos. The castle was an authentic relic of medieval Japan.

They stopped in a supermarket on their way back to buy ingredients for dinner, since visitors were allowed to use the guesthouse kitchen. They bought three kinds of fish, clams, vegetables and greens to cook for their hosts and whoever might show up. Dinner started with the clams, steamed in their juice with a little sake. They were sweet and tasty. The main dish was steamed vegetables and various cuts of fish, which were pan-seared and laid out on salad greens. French guests appeared, so they were eight around the table. Their hosts, a young American and his Japanese wife, provided homemade beer. Japanese neighbors came and went during the evening. Conversation bounced around in English, Japanese and French.

In the morning, they visited the shrine just up the hill from the guesthouse, where the cherry blossoms were at their glorious, ecstatic best. An elderly Japanese woman climbed the steps to the shrine as they were descending. Something about her made them stop and turn. She also stopped and looked at them quizzically, and then she took a framed photo from her bag. She was taking her deceased husband to see the sakura. The picture showed him with blooming cherry trees. They had been married for fifty years until he died three years before. She said that he loved these cherry trees, so now she takes him every spring to see them.

They left Matsuyama by train to avoid biking through the urban sprawl. There was time to talk.

"I was so moved by the lady in the shrine that I almost cried. She wanted to share her pain and joy with us. She wanted us to remember how fragile life and love can be. She was saying to take it and live it when you can, for it's a short-lived, sakura happiness."

"She had fifty years with her husband, but if it had been a thousand, it would have hurt even more to lose him. You can't get or give enough love. As the Cole Porter song says, 'What is this thing called love?'"

"You're a poet and you ask me, a doctor, to tell you what love is?"

"You're right. I should be asking you what life is…"

"Happy to oblige, but only if you'll do the same for love."

"It's a deal, doctor. Please go first. There should be plenty of time before we arrive."

"OK. What's life? That's an important scientific subject. One of my professors was an astrobiologist. After taking her course, I did my senior thesis with her on the definition and origin of life. I'll give you a short summary of my seminar.

"We can only describe our life here on Earth, since we've not found it elsewhere. Before defining life, we can simply ask if it evolved on Earth or was imported from the outside. We know that all life on Earth uses DNA to store the information that defines life, and essentially the same genetic code is used by all the organisms so far studied. So the life forms we know likely came from the same source. Also, fossil bacteria are found in the oldest rocks known on Earth, dating from more than 3.5 billion years ago. The

Earth was formed 4.6 billion years ago. So bacterial life was here from almost the beginning. All of this doesn't define life, but it supports panspermia, the idea that life came to Earth from elsewhere, perhaps as bacteria hiding in rocks or comets.

"Another possibility is that life formed spontaneously from chemical precursors. This has never been observed, but the basic chemistry of life is spread through the universe, and given time and the right environment, a primitive life chemistry might have evolved on Earth and elsewhere.

"But the question of the origin of life still doesn't lead to a definition of life. Defining life is the subject of biology, which describes life as populations of organisms, their cells and their chemistry. Much is known, including the sequence of words that form the information encoded in the DNA."

"You mean the nucleotide sequence. In my former incarnation as a chemistry student, I was interested in the structure of DNA, described by Watson and Crick, and the defining of the genetic code. My father was a physicist, and my mother was a biochemist. They were first generation molecular biologists, so I grew up with the vocabulary, and I've kept up with the DNA sequencing story."

"Oh! That changes everything. So we speak the same language?"

"My knowledge is rusty. But I see your point. DNA defines life."

"At least it has the potential to define life, but even that's conjecture. Maybe there's much more — perhaps in the realm of poetry."

"OK. My turn. Life has end points. We see organisms like us die. We become inert. Breathing stops. The heart stops. We're eaten by microorganisms — we rot. That's pretty dramatic. Life stops. But does it start? When? How?

At conception? At birth? So we can't see a precise starting point for life, and even the end point is complicated. What happens to our DNA when we die? Does it get recycled by other organisms? Do we die or are we just fragmented?"

"I think we're fragmented and recycled, because some of our DNA survives in our children, and if we don't have children, fragments are carried by the children of our relatives."

"I agree, Sara. Maybe we're a patchwork that covers our species and is part of a larger fabric that blankets the Earth. Death would only be complete if it applied to all life forms on Earth and elsewhere."

Their philosophical exchange was interrupted by their arrival in Uchiko, their destination, chosen for its Kabuki theater, which turned out to be a gem of a wooden building. They were guided in English by a young Japanese woman, who carefully explained the history of the theater and how it functions. There were no performances that week, but even without actors the theater was a show in itself, with elaborate stage machinery, trapdoors and hidden passageways.

They decided to bike southwest to Yawatahama, a port town, which would position them for exploring the Sadamisaki Peninsula, a long finger of land pointing toward Kyushu, the third of the main Japanese islands.

The ride took them through a tunnel with a narrow sidewalk on one side. It was a relief to finally see a distant point of light at the end, but getting there was slow, and the sound of each passing vehicle resonated long before and after it passed. The light grew and then exploded as they rode out into bright light. What felt like high adventure on a bicycle would have been mundane in a car.

In Yawatahama, they found a small hotel in the port and ate dinner in a shokudo. It rained all night, and the storm intensified toward morning.

He is awakened by gusts of wind hitting the building. Sara sleeps, oblivious to the storm. He tries to mute his hearing and redirect his mind toward sleep, and then he enters a no-man's land. As he stumbles through this barren landscape, it expands forever before him. He wants to hide from the wind, but he cannot stop. It catches the hollows and spins around the rocky outcroppings. A human voice comes with it, saying only one word: "Now..." and again at a higher pitch, "Now..." Again and again he hears this single word as the wind slams into the landscape. Finally, he is fully awake.

Now.

He slips out from under the down comforter. In the bathroom, he opens his bag of toiletries, and finds the leather case. He removes a sealed plastic pouch, which he puts in the sleeve of his *yukata*. In the hallway, he finds the stairs to the roof. He opens the door, removes his slippers and walks barefoot across the wet rooftop. The rain has nearly stopped, but the wind is fierce, pounding his back in gusts. He comes to the edge of the building, and looking east, he catches the first hint of dawn. Not really dawn — just a few photons sent by the sun to scout the horizon for a break in the clouds. There is no opening. The storm has commandeered the sky, but even so, the dawn is there in diffuse grayness.

He takes the plastic bag from his sleeve and rips off an edge with his teeth. He feels an astringent rush on his tongue and lips. He enlarges the tear with his fingers, hesitates, and feeling the urgency of the coming light, he flings the white powder upward, into the wind. It vanishes in blackness, born eastward toward the horizon, to the first hint of dawning light.

He waits and watches, as the sky breaks in the east, glowing white against the black. He battles the wind back to the staircase door and descends with wet feet, carrying his slippers. He enters the room as quietly as possible, and realizes he is deeply chilled. As he steps into the hot shower, he licks his lips. The astringent taste hits as a gust of silent wind. His fingers carry a film of white dust. This he carefully licks off, reveling in the exotic taste. Then the hot water washes everything away, even the tears that flowed with the flight of her ashes.

Over breakfast in the hotel they took a look at the general map of Shikoku.

"Sara, how do you feel about riding in the rain or waiting for it to stop or maybe changing plans and taking a train out of here?"

"I don't mind riding in the rain when necessary, but starting out in the rain with the prospect of a long, wet day dampens my spirits. This feels like a major storm, so to ride the peninsula we should wait for better weather, and the forecast is rain all day. It might be nice to have a day off, but then there is so much to see… I already feel the time closing in.

"I've been looking at the map. We could take a train toward southern Shikoku, and ride through the Shimanto River valley. Cape Ashizuri has small roads, and the southwestern coast is cut out with capes and islands and served by secondary roads close to the coast. The other choice for a southern ocean experience would be the Muroto Cape, farther to the east, but I see only a relatively major coastal road."

"I'm for small roads. Yesterday's ride was mostly through populated areas. The tunnels were exciting — maybe a little too hostile, but it was worth the detour to visit the Kabuki theater. I was most impressed with the lone pilgrim we saw just before we entered the long tunnel. He had just walked through it, with the passing cars and trucks. In spite of the noise and narrow walkway, he was full of smiles under his conical hat. Next time, I want to walk the 88 Temple Pilgrimage. It's 1500 km, but worth it to wear the hat and carry the staff."

"Did you notice he limped, and he was using a cane, as well as the staff? It made me feel like a lazy, high-tech bicycle sleaze. It puts things in humbling perspective."

She poured more tea. The rain was hitting hard outside.

"There is a something I'm curious about. Do you sleepwalk?"

"Sleepwalk? You mean the shower I took early this morning?"

"It's more the wet tracks in the hallway. They seemed to be coming in, but not going out. You don't have to tell all, but I'm a bit curious. Did we have a one-way, barefoot visitor last night?"

"Well, sort of… to be honest, I woke up early and took a walk on the roof to see the dawn, but I was fully awake. I went barefoot on the wet roof so as not to ruin the slippers, so I returned to our room barefoot. I hope you're not jealous."

"I am — very jealous. But I can wait for a full explanation."

They put on their ponchos, made a dash for the station, and soon found themselves in a cozy little train, headed for Ekawasaki. The two-car train ran on a single-track line, rocking gently. It felt more like a magic bus, with the driver next to them. They stood in the front and watched the tracks coming toward them, with tunnel openings, bridges and villages slipping by. The train was part of the landscape, hardly making a mark as it passed. The rain abated to a drizzle. He began to wonder about Sara's sixth sense. There was no hiding from her.

"Sara, I have a confession. The episode last night with the footprints... I need to tell you the whole story."

"You mean the plastic bag, torn open at one end that I found in the trash can?"

"You're way ahead of me!"

"I heard you shower during the night; then I saw the footprints this morning, and I happened to notice the torn bag in the trash. It had contained a white substance."

"So you think I'm a drug addict?"

"You're not a drug addict. I know what was in the bag. You're a love addict. I've been there too. I've spread my share of ashes."

"You amaze me. She wanted her ashes spread in Prospect Park, with some saved for Japan. So when you mentioned a wedding in Kyoto, everything fell into place. I wanted to come to Japan to be with you — to get to know you — and to spread the last of her ashes. I've been fighting off ghosts, and you're my only weapon. I need your youth, your strength and your compassion."

"And I need a discourse on the definition of love, since I did my bit for life in the last train."

He watches the passing blur of foliage and fields, hesitates and says,

"OK. Poet or not, I haven't a clue. All roads lead to love, yet we don't know much about it, even if we can enumerate its forms. For some people, it's a mirage that flees before them. For others it comes easily and gracefully — at least for a while. We know when we have it, and we know when we don't. When love is true, we can't define it, create it, manage it, buy or sell it. The nemesis of love is death. So love is closely allied with life. Perhaps love is both the origin and the definition of life?

"Carmen says that love is the child of a gypsy, and that it

knows no rules. '*L'amour est enfant de bohème. Il n'a jamais, jamais connu de loi.*' She's right. It lives in its own time and way. Love is a livelihood for poets and songwriters, but do we so-called artists know any more about it than sex workers? We talk about 'romantic love,' when we mean it involves sex or aspires to it. Other forms of love abound, like our love for our family, friends and pets, but are they really different? Romantic lovers 'make love,' and romantic love makes life, so love must signify the making and the nurturing of life, and that would explain the relationship with food. But music is also involved. Music is the language of love. In the words of Henry Purcell's lyricists,

> "If music be the food of love,
> Sing on till I am fill'd with joy;
> For then my list'ning soul you move
> With pleasures that can never cloy,
> Your eyes, your mien, your tongue declare
> That you are music ev'rywhere."

"That's my favorite Purcell song. Maybe there's something in your own poetry that defines love."

"You're right. Why am I going on like this? Let me think… OK, here's a love poem from many years ago. It's based on personal experience."

Love on high, high on love

Synthesis of light, water and air
There is nothing like an apple
High as Icarus, yet firmly attached
Rosy with hot sun, full of sweet juice
Big and round and hanging from a branchlet

High, near the sky, clean from rain
Tempting as the goddess of love, naked and beautiful.

Oh, to get a hand on it!

Nothing prevents me, but this ladder,
One rung too short, yet, maybe
Just tall enough, if I take the risk.
One more rung. Don't look down.
One more step to paradise, one more
Breath of clear courage, and a stretch
To heavens, to touch perfection, to deliverance
From desire, to total satisfaction.
Just another inch to go.

And the breeze waves the branches,
And the ladder, over-stretched,
Sighs and protests. And my arm,
Over-stretched, aches, but not so much
As the desire in my fingers
And the folly in my brain.

I touch the red green skin of my beloved,
And she slips away. I dare another and another,
And she still mocks me.

"One more inch, one more rung,"
And I am lost forever in this insane
Need to possess beauty,
In this doomed enterprise.

Then the breeze moves, swings so slightly
An unsuspecting, unnoticing, perfect
Object of desire… the needed millimeter.

And I spring, and current flows through my
Fingers, down my arm to my heart, as I cling
One foot on the ladder, one hand on love.

I am the happiest man on earth and in heaven.
Split between the worlds of life and after life.
This is the ecstasy of doing and undoing.

Yet, she yields not, and I am trapped.
In love with no way out, down or up.
Infatuation doubled by the cool feeling
Of juicy flesh between my fingers.

Yet she cannot yield, for she too
Loves and sees the hard cold sense
Of my predicament: Falling is forbidden.
Flying is out. Certain punishment waits below,
So we hang together, balanced on nothing,
Held in place by a thin apple stem.
And one foot on a ladder's rung.

Though slow of brain, I finally sense
The only dénouement. Marriage!
Thus a proposal I cast. First a whisper,
Then an exclamation and proclamation.
Then a shout for joy, MARRIAGE!

Then a scream, as agitation ruptures balance,
One safe foot slips from ladder's rung.
And like a ship casting off from pier,
In slow motion backwards I fall in
Full somersault, eyes open, admiring
Passing leaves and branches, sky, chirps of
Frightened fellow flying creatures, not

Used to large specimens, such as me,
Cavorting in their midst.

But ladder and I are old friends,
And I am caught in its rungs by
My cleverly bent knee, as if rehearsed.
So back to reality, but inverted,
I am stopped in my delirium, red-faced at my
Performance so ungainly, with my prize clutched,
But not too tight for fear of bruising.

I hear faint applause, and perceive, far below
A youth watching as if a circus were setting up
And the acrobat had begun his warm-up
As if I had planned a show!

But no, this is life and I am saved, hugging love.
I untangle my limbs from those that braved me,
And find a perch on ladder's top, safe, with
Heart pounding and head dizzy from fear and passion.

From this roost I ponder my next move
Or how to prolong the feeling of conquest,
Of manly proof of power over nature,
Nasty tricks of gravity vanquished.

I ponder life saved and love attained,
And the beauty of my catch.
A perfect blend of youth and ripeness
Blushed with color, ideal in shape,
So large, such a handful!
So cool to touch and warm at once.
This is the meaning of perfection.

This is the meaning of love.

With passing summer sky sheep
To witness, I consummate our marriage,
For this is my reward for bravery.
The first tooth mark, then the
Breaking of skin and the rush of
Cool sweet apple juice. Ecstasy.
 I take my time, but all too soon
Am left with echoes of ringing bells,
Lingering perfume, the memory of all that,
And an apple core as proof.

This I also consume, my passion
Still not quenched, and then I
Eat the last remaining vestige,
The stem over which I triumphed.

They set up their bikes at Ekawasaki station, in a small village with the Shimanto River running by. The rain has stopped and the road nearly dry. There is clearing to the west, bringing afternoon sun and warmth. They phone an isolated, country youth hostel to make sure it is open, since there are no towns for a long distance along the river. A stop in a food market turns up fruit and a local tofu cake, which they save for later.

The road follows the river valley with short climbs over ridges and headlands. The air has a just-washed-and-dried texture, and it feels good to be back on the road. The youth hostel is on the far side of the river, reached by a small road that, according to the map, can be accessed by a bridge, but the map doesn't say it's an unusual bridge. When it comes into view, they don't realize it's a public road bridge. It's one lane, set on concrete pillars, and there are no guardrails, no shoulder — just painted white lines on either edge of a narrow, asphalt lane. The bridge surface seems almost continuous with the gray surface of the river — as if they could bike off the bridge and continue on the river. Riding the bridge seems like walking a taut wire, slowly to savor the view of the quietly rushing river, full in its banks and happy.

They stop in the middle, put down their bikes and sit on the warm pavement to eat their snack of apples and tofu cake. The sun is close to the mountain horizon, and shadows are long. She is pensive.

"So you were no better at defining love than I was at defining life. How can you know when you're in love or alive?"

"If you pinch yourself and it hurts, you're living. But you're not really living until you're in love. Nothing can hurt when you're in love. All of the clichés about love are true."

"So if it hurts when I pinch myself, I'm alive, but if it doesn't hurt, I could either be dead or in love. Here goes, are you ready?"

She pinches herself. No reaction. She pinches harder. She waits and looks at him. She tries again in a different spot.

"No pain! So if I'm living, I must be in love!"

"And if you're in love, you're living as never before, and nothing can hurt you or dilute your feeling of joy."

She stands, extends her hands to pull him up from the pavement in the middle of the bridge without guardrails.

"I'm sure of it for me. How about you?"

"I've been pinching myself for months — every time I'm with you. I feel no pain, just happiness — unlimited, high-flying, endless joy. I'm in love. Wildly, desperately, crazily in love with you!"

The bridge begins to slowly revolve around its center, and they slowly come closer and closer, and as the bridge turns faster and faster around them, swirling the river, mountains and sky, they come still closer, and as the cool night air surrounds them, they share in each other's warmth, pressed together, one being, alive in the vortex of the universe.

The narrow road on the other side of the river was a cyclist's dream, climbing and dropping in small doses, with the river to the left and the mountain above, on the right, through cedar forest, bamboo groves, isolated orchards and farms. One farmhouse had the youth hostel sign they were looking for. They arrived just at dark.

Dinner was ready, so they sat down with their hosts and the only other guest, also a cyclist, who was on a three-week, self-guided tour of Shikoku. They learned that their hostess was a river guide and that their host built wooden canoes. The dinner was delicious.

Their room was for four, without the other two people. They took their "his and her" baths; then talked with the lights out. Her voice was radiant.

"Do you feel sleepy? I do. Sleepy and satisfied. But wondering what happens next for us."

"Time takes its time. You said in New York that there are all kinds of love. Let's let it evolve, see where it leads, what it teaches — hoping and building, but not rushing. Gently down the road — no racing. We have so much to learn, and we have time. Time is ours — this is our time."

Breakfast was Japanese, except for a fried egg, in the shape of a heart, with a shiny yellow yoke in the middle.

"Oh. Look at that! How sweet! Do you think she sees something between us?"

"I doubt it. She sees we're happy cyclists, obviously father and daughter. Maybe she sees a lot of happy cyclists, but not often as happy as us…"

They continued down the small road, crossed the river on

a red bridge, took the slightly larger road, and then crossed again on another bridge without guardrails. Again, they stopped in the middle.

"I just realized what these minimalist bridges are about. They must be submersed in high water. Guardrails would catch anything drifting down the river in a flood. This way the bridge stays clean and whole."

"That makes sense, and the converging lines draw you to the other side. I wonder what happens when cars confront each other. Backing up would be dangerous. Long live bicycles!"

They bought lunch supplies from a van making the rounds of the farmhouses and hamlets. There was a third submersible bridge; then the valley opened up, and they stopped for their picnic lunch, perched on a bench overlooking the river.

They continued through farmland and into the town of Shimanto, where they found a phone booth, called Mamasan and reserved in a ryokan on Ohki beach and recommended in the guidebook. To get there, they picked a series of small mountain roads, rather than take the more traveled coastal road and a long tunnel. Finding the beginning of the first road was difficult, and it involved riding through a commercial strip with garish signs and empty parking lots. But once on the small road, they rode along a stream through cedar forest, and then the one lane road climbed steeply — at times at grades around 15%. They were in a long, slow wrestling match with gravity.

When they finally won, they had climbed over 400 meters through forest of all kinds, with flowering wild cherry trees punctuating the mountainsides. They followed ridges and descended back to the coastal road.

They were the only guests in the ryokan, which was minimalist with an ecological purpose. The owner suggested they visit the beach both at sunset and at sunrise. Ohki beach was reached by a steep path, and it was a gem of fine sand with dark rocks and big surf. They walked its length and back, wading in water warmed by the Japanese current. The sand was a mixture of grains in shades of white to gray, orange, yellow and full black. With these colored elements, the moving water had painted complex and sometimes symmetrical patterns on the surface.

Back in the ryokan they each retired to the appropriate bath facility. The hot pools were heated by a wood-fired boiler, and minerals had been added making the water feel silky and leaving a smooth layer on the skin after drying. Their room was large, finished in cedar, with views over the ocean. They ate their stash of snacks, listened to music and talked about events in their lives.

"You mentioned an astrobiology professor, Sara. I think I remember her. Was there a controversy concerning her?"

"Indeed there was, and I was there. I was lucky to take her astrobiology class. Part of it was about the origin of life, as I mentioned, and it was in this class that we watched sea urchins release eggs and sperm. We saw the sperm fertilize the eggs, and we followed the development of the embryos for a week. While we were watching all of this under phase contrast microscopes, somebody... OK, I admit it... I started the whole thing by asking our professor about fertilization in humans. She said it was similar, but the human eggs were smaller, and she thought that human spermatozoa were differently shaped. She said she would have to look up the differences, but then she had an idea. She said that if one of the students would provide some sperm, we could compare the two directly. We could even see if the human sperm was attracted to the sea urchin eggs."

"I suppose she said all of this spontaneously, without any forethought."

"Of course, it was unplanned. She was just a scientist with an idea. She was already enthusiastic about the experiment with just the sea urchin eggs and sperm. There were at least ten boys in the lab, including several strutting macho types — you know, the weightlifter, tight tee shirt variety. The professor pointed out that men produce plenty of sperm, but women have only a limited number of eggs, so it was up to the boys to come up with the goods. At this point, you could see she was teasing, and the boys in the room were terrified.

"So she's looking at the class and waiting for a response, smiling ironically; then just as she is about to go on to another subject, a big grin breaks out on her face, and she points to a guy in the back with his hand up and thanks him for being a brave warrior.

"It's the boy with no flash or pizzazz. He sits in the back of the class and gets good grades. In a second, he goes from being class nerd to class hero, and the macho fraternity types are crawling out from under their chairs — envious. The girls (me included) are thrilled. Everybody's looking at him like Superman just flew into the room. So he walks to the front of the teaching lab, just as natural as can be, and picks up a plastic centrifuge tube from the shelf, smiles at everybody and walks out.

"He comes back about five minutes later, hands the tube to the professor, smiles at everybody and takes his seat. Big applause. The professor holds the tube up to the light and says, 'Not bad, really very good, thank you for your contribution.'

"So the professor puts the tube of semen on ice, and we discuss what to do with this treasure. We measure the volume of the ejaculate, weigh it and calculate its density. Next we determine the sperm count, using a series of dilutions in physiological saline solution and counting under phase contrast, using a known volume and a Malassez hemocytometer.

"The spermatozoa were swimming like crazy, so we added ethanol. Drunk sperm don't swim well. Otherwise, they had amazing energy. The sperm count was almost 160 million per milliliter. Nearly 700 million spermatozoa were contained in the ejaculate. Talk about virility! The girls in the class were seriously turned on. The boys were probably wishing they could at least see their own sperm.

"We compared human and sea urchin sperm, and found they were similar in size. The sea urchin eggs were about 100 microns in diameter, which was about twenty times the length of the sperm, not counting the tails. The human spermatozoa were not interested in the sea urchin eggs. We learned that the chemoattractant released by sea urchin eggs is a peptide, and in humans there is probably more than one attractant, including the female hormone, progesterone. Human olfactory receptors on the sperm are probably involved. Over the following days, we came in at our leisure to record the development of the urchin embryos and to compare samples of human and sea urchin sperm that had been left at room temperature or kept in the cold.

"Anyway, toward the end of class, the professor thanked the sperm donor. He replied quite calmly that it was no trouble for him, because he regularly contributed sperm to a sperm bank, and this was a tax-deductible contribution to science. The professor asked him how many children he had fathered, and he said he didn't know, but there was no limit in the USA. There ensued an interesting discussion about sperm banks and the danger of incest between half-siblings who share a father without realizing it.

"As I walked out of the class, I noticed somebody had written a phone number on the blackboard. I called it the next day. It was of course the sperm donor. We had coffee together. He turned out to be really cool, but nothing came of our encounter. I did notice he beat me for the best grade in the class.

"Of course word got out, and the professor was called in by the dean, but she explained the context and agreed not to do it again, so nothing came of it, but the professor found another job soon after she got tenure. I was so impressed that I asked to do my senior thesis in her lab."

"Was seeing sperm an erotic experience?"

"Yes, very erotic, and seeing the egg being fertilized was even more exciting. Imagine seeing the beginning of a life! You men are lucky. You make lots of gametes, and you can see them, assuming you have a phase contrast microscope handy."

"I gave sperm once…"

"Do tell…"

"Well, it's far in the past, and a long way from this ryokan. We wanted to have a child, and it was fun trying, but it wasn't working, so we went to a fertility clinic. I was supposed to donate sperm to have it counted and checked for motility and morphology, with the aim of using it for *in vitro* fertilization. OK, sounds easy. I get to the clinic on a warm summer day. It's early and still cool. I walk into a large waiting room with rows of seats, but no people. There's just a desk and a woman looking at me. She's not wearing a white coat, so I figure she's the receptionist, but what a babe! Short skirt, low neckline — beautiful! I tell myself this is going to be falling out of bed easy. She gives me papers to fill out, and I'm checking out her low-cut dress, large brown eyes and the rest, and she's being nice and friendly… then she asks me to sit down. I sit where I can pretend to read a magazine and steal glances at her. After a while, a door opens and a guy in a white coat enters, carrying some stuff. He calls my name, even though there's nobody else in the room. He asks for photo ID, which he checks carefully, and then he asks me to follow him. We go through a door with a small window in it and right into some kind of examination room. He hands me a plastic conical centrifuge tube with graduations. Then he gives me some tattered girlie magazines and walks out.

"So there I am in this most unromantic place with some sad magazines and a plastic, screw cap tube. Ouch. Things are looking difficult. Then I get an idea. I turn off the room lights and stand where I can see the waiting room, with a clear view of the receptionist through the small window in the door. Who needs magazines, when you have a beautiful, sexy woman, lightly dressed on a warm, summer morning? In no time at all, I've done it, like falling out of bed. Just needed to imagine myself falling into bed with the receptionist!

"So I hold the precious tube and wait for something to happen. The ejaculate is sliding down the side and filling up the conical bottom. I swing it at the end of my arm to bring everything down, so I can read the volume. Finally, there's a knock, and the guy in the white coat opens the door. I give him the tube, and follow him into the waiting room, which has filled up with people. He holds the tube up to the light, and says in a loud voice, so everybody can hear, 'Not bad, over four milliliters — really not bad at all, definitely above average,' and he flashes me a satisfied look. I don't know how to react, but then I see everybody in the room is staring at me. I become extremely embarrassed and decide to get out of there as fast as possible."

"What was the result of your valiant efforts? Did you get the receptionist's phone number?"

"As I walked out, I smiled and thanked her for her help. You're not going to believe this… she said, 'You're most welcome, anytime,' and she winked at me."

"I believe you!"

"Thanks! But then I was really scared. I'm a monogamist. It's not quite a religion, but it's a strong tradition. That receptionist was dangerous. Anyway, the experience in the clinic made me realize what people go through to have children. And after all that, it still didn't work for us, but the sperm check was fun."

They got up before dawn and walked to the beach with a bicycle light. They sat on a rock, feeling the first hint of colorless mist surround them. The light quickly took form and color. The sky went from black to gray, to gray-blue and to a clear bluish hue, but it was still the embryo of a day. The gold was slow to come. It propagated first on the sand, invaded the surf foam and finally climbed the rocks along the shore and caught the trees. Real light sent shooting rays into the air above the sea, streaks through the distant haze, and the low clouds picked up the theme and restated it in pink that quickly turned vermillion. Finally, the first hint of a red disc peeked above the horizon, and a new day was born.

They had taken towels and worn their swimsuits. The air was cool. The sky and water continued their light show with reflections in all directions. Waves were hitting high on the beach, because the tide was climbing fast. They went in anyway, and dove under the breaking waves to get beyond the surf. They bobbed, sometimes holding hands, sometimes drifting apart. Getting cold, they headed back to shore, trying to make a dash between waves, but the tide had come in even more, and the beach was steep, so with each wave, they could not quite escape to high ground, rolling instead in the sand, foam and water mixture. Finally, in the wake of a breaking wave, they found each other and locked hands, and as the next wave hit, they sprang for the beach, just making it out of the water before the wave's eroding retreat collapsed the beach and washed them back to sea. They were covered with sticky sand, but safe and happy. They dried and walked back to their room where showers washed off the remaining sand. It was not a near death experience, but it might have been nasty — had they not lunged upward at the right time.

The road south to the Ashizuri cape was good riding, and there were alternatives that took them on narrow lanes that closely followed the coastline. They encountered pilgrims, walking along in their white shirts, conical hats and using a staff. They stopped in a village and watched the unloading of a small fishing boat. All kinds of sea creatures could be seen, including vibrantly colored squid. They snacked on mackerel sushi, reconstructed to look like a whole fish, but with sushi rice inside. One village seemed to be a squid fishing center. Squid were drying like white shirts on clotheslines.

The tip of the cape afforded ocean views from high cliffs. They admired the lighthouse and discovered a large statue of John Mung, a local fisherman who accidently found his way to the USA in the middle of the 19th century. They visited Kongofuku-ji temple, number 38 in the 88 Temple Pilgrimage. A light rain enhanced the beauty of the temple grounds, which included a large pond, decorated for the occasion by the falling rain drops. The temple was surrounded by approximately seventy large bronze statues of religious figures sitting cross-legged. They were intricate, varied and clearly influenced by Indian bronzes. There was also a statue of Kobo Daishi, the priest who brought esoteric Buddhism to Japan from China in the ninth century. He was the original pilgrim, usually depicted in a conical hat, wearing a cloak and carrying a staff.

They had a late lunch of noodles in a cafe across from the

temple, sitting with a pilgrim, who seemed carefree and content — like them — happy to be on the road. By the time they left the restaurant, the light rain had turned heavy. They were tempted to find lodging nearby, but instead they put on ponchos and wind pants and rode into the rain. It was cozy and mostly dry under the ponchos.

The rain made the subtropical vegetation shine. It intensified with blowing gusts — real ocean weather. Biking over headlands was a challenge, and the small towns and ports seemed to be hiding behind their sea walls. They pushed on, not to be intimidated, but each secretly wondered if it was worth it.

The rain in Spain. No rain, no gain, no plain. And still rain. Water fills my shoes. The cloud dam bursts. This poor poncho is a flimsy shelter from desire. She doesn't notice, but it's pouring desire. She's dry, protected by her youth. I'm drenched. Gentle on curves. Fast on straights. Coastline through the mist. I hear waves breaking. A sloshing car. Dark forests, and the wind returns against me. She's protected, impervious. I'm the ancient mariner, the old man and the sea. Can I haul back my catch? I stay the course, on the road with water flowing over to meet the waves. But climb I must, climb against the blowing rain, desire unquenched.

Then without warning they saw a large building with the words, John Mung Museum, written in English on the side. It looked like a perfect refuge from the storm. The museum was open, and the receptionist seemed happy to have dripping visitors.

The museum told the story of John Mung, a fourteen-year-old fisherman, blown to sea in a small boat with four companions in 1841. They were rescued from an uninhabited island by an American whaling ship. Captain Whitfield took John (real name Manjiro Nakahama) and the other fishermen to Hawaii, and realizing John's generous nature and intelligence, took him home to Fairhaven Massachusetts, where he received an American education. In ten years, he learned English, shipbuilding, mathematics, surveying and navigation, and he was exposed to new ideas, including democracy and gender equality. He served as first mate on a whaling ship, and while in California during the gold rush, he earned enough money to get to Hawaii, where he was reunited with his fishing companions. He managed to return to Japan with them in a small boat in 1852. The Shogun, Hatamato, used John Mung and his knowledge of the United States in his dealings with Commodore Perry. Mung became a professor in Japan's first naval academy, where he taught surveying, navigation and shipbuilding. His life was devoted to informing the Japanese about Western culture, and his activities as a diplomat and teacher contributed to the opening of Japan to the West.

The rain did not abate while they were in the museum, so they rode on in their ponchos, eventually finding a *minshuku*, a family-run guesthouse. Their hosts spoke no English, but Sara's Japanese was progressing, and their hosts were friendly and not concerned about their dampness. The dinner was generous, including tuna sashimi, langoustines, abalone, salad, diverse cooked vegetables and pickles. They had hot sake with dinner. The *minshuku* was decorated with beach artifacts, including glass floats. The baths were hot, and they were feeling mellow. It had been a long day, but they still had the energy for their evening talk. He was curious about her religious leanings.

"What do you make of Kobo and the 88 Temples?"

"It's strong stuff. There's no doubt about that, and I'm interested, but I've never been a believer. I did enjoy our temple visit. The statues were exquisite. I would like to see more."

"This is the first time I've been so aware of the influence of India on the rest of Asia. I have everything to learn about the origins of Buddhism."

"I hope we can visit Zentsuji. According to the guide book, it's a temple not to miss: the birthplace of Kobo Daishi."

They found it on the map and roughly planned a route to get there via the Iya valley, known for its wild mountain scenery.

"If the weather improves, tomorrow should give us a full dose of ocean on small roads with few towns, but with lots of climbing over headlands. I'm always up for a day of climbing."

"And I'm game for a long ride tomorrow."

"Are you feeling sleepy?"

"Yes, what are you thinking about, Sara?"

"Just reliving the bridge."

"I see more bridges down the road — some graceful and long, some narrow and exciting, without guardrails."

"And climbs to mountain passes that cross into new watersheds, transitions between worlds."

She sings the spiritual, "Deep River."

"Deep River,
My home is over Jordan.
Deep River, Lord,
I want to cross over into campground.
Deep River.
My home is over Jordan.
Deep River, Lord,
I want to cross over into campground
Oh, don't you want to go,

To the Gospel feast;
That Promised Land,
Where all is peace?
Oh, deep River, Lord,
I want to cross over into campground."

The morning brought moving sunspots and clearing sky. The family of the *minshuku* came out to send them off. They were back on the road again, moving in rhythm, drawn forward by converging lines, along beaches of sand and pebbles, alternating with rocky outcroppings, peninsulas and islands. The headlands were cut through by tunnels, so they often took the old road, making a detour around or over. The air was freshly scrubbed and shiny, and the road was smooth and fast.

They followed the coastline, cut inland with the main road and back to the coast on a small road, close to the ocean. It was ideal road biking. She frequently rode ahead to double back and climb a second time. He pushed himself as far as he dared. They often stopped at viewpoints.

The *Touring Mapple* recommended a hotel slightly inland. It turned out to be clean and cute. They had a small tatami room, with a *kotatsu*, the low table with a blanket closing the sides and an electric heating element underneath. They enjoyed the warmth, while they had their arrival tea, before their baths. They ate in the hotel: simple, fresh, tasty and copious. It was the perfect meal after a day on the bikes. She was glowing from the ride.

"The rocky shore was so attractive and enhanced by the winding road and the changing views."

"We had a perfect day. You're right, Sara, the variety was special. We had mountains and ocean coming together under us. There were no tourist monuments today — just spectacular scenery, and being on a bike adds a dimension."

"Yes. Riding is a reward in itself, beyond the scenic and cultural interests. What a privilege. I see you're climbing faster, and I feel stronger and wiser about using my energy and oxygen. The air is so clean. I'm enchanted with Shikoku. You're right. It wouldn't have the same impact without the bikes. On the other hand, I admire the pilgrims who walk the 88 Temples. Maybe that's the ultimate way to see this island?"

The hotel didn't provide breakfast, so they rode until they found a market with breakfast bentos, and they bought oranges from a roadside honor system stand. They ate sitting on a warm rock wall, beside an estuary, watching gulls and crows. He felt bliss.

"What a life. Nothing is planned. We're never late and never early. We intend to take a train today, but we're not worried about the schedule. Tonight we have no lodging reservations. We're just going into the Iya valley. We don't even know if there're hotels there. Things will work out for us. It's our vagabond way of life."

"Here we are, eating breakfast outdoors on another perfect day. The sun is warm enough to ride in shorts, even in the morning."

"I've disconnected from the past and future. I'm here with you, and that's all I want. Tomorrow is not just another day. Tomorrow is today."

They rode to Sukumo and discovered that a train was leaving for Kochi in forty-five minutes, giving them plenty of time to bag their bikes. It was a cutely painted, two-car train, running on a single track that took them through farmland to Shamanto, and then up the coast. They changed trains in Kochi and bought sushi bentos in the station. At first, the train was full of schoolchildren in uniforms, and then it slowly emptied as it climbed into the mountains.

The descent on the north slope followed the Yoshino River, which looked like prime whitewater boating.

It was late afternoon when they got off the train in Iyaguchi. They crossed the river on a suspension bridge for pedestrians and bikes, and rode up the Iya, a stream flowing into the Yoshino River. They were in a deep valley with steep sides, carpeted with vegetation of many shades of spring green, marked with wild cherry trees in bloom. The sun dropped behind the ridges, but the climbing kept them warm. The road was narrow, and there was no traffic. The day was ending with the mountain chill sliding off the peaks and into the valleys. The route left the dark water for the lighter sky, but that too was losing luminance. They climbed, believing in luck or fate or just not thinking about anything beyond the turning of the wheels. Standing, sitting and standing again, against the steepness. The road climbed relentlessly. They were still warm in the cooling air, but soon they would need lights. But to go where? It didn't matter. They were free to accept what the road would bring.

"How're you doing? Warm enough?"

"Fine here, but when we stop to put on lights, I'll get out my tights and jacket."

"Where does this road go, Sara?"

"The map shows villages up the valley, which is on the tourist agenda, so we can hope to find a place to stay in one of those villages."

"What's that hanging on the mountain ahead?"

"It's like a building glued to the cliff. Looks like the road takes us there. We'll soon see."

It was nearly dark when they pulled up in front of the building. A sign said Iya Onsen.

"Iya Onsen! It's a famous place. I read about it in the guidebook, but I thought it was in another part of the valley.

They have a cog railway down to an outdoor hot spring. I sure hope they have a room!"

Once inside they found a lobby with a reception desk attended by a young woman. She seemed surprised to see them in their biking gear, but she remained composed, saying "*Chotto matte kudasai.* Wait a minute, please." She returned a few seconds later with a man in a business suit. They asked for a room. He looked at them smilingly; then consulted a reservations book.

"OK. I think we have a room, but I have to double check. Please sit down."

They sat on a comfortable sofa feeling lucky and happy. This was clearly not an ordinary *onsen*. There were elegant furnishings, and they could see the raised entrance to a classy dining room at the other end of the lobby. Unlike ryokans, *onsens* are open to drop-in guests, even for dinner, and dinner sounded good. The manager returned.

"Please excuse me. The room I mentioned is not available. It was our last standard room. I'm sorry to have misinformed you. However, I see you're on bicycles, and it is dark outside. Therefore, may I suggest another room? It is our special suite, but at twice the price of the standard room. However, you can have it for one night, but only one night, at the standard price."

Jubilation. They unloaded the bikes, and their bags were taken by a porter, who showed them the room. It could not have been more different from the room the night before. It was indeed a suite, but with the different parts open to each other. The walls were mostly glass, with now darkened views down the valley they had just climbed and the mountainside across the valley. There was a large terrace with an outdoor wood and tile bath, separated from the room by a wall of glass, and there was a bench with a footbath. The suite seemed designed for natural intimacy. The decor was luxuriously simple. There was also a sound system, a supply of CDs, easy chairs and a massage chair. In the main room there was a large *kotatsu*. They changed into *yukatas* and haori jackets and descended to the dining room, where a special table in an alcove was ready for them with the same double direction view as the room.

The dinner was served by a woman wearing a kimono, who explained how to eat the local dishes. Feeling thirsty, they started with beer. Dishes appeared, including an oblong plate, containing four taste treats, plus a separate white bowl with a pinched rim, holding a pale green square with a slice of red radish on top. In the center of the oblong plate was a small bowl, sitting on a square of origami paper. Inside were cooked spring vegetable greens, which they could not identify, mixed with pieces of carrot and mushrooms. A sprig of sakura buds lay across the top. To the right of the central bowl was a pink, brown and flat unknown that had been cooked on a bamboo skewer, and farther to the right was an unfamiliar, dark green nut-like object. To the left of the central bowl were two stuck-together rectangles, cut from what resembled a vegetable flan, and leaning against these were two long, thin, freshly grilled bamboo shoots. There was a glass of aperitif wine, a bowl of dipping sauce, and two alcohol-fired *shichirins* (braziers). One had a wooden steamer on it. An exotic salad was artfully displayed on a round silver wire grill in a black ceramic bowl. It was composed of two kinds and colors of gelatinous strips, a decorative carrot slice, a *shiso* leaf, three slices of bamboo shoot and a slice of cucumber under a dollop of an intriguing green paste.

"Well, this is the sumptuous après-bike meal of my dreams!"

"Mine too, Sara, but we haven't seen any fish or meat, so this must be just the first course!"

They lifted their wine glasses, and made a silent toast, speaking only with their eyes and smiles. He reached across his chest and pinched his arm. He closed his eyes, and when he opened them, she was still there — a miracle. He felt waves of joy and tears coming. A tear rolled down her cheek, and she smiled a grand and girlish grin. She pinched herself and said, "I'm in love. There can be no greater happiness than this — our happiness together here, in this splendid place, with this work of art for our dinner."

She leaned forward, took his hand and sang to him in an ethereal whisper, that only he could hear:

"Drink to me only with thine eyes,
And I will pledge with mine;
Or leave a kiss within the cup
And I'll not ask for wine.
The thirst that from the soul doth rise
Doth ask a drink divine;
But might I of Jove's nectar sip,
I would not change for thine."

Their image was reflected in the glass wall, with the wild cherry mountain beyond, invisible, but they were clear against the dark night. They began to eat, lifting their chopsticks from their ceramic holders, placed in front of the array of dishes.

"Oh! The bamboo shoots are fresh and tender!"

"And the salad is too beautiful to eat, but here goes a piece of this green, rubbery stuff into the sauce. It's cool and soft, and the sauce is soy-based and salty. Now I see. The green paste on the cucumber is freshly ground wasabi for the dipping sauce!"

"And the strange skewered pink paddle has a vegetable interior."

"The green square seems to be a lime-flavored bean creation, with a glaze topping."

"Try the vegetable and mushroom center bowl. There is something rolled up underneath, but it's a new taste for me."

"What looks like a nut has a soft interior. It seems to be made from a nutty paste and formed to look natural, but it's a salty confection."

A waitress came to light the flames under the steamers, and empty dishes disappeared and were replaced by full ones. The second braziers were lit and iron pots placed on them, containing greens, meat and mushrooms — so they each had two braziers cooking away.

As they finished the array of first courses, the last plates were replaced by a basket containing two small trout on skewers, sitting vertically with their tails in a white bowl. Between the trout were two more skewers with a lollipop-shaped slice through a coil of something dark with a white skin. The basket was decorated with sprigs from a bright green coniferous shrub. The waitress indicated they should each take a whole trout and eat it bones and all, directly from the skewer — the way the mountain people do.

The trout were succulent — crunchy and salty on the outside. The lollipop on a skewer seemed to be made from their roe. It was pungent and salty. All was eaten with gusto. The bamboo steamers contained a ceramic bowl holding a square paddy of sticky rice in a light sauce, topped with an exotic leaf and kale buds. The contents of the second brazier had cooked into a stew, and two eggs appeared for breaking into a bowl, shaped like a large spoon, and decorated with blue and white sectors, radiating out from the center. The broken eggs were mixed, and they were instructed to dip the meat and vegetables from the stew in the raw eggs. They were also served a simple shallow dish containing a metal grater and a large lump of pink rock salt.

"What do you think the salt is for?"

"It's good with the stew, and the broth is nicely balanced between the meat and vegetable worlds."

While they sampled the just-cooked brazier dishes, each was given a basket lined with thick paper, with a maple leaf motif printed on it. Tempura sat on the paper. It was hot, not oily, and it included fresh, still-furled fronds of a young bracken fern and slices of a root vegetable, lightly battered and tempura-fried. The tempura was followed by a bowl of local soba noodles in a clear broth, with thin slices of something probably egg-based. Finally, there was a dish of deep purple eggplant pickles, accompanied by another type of pickle, decorated with a tiny zest of something red. Perhaps a red pepper? The last dish in this series was a hexagonal bowl, containing a custard-like cream, topped with finely sliced and diced green onion leaves. And as if that were not enough, there appeared a most unusual square of layer cake, with a second piece of a different cake, seemingly built into it.

"Sara, how can we eat such a beautiful object, as if it were a Twinkie?"

"No problem, it doesn't taste like a Twinkie. It's divine, particularly with the two perfect strawberries and the white flower made of whipped cream."

A perfect scoop of vanilla ice cream lay peacefully in the bottom of another bowl with a lotus flower bas-relief on the inside.

And so the long procession of dishes came to an end. Sara was not yet satiated.

"Wow. What a feast for the eye and the palette! What's next? Hard act to follow. Perhaps we should take our evening bath below, by the stream? I see it's open late."

The ride on the steep funicular was between two lines of illuminated cherry trees in full flower. At the bottom of the canyon was a small building with the usual division of sexes.

"I'll probably be fairly quick, since bed sounds very good, so please take your time. I'll leave the room unlocked."

He did take his time, and it was worth it. The bath was a large pool, just above the stream. Hot water fell continuously into the pool from a stone pillar. The pool was irregular in shape, naturally fitted among the rocks. The bottom was flat stone. The water was hot and the air cold. He was alone, massaged by the hot water falling on his neck or, when he got too hot, lying nearly submerged or sitting, steaming on the rocks. He returned to the room to find Sara sound asleep.

He spent a moment on the terrace, listening to the stream below and wondering how this had happened.

Did she plan the whole thing — even getting the suite? No, no pinching necessary. It's all I could dream for. I'm high, high in the mountains in Japan. I'm not alone, not afraid and totally in love with this young woman, sleeping here. We had an exuberant climb with just us on a windy, narrow road. Just us going up with no destination — but higher, toward the fading light — just believing, and suddenly there was the strange building hanging on the cliff, and a room was waiting for us. We had a show-stopping dinner, looking out on the black mountainside, and a bath in an outdoor hot spring. It's hard to imagine how it could get better, but the sky's the limit, and tomorrow is not just another day.

He is dreaming music. Bach's cello suites. They are perfectly rendered and present — too real for a dream; then he hears the faint sound of a teacup settling onto its saucer, a gentle clink, and then the sound of pouring water. Hot water. He is awake. She is handing him a cup of tea. He sits up against the pillow, and takes the cup and saucer. She stands in silhouette before him, and behind her, he sees light hitting the mountainside, with its coat of many greens, fresh spring leaf greens and the brilliant, off-white, wild cherries. She says nothing — just smiles, turns, walks toward the terrace and slowly opens the glass door. She is in silhouette, facing away from him, gazing at the mountainside. Beside her, steam is rising from the outdoor bath, and he hears water flowing. He sees the *yukata* coming off and hanging on a peg, and she sits turned away from him, on the wooden stool, running the shower water over her head and down her back, the back he is seeing naked for the first time.

This must be the hallucination of a starving traveler, desperate for food and drink, imagining a full meal before him.

But she is real; soaping and scrubbing, rinsing and stepping into the bath, still in silhouette with her back turned toward him. She soaks, moving her head from side to side, stretching. She brings her arms up, locks them and stretches, and then settles back with her head on the edge of the wooden bath. She doesn't move for many minutes; she stands slowly and turns, stepping out of the bath. He sees her in profile, and he is flying. Drunken flight through time, over the wild cherry mountainside — back through all his years of being, decades of living — back to the moment of his birth.

She has turned toward the mountain, drying with the bath towel, which she wraps around her hair like a turban. All is slow motion, a tea ceremony, an offering of love. She comes through the door, wearing only a white turban and a Mona Lisa smile.

He rises, and they pass in the middle of the room and touch hands and eyes. He continues to the terrace, where he repeats every move she has made, including removing the *yukata*, the washing, the bath, the slow turn into profile, the turban and the return to the room. The music has stopped. She is lying on her bed, which is now pushed against his. She watches him, and she turns onto her stomach as he nears. The comforter barely covers her lower body. The bath towel is on the floor. He drops his towel turban and pulls the comforter down. She is as beautiful as he had imagined during those many hours of watching from behind as she stood on the pedals, *en danseuses*. He kisses the bottom of one foot, then the other and slowly moves up her body to her neck. He is hanging above her. Very slowly he settles onto her so that they touch, slowly melt together and meet for the first time. She rolls over and they kiss so gently and longingly that time stops forever. The summit is there, within reach — to savor and reveal in slow motion, in new dimensions and universal truths.

The air is cozy warm, but with prickly cool places. The stream sounds are distant. The mountain changes with cloud shadows passing fast. Cloud caresses. They have been asleep. She rises and puts on her *yukata*, hesitates, then lets it drop to the floor and returns to him. The air has cooled. A patch of fog blows up the valley, across the mountain, engulfing wild cherry trees. They rise together and make their way to the terrace bath, together, and settle into the hot water, together. They watch the weather changing, the passing of low clouds and the coming of rain. A gentle tsunami of fog sweeps along the steep sides of the Iya valley, clinging to the ridges and filling the low places, leaving patches of mottled light in its wake. They soak, caress and dry each other the way a mother dries her baby — fondly, lovingly. They dress in their *yukatas* for breakfast.

From their alcove breakfast table, they saw the entire mountain with the valley below, filling with fog. The rain was starting to hit the window. Breakfast together in a mountain refuge.

Each was served a large woven basket platter, holding seven dishes, including fish and various mysterious treats, a salad, a miso soup and a vegetable stew, cooking on a brazier. Other dishes, each a ceramic masterpiece, contained tofu, pickles and the unusual and unidentifiable delicious tastes. There was even a glass of milk.

Leaving the breakfast room, they encountered the manager. They exchanged bows and "*Ohayou gozaimasu.*" They said they would pack up and be out of the room soon. He nodded his head. A few minutes later they were back in the lobby with their bags and ready to pay their bill. The manager was at the desk. He said that it was a big storm, and not a day for cycling. He proposed a second night in a standard room with a generous discount. A few minutes later they were led into another room on the same floor.

The room was more traditional, with futons, a central *kotatsu*, the usual amenities, a wall of glass and a terrace. The prominent feature was a luxurious white porcelain bathtub in the center of the room, separated from the living space by floor-to-ceiling glass, looking out on the mountainside. The bath space included a hand shower and a wooden stool. The furnishings were of the same refinement as the suite: simple and luxurious.

"Shall we take a walk in the rain with our ponchos?"

The rain is driving, with intermittent gusts of wind. Walking along the road is the only choice, since the mountainside is a cliff, and no trails are evident. Their feet are soaked by the sheet of water flowing over the road. They come to a construction zone, where the road narrows to one lane. A dripping flagman directs the nonexistent traffic. He is happy and amused to see them. They continue until they have a view of their *onsen* on the cliff, just visible through the low clouds. The rain lets up for their walk back. The flagman is even happier to see them return.

They change into their *yukatas* and take the funicular railway to the outdoor hot spring. The baths are empty, and the stream and valley floor are partially obscured in fog. He is alone in the large outdoor men's bath, with the stream rushing just below. After soaking in the hot water, he returns to the dressing room and takes something out of the sleeve of his *yukata*. He walks naked — his body steaming in the cold air — to the edge of the bath terrace, where he uses his teeth to tear open the clear plastic pouch. After enlarging the hole with his fingers, he holds the bag between his teeth, while he climbs over the railing and down into the creek. Standing in the freezing water, he slowly pours out the white powder, which partly sinks and partly floats away, swirling on the surface and dissipating with the sound of falling water. He licks his lips and hand and feels the astringent taste again. He is shivering when he climbs back to the bath to warm up before regaining the dressing room.

Back in their room they use the massage chair, listen to music and watch the storm clouds blow across the mountainside. The rain is back, but intermittently. The light starts its fade to day's end — early with the thickening fog. They watch the slow show beyond the windows. He is in an armchair, and she on the floor between his legs, leaning against the chair, arms around his knees. The clouds caress the wild cherry trees and sift through the conifers. His hands cup the sides of her head and her hair, feeling the contours of her face, her ears and down to her shoulders. He leans forward and kisses her forehead; then reaches down and touches her breasts. No sounds are audible. They are alone. Time and place are suspended. The only contact is between them, through their skin and warmth. She turns onto her knees with her head in his lap. He is bending forward, caressing her back. She spreads open his *yukata* and takes him in her mouth. They slide slowly to the floor, locked together, with the armchair sliding back and away, leaving them alone to discover and rediscover the origins of life and love.

They ordered a bottle of wine with dinner. Their toast was a simple "*Compai*," but their eyes and smiles swirled with meaning, drifted through rapids and floated over calm waters. Words had faded with the evening light. The sounds of the dining room were muted. Colors faded into the night. But their faces were clear with eyes alive and seeing. They ate and watched each other eat, tasting the food in the other's mouth. They became identical twins, knowing all without words. Connected by light and time.

The first course was served on two principal platters for each of them. One was a square, flat basket, with bamboo hoops connecting the four corners in arching handles that crossed in the middle. Origami papers were placed on the woven square, forming another square, turned so that the corners protruded along the straight sides of the basket. In one corner were two small, glazed fish, lying on a sprig of a scale-like conifer branch, and next to the fish was something round, sitting on a slice of cucumber, encrusted with what seemed to be roasted barley, but the inside was a mysterious ball. Just beyond was a small celadon bowl, with pieces of something green that looked like avocado, but was not. To the right was a bamboo skewer through a flat blade of brown crusted tofu with thin *nori* strips on top, and farther to the right there was a smooth ball of what seemed like glutinous rice, slightly pink in color, with a spicy leaf wrapped around it. To the upper left of the square basket was a tulip-shaped blue bowl, which, when uncovered, revealed cooked or pickled spring shoots of Japanese kale, and just beside it was a small bowl, containing a green liquid that resembled matcha tea. In the front was a glass of white wine.

The second platter was a sashimi masterpiece. A fish had been transformed into bite-sized morsels, presented with a bamboo twig mat covering the part of the fish where the sashimi had been, but leaving the head and tail on either side. The sashimi was set on *shiso* leaves and shredded daikon with a cup made from a piece of cucumber holding wasabi for the soy sauce dip. The platter was further decorated with a slice of carrot in the form of a flower and a piece of lime, carved to produce a tail with a knot tied in it, and two slices of lemon. The square platter was white with a design in blue and a light brown rim. The fish was held in a curved, swimming position by a bamboo skewer.

"Sara, have you ever seen such a sashimi presentation? It's a case of having your fish and eating it too: a tribute to the fish and a taste privilege for us."

"Never… and I'm fascinated by the abundance of unknown foods. Each one is a new experience."

They slowly worked their way through these wonders, exclaiming and guessing at each one. Braziers came out with plates containing pieces of red meat, broccoli, onion, tofu and a slice of something yellow — all to be grilled on the brazier. In the meantime each was given a large bamboo tube, which was split lengthwise. Inside was a hot grilled trout, lying on a long leaf, with hot white pebbles beneath. A fresh, vermillion ginger shoot was laid across the fish, near the tail, which was covered in salt. It was finger food, and they each admired the spectacle of the other's enthusiasm for the succulent fish. Meanwhile, the grill had nicely browned the red meat, onions, tofu, etc., which they also ate with gusto.

"What appetites we have, Sara, and we didn't bike today!"

"Yes, but we got lots of exercise — even before we got out of bed!"

As they finished their meat and vegetables, another set of dishes appeared. One was a light, pinkish bowl, containing rice mixed with beans in a sauce, decorated with a large pink sakura blossom and a small green and yellow maple leaf — both confected from unknown substances. The tempura plate consisted of shrimp, with a *shiso* leaf leaning against them, and in front of that was a slice of Japanese eggplant, also lightly battered and deep-fried. The black skin had been sliced through to let the batter and oil enter and cook the inside. It looked like undersea kelp, moving with the currents. There was also a bundle of soba noodles, wrapped in what was probably nori. They had been pre-pared as tempura and cut in half, showing a cross section. The last tempura item was a slice of a succulent root veg-etable they could not identify. All of this was laid out on absorbent paper, but not a drop of oil could be seen.

A small dark bowl contained a thick liquid that was prob-ably derived from taro root, with chopped green seaweed on top. Another blue and white bowl contained two slices of dark purple, pickled eggplant, leaning against a finely grated, white vegetable, something like daikon radish, but not. They were also served a bowl of soba noodles with chives and thin slices of tofu. A bowl of perfect Japanese rice, light, fluffy and slightly sticky, announced the end of the main part of the meal. Dessert was three small treats served on a long rectangular black lacquer tray. On the left were two pieces of chocolate layer cake, consisting of dark, white and milk chocolate. In the middle was a perfectly round ball of vanilla ice cream, and on the right, in a glass bowl with blue sectors, was what appeared to be a slice of lemon, but it was a dense lemon custard, contained in a skin of something sweet, sour and delicious. All was placed on squares of origami paper, printed in a red and white sakura design. A small spoon and fork were the utensils.

"It's symphonic! How did they make this? So inventive and delicious!"

"And exciting for the eye."

They fall asleep in full body contact. The night is silent and long. Morning comes as a hint of white cherry blossom against a black mountain. He is awake, rolling silently off the futon. She dreams of birds, flying through the valley, grazing the trees, turning skyward, chattering. She is one of them — free of gravity and all burdens — free to dive and soar. She drops to the valley floor and swoops along the water, hearing it call to play, sing and dance in spray and sound. Something foreign intervenes: the soft clink of a cup on a saucer. She is awake, and he offers her tea. They sit against their pillows and slowly sip the hot drink.

"I'm the happiest woman on Earth. I'm the only woman on Earth, the only one to have the greatest lover in the universe. You've taken me to the summit of happiness, after the longest, most loving seduction in the history of love. I'm all yours, body and soul."

She rises and walks slowly toward the mountainside, reaching out to the wild cherries, opening the door to the bath area, where hot water is waiting. He watches every move in this ballet, memorizing every gesture. She faces him, soaping and scrubbing, rinsing; then she steps into the bath. He sees her serene face, her outstretched arms — her hair, wet, and the steam rising from the hot water, clothing her body in moisture. When she gets out, he is there to dry her lovingly, caressingly — as a lover. He repeats all of her gestures, as she watches and waits for him, sitting in the armchair. She is there to dry him, and they embrace as lovers who know each other, and she leads him by the hand across the tatamis to the futon.

And that is how their pasts erased, without them realizing what was happening. Everything before fell away, leaving the present with just each other and a song, suggested by a low hum or a drawing of breath, a moan, a wily glance, a touch of lips, a mouthing of words. Their memories were thus reset to zero. They became primitives, alive at the deepest root of life. A new meaning emerged from this primitive root: the meaning of now and a rebuilding of the future in past-less time.

The sun grazed the mountainside, alighting on the cherry blossoms and young leaves. The sky was clear. The storm had passed, leaving the mountain finely scrubbed and clean. They stood together on the balcony admiring this new world and each other.

"Can you see what I see, Sara? We've crossed the pass, and the other side is paradise. I've flipped, gone crazy in love. I want to be with you every second of the day. The definition of life is simple: it's being with you — just us together, anywhere and everywhere."

"Yes, I see a beautiful mountain scene, freshly renewed by rain, with cherry trees in bloom. I see a beautiful, generous man beside me. I feel his warm body, and I feel whole and fulfilled. Yes, we've climbed to the pass, and on the other side is paradise with just us in it, holding hands. Thank you for waiting for me. Thank you for waiting for me. Thank you for waiting for me."

Breakfast was in full view of the mountain, with them facing each other, legs touching. It was different from the day before, but similar in design. They were hungry, devouring everything.

The flagman was there. All smiles, waving them through with exaggerated, enthusiastic gestures. The road descended gently from the hotel high point, giving them views of the *onsen* and the meanders of the valley; then it reconnected with the stream in a small town. They stopped to cross a footbridge made of kiwi vines, reconstructed for visitors to demonstrate the ingenuity of the mountain people. They continued east, having lunch in a restaurant specializing in homemade soba noodles. She was planning their route.

"The map shows a small road, Route 44, leading north from here, over the mountain pass above us. It descends to another small road, climbs a second, lower pass and drops way down to the Yoshino river valley, well below the village where the train left us. From there we could cross another range of mountains to Zentsuji."

"I'm all yours. Lead me anywhere, but down."

So they climbed to Ochiai pass, by thatched hillside farmhouses — through valleys, canyons, conifers on mountainsides, wild cherries, meadows, crashing streams, patches of snow and thinning air. Always up, relentless up. Standing on the steep stretches, sitting when possible, stopping to snack and for views far down into the Iya valley, from where they had come. He couldn't believe his luck at living a prime cycling experience with the woman of his dreams.

"This is better than the Alps — we haven't seen a single vehicle. The road is perfect — pure mountain. It's a cycling dream come true and with you. But you're not doing your intervals!"

"I'm staying with you on this one."

"I'll do my best. The grade is steep, but within reason. I wonder where the pass is? The map showed a series of switchbacks. We should recognize them easily when we get there. The last part is a long traverse."

They climbed through the switchbacks, feeling the urgency of the sun moving westward. The road rounded the top of a valley, and they were in the long traverse. Below was the river valley and ranges of mountains, lined up one behind the other. He was leading and picked up the pace and the rhythm of his breathing, trying to collapse and expand his lungs fully with each breath. He stayed in the bottom of the gear, spinning just enough to stay aerobic. She was riding behind him; then she came alongside.

"Do you think we're in the final traverse?"

"I hope so. It's quite a climb. I can feel the altitude. Please lead for a while. I like the rear view."

She went around and stood up on the pedals, but without changing speed. She looked back at him and winked.

"Now I'm really inspired."

He sped up slightly, closing the gap between them, but she sensed his presence and increased her speed. She could hear him breathing and kept the pace; then pulled out and fell back beside him.

"You seem to be full of energy. Must have been the noodles for lunch."

"I feel good, but it's not noodles. It's you in those lycra shorts, and now that I know what's underneath, the view from back here is even more exciting. Riding with you is like chasing a rainbow, except you're more beautiful."

The grade increased suddenly, and they both stood up, breathing harder. It was a one-lane road with good visibility, so they rode side by side, in synchrony. The air was cool, but they were hot from the effort. He pulled out his water bottle, handed it to her, and took a drink himself.

They pass a small shrine with a statue of Kobo Daishi. The top of the ridge is within grasp. They accelerate, standing, sprinting. He jumps ahead; she catches up. He pours on more coal, and his muscles catch fire with pain and exhilaration. She drops behind him, close. Their lungs and hearts are in the red zone — maxed out, off scale — then he turns on the afterburner and shifts up into superman mode, where pain does not exist, where muscle fibers defy the laws of physics. He jumps forward and accelerates up through the gear, right to the top of the pass and onto the grass, dropping the bike, staggering to stay on his feet.

She is right behind. Her bike on the ground, they run for each other, arms open, and embrace, breathing desperately. He bends down, locks his arms behind her thighs and with his last fragment of strength, he lifts her toward the sky and screams, and she reaches skyward and screams, and they spin like a helicopter, rising slowly at first, and then climbing fast and disappearing into the clouds.

When they finally come floating down, she collapses over his standing body, with his face buried in her belly. Suddenly she shrieks and bolts straight upright, flailing her arms and kicking; then she hits his back with her fists, pulls his hair, grabs his neck, wriggles in all directions. He holds tight, loses his balance, and their edifice collapses to the ground.

They are both laughing hysterically, rolling on the grass. They finally lock hands and find each other. He pulls her close to him, caressing her hair.

"You bad boy! You rascal! Not only you beat me to the top, but you discovered my greatest weakness! Now I'm your slave forever. You have complete power over me. I give in totally. You know my secret. Now you really have me, body, soul and…"

"… belly button."

"How did you know?"

"It was so delicious. Slightly salty. I couldn't resist. It tickled my tongue."

They lie together on the grass, laughing and drying their eyes. Two crows watch them warily, wondering what to make of these crazy humans.

"Never seen anything quite like it before," one says. "They seem to be having convulsions. Strange behavior, even for humans. It must be their mating season. Maybe they'll take out their snacks and leave something for us to eat?"

Recuperation is slowed by flights of uncontrollable laughter, set off each time they look at each other. They finally cover their eyes. When they fully recover and roll onto their backs, holding hands, she says, "I don't want to go down. I want to spend the rest of my life right here with you, watching the clouds go by. Please stop time right now."

"I could smash my watch for you, but I don't have power over time. We can spend the night here. I'll build a fire… but there is very little wood at this altitude, and it will be cold and dark tonight. I saw a couple of crows… they're hard to catch and not very good eating, so dinner might be a little lean."

"OK. If I go down, do you promise me a nice dinner?"

"I promise you a nice dinner, and I promise you that we'll descend in altitude only. We've crossed into a new watershed. This is the doorway to a new life. I promise to do everything possible to keep us here, high on the summit — to never go down. That I can promise, but time has powers of its own. I can't stop time. Some compromise with it might be necessary."

"I understand. I really do. I accept your offer and timely conditions."

They took the descent carefully, dodging fallen rocks, branches and road washouts. The grade was steep with winding traverses, switchbacks in series and contours above cascading streams through cedar forest. They rode through a high valley with a few farm buildings, and then they started up to Sajiki pass, which was a strenuous but easier climb. They didn't stop at the top, and waited until they had a view over the deep and distant Yoshino valley. The sun had dropped behind the next range of mountains, lying between them and Zentsuji temple, and they were feeling the chill. The descent was long. They finally saw farmhouses, and as the road widened, they picked up speed. They arrived at the bottom just as darkness was complete, stopping in a grocery store in Mikamo to ask for directions to a hotel or *minshuku*. The owners took time to draw them a map. The hotel receptionist directed them to park their bikes in the lobby, and suggested a nearby restaurant. They had a standard western style hotel room with their own bath. Freshly bathed, they walked to the restaurant and ordered a copious meal, including local soba noodle specialties, tempura and Japanese beer.

"You look happy!"

"I am very, very happy. What a day! You sure poured on the juice in the sprint for the top of the pass. I didn't know you could do that sort of thing."

"I didn't either, but it felt good. I was high. High on you! I went over the top into a new existence. I'm still there, and I'm staying. It wasn't the climb or the altitude or the mountain scenery or the physical effort. It was being with you. Really being with you with no restraints. I feel liberated, ecstatic to know you, to be alive and in love with you."

"And you acted like a mischievous ten-year-old boy!"

"Ah, you have a point. I have acquired inside knowledge that could be used in the future…"

They walked back to the hotel. She entered the room first, turned on the lights, and on her pillow she found a folded piece of paper with her name on it.

Shore break

The wave breaks, forever
No tears. Others come
One by one to a broken end.
Glorious sound spray. Once.
Each in turn, endless lines
Night and day, shore rake.

Hearts unwoven broken lives
Blended sand foam, atomized.
Diminished and left to coast,
Backwards into oblivion depths
Meanderings of current aerated
Energy dissipated in sound.

Rhythm furious, many amplitudes
Where from, these soldiers of lost
Fortune and steady supply?
Destiny? Entrained wind tide?
Floating riders wave, sitting
Standing, sitting, standing.

Upon this shore confronted
They break, wash up, ruined
Remnants, reminders of
Comets, Naga nymphs,
Interstellar condensates.

And into this chaos
From order we plunge
From fine sand beach,
Sand, suspended in foam
We swim, cling the floor
Crashing thrashing above

David Tepfer

The struggle to Nirvana
Safe haven beyond the break
Order over disorder, chaos
Solitude and mind peace
Just bobbing gentle bubbles
Clear above, cloud wisps

We talk above surf's roar
We bob out of sync, losing
Sight and mind contact,
Then clinging, swimming
In unison we contemplate
The future of body surfing.

Riding wave in is out
Shore break neck break
No question, but to
Sneak through from behind
The forces that be
Then swim like mad.

We procrastinate drift
Shorely, surely into chaos
Watched by gulls, keen
On a future meal, and
We hesitate, as if lost,
But nothing of the kind.

We listen to the breaking
Fury on the beach, illicit
Anger of gods, unnatural
Powers of nature focused
On water and gravity
And us, the wary ready.

We close in on shore,
Watching for oversize
Outliers, then try our
Luck. A friendly one?
No, wait! Next one. Go!
Swim for it! Go now!

The tide is in, so
The breakers hit on
Steep, eroding sand.
Just behind the wave
We land in foam and
Rolling with the flow,
Back to sea we go

In time for the next
Mercenary wave to
Clobber us against
The beach and roll
Us homogenized up
Then back to Neptune

The third wave is larger
And we roll harder, twisting
To find ourselves together,
Standing we lock wrists
And the beach collapses
Into suspended particles.

We sink. The fourth wave
Hits and I feel the floor
Hear the crash and
Lunge with you, upward
Anywhere but down
Exploded thrown recoiled

Hands and knees hit solid
And we scramble up
The sand embankment
Safe from the charge of
The fifth wave and
All others waiting behind.

And I had thought we
Would roll forever in
Sandy foam, leaving our future
To sea gulls and sandy loam.
But the fourth wave saved
The day and even the night.

We are breathing hard
And laughing. What a ride.
The tide rose fast, and
The beach was so steep
What a surprise, but we
Made it made it made it.

Sand in ears, hair, everywhere
Sun is bright, as we dry
Then take a walk, holding
Hands gently, I see your
Wrist is bruised, where
We clung together in love.

After breakfast in the hotel, they crossed a bridge decorated
with statues of fish and another bridge with local images
chiseled in black granite. They rode upstream on a bicycle path, high on a dike with a forest of bamboo between
them and the river. They stopped to buy strawberries at a
stand beside the road below them. The seller wore white

gloves while inspecting each strawberry before adding it to the paper box. They were shiny red, with long green stems, carefully packed with special wrapping. They ate their strawberries sitting on the dike, facing the bamboo forest. They were juicy and pungent with just the right sweetness — produced in a nearby hydroponic farm, which explained their perfect exteriors and long stems.

She dangles a large, bright red, pristine strawberry in front of her mouth, looking at him mischievously. Her tongue darts out, sending the strawberry swinging. She inches it toward her mouth, teasing her tongue with it. Then her tongue attacks again; she just barely pulls it away, keeping her eyes on him and the strawberry. After several attempts the strawberry pretends to succumb, and her tongue and lips engulf the juicy fruit. She seems to chew and swallow it, but after much struggle, slowly pulling on the stem, it finally pops out of her mouth, whole, wet and triumphant. She dangles it in front of his face, and with a wolfish grin, his mouth snaps it away, chews and swallows it, stem and all, emitting a moan of pleasure.

They explore the bamboo forest on foot, walking to the river, which is clear and fast. Later, when the bike path ends, they continue on the road, riding close to the river. They come to a town, buy bentos for lunch, withdraw cash from the machine in the post office, and Sara makes her weekly call to Mama-san. They leave the valley to climb the range of mountains between them and Zentsuji temple, ascending through a steep valley. Light glistens off the new leaves with the intensity of fall colors, punctuated by wild cherry trees in full bloom.

The grade is constant, unabated upward. He feels strong and spunky.

"I see you're not doing intervals today. Mind if I try some?"

"I would be delighted to see your grinning face as you pass me coming down."

He rides ahead, while she continues at a leisurely pace. He is soon anaerobic, feeling pain in his legs. He kicks into accelerated breathing, trying to expand his diaphragm on each inhale. He holds his own against the hill; then the grade gets steeper, and he shifts down, spinning and breathing hard. He recovers, stands on the pedals and shifts up as the climb subsides for a short distance. When it steepens again, he tries to keep the pace, but runs out of oxygen and strength. He finally turns around and heads down, sucking air into his lungs and feeling relief in his legs. He manages a grin as he passes Sara.

He continues to descend fast, thinking about how far he should go and still be able to catch up with her on his second climb as she nears the top. When he turns around, he realizes he is far down the road. He starts slogging upwards again. He imagines her doing her intervals and wonders once more at her ability to climb impossible grades with seemingly little effort. Is it her weight? Does she have some extra-human ability to transport oxygen? He tries to goad himself into similar performance, but the pain and breathing are intense, and he feels weak. He realizes he is hungry, but Sara has the snacks. It's all the more reason to catch up. He sweats, breathes hard and his tongue and lips tingle.

Just ride through it. So I'm low on blood sugar. Big deal!

He stands and hits the pedals, but there is nothing to burn. The road goes out of focus, and he barely gets his right foot down as he rolls to the pavement. Everything is spinning. He manages to drag himself and the bike off the road, where he lies, looking at the sky, blurred clouds and soaring birds.

The buzzards are after me.

Minutes go by and he sits up, feeling weak, and then Sara comes flying around the corner, slams on the brakes, drops her bike and rushes over.

"I think I bonked."

She has her ear on his chest, while gently lowering him onto his back. Then she is looking at him strangely. He can't quite focus on her.

"Say that again."

He has trouble saying, "I bonked."

"OK. Your speech is slurred. Diagnosis is simple. Take some sugar. Hold it under your tongue. If it's hypoglycemia, you'll start to recover shortly."

She fetches sugar cubes from her rack trunk, and she sits beside him, taking his pulse. He sees blue sky, clouds and the same soaring birds. They seem to be coming into better focus. She gets something from the bike and helps him sit up.

"Drink some water and eat some peanuts."

He sits up and, the sugar gone, he chews the peanuts.

She puts her arms around him.

"Speak to me, please. What happened?"

"I got carried away; went too far down. On the climb back up, I started feeling weak, and tried to catch you; I got extremely dizzy, almost crashed, but I'm starting to feel better, so it must be the bonk."

"Well, that sounds more like it. Your speech is normal. Are you still dizzy?"

"Not really. Just hungry."

"You picked a perfect spot for lunch! It's almost noon, and our only snack was strawberries. You ran out of blood sugar. I'm so sorry I didn't think of dividing the food with you. I won't make that mistake again. By the way, how long has it been since you've had a physical?"

"I had one a couple of months ago. Everything was normal."

They eat their bentos overlooking terraced fields, with a mountain of multicolored foliage in front of them. The light glistens off the new leaves with the intensity of fall colors, punctuated by wild cherry trees in full bloom. He is starting to feel normal.

"I forgot to ask you, how was your talk with Mama-san?"

"She said I sounded '*genki*.' She could hear a change in my voice. She said there was music. She's right. I've been thinking about 'All the Things You Are.' It's one of my favorite standards."

She claps her hands together and listens intensely to the echo. She stands and sings full voice toward the mountain and its robe of vibrant leaves, with the power and feeling of spring love. She sings of seeking adventure and finding it in his love. Touching his hand is the excitement she desires. He is springtime's promise, the quiet of the evening… She longs for the moment when he is hers…

He is convinced a bank of speakers has been introduced into the trees. Her sound is clearly being amplified, but how? Each note is a succulent fruit, and the sculpted phrases reflect multiple facets of meaning. He is so surprised that it takes a moment to find words to express his wonderment.

"Sara, I can't imagine how you did that. I'm dumbfounded. You're a sorceress."

"I just had a hunch, and it worked out. Leafy trees can be good sound reflectors and diffusers. In the right configuration, they resonate and blend. I clapped to test the reverb, but I was already pretty sure it would work. I just had to adjust my overtones and volume to hit the right frequencies in the amplifier."

"The what? You know how this happens?"

"Sure. That's how acoustical music works in large spaces. Opera singers do it instinctively. You don't need to know the physics — just how to make the acoustics serve the music."

"Do you sing opera?"

"Are you a fan?"

"You could say that…"

"So who's your favorite opera composer — whose music would you take to a desert island?"

"Well, that's easy — Puccini. What's his first name? Guacamole?"

Sara advances — hands in strangle mode…

"I take it back! Don't kill me! Giacomo, OK, Giacomo. Help!"

She pushes him back against the grass. Her hands are on his neck.

"Repeat after me: Giacomo Puccini was a genius, the greatest genius who ever lived! The greatest opera composer of them all!"

He pretends to cough and gasp, finally repeating the phrase after her, feigning death in his last word.

"Now that you've almost killed me, please tell me… no, please sing for me your favorite Puccini aria. Wait! Let me guess… you're the perfect Mimì. Of course! But you'll always be my Butterfly, my Cio-Cio-san!"

"Which aria do you want? I know both roles."

"Well, in that case please sing, '*Sì, mi chiamano Mimì.*' I'll save Butterfly for another special moment. The stage is yours, Mademoiselle."

Sara sings to him and the hillside tree audience.

"*Sì, mi chiamano Mimì
ma il mio nome è Lucia.*"

With this unforgettable phrase, Mimì introduces herself, responding to Rodolfo's declaration of love. She connects without artifice, directly to Rodolfo's soul, with the hillside audience as witness. She embroiders sweet odors of spring, love itself. She is Mimi working alone in her room, but when spring comes, the first sun is hers, like her first kiss… He is transfixed, but remembers to sing Rodolfo's "Si" at the right moment. She is the total Mimi: natural, musical and profoundly beautiful, without artifice.

"So now I know how Pavarotti felt the first time he sang *La Bohème* with Freni! It's heaven. I'm reliving my first Mimi. You're there. You have it all."

"Seriously, you heard Luciano Pavarotti and Mirella Freni sing *La Bohème*?"

"I did, and I couldn't sleep for nights after. Now I won't sleep for weeks."

"And your Rodolfo came in perfectly. How exciting to know you know… It's a new world for us to share."

They continued climbing at a reduced pace and stopped to visit a wooden shrine, decorated in finely carved dragons and cranes. The roof had the traditional turned-up corners, and they could see a large tatami room inside.

The road was smooth, and after the pass they descended through forest, which gave way to farms, villages and many traditional houses. Women were working in the fields, wearing large sunbonnets. The landscape was dotted with conical, volcanic hills, rising several hundred meters above the plain. They encountered pilgrims as they neared Zentsuji temple; then they saw the five-story pagoda and entered into the temple grounds at the gate beside a massive camphor tree. A nun with a shaved head greeted them at the temple lodgings. Their room was traditional, in a contemporary building. After their baths, they walked through the grounds, admiring the many buildings and statuary. Dinner was in a nearby *shokudo*, where they sat at the bar and watched the two chefs: one for the yakitori grill and another for everything else. They were young, and full of energy and good humor. The food was inventive and delicious, with a large choice of yakitori, soups and salads. It was starting to rain when they walked back to their room.

"I feel a strong kinship with the women we've seen working in the fields, who appear to be at least in their seventies. They seem so happy. I envy them, weeding while kneeling on the ground or sometimes lying on their side. They're in direct contact with something real and important to them. And they have their fashion statement: no skin exposed, except for faces, which are protected by bonnets. I like their pants and boots... and the gloves. This is the side of Japanese fashion I admire. But most beautiful is their reaction when you smile at them. They light up with pleasure. We couldn't be more different: me in my cycling attire and them in their farm clothes. But we understand each other as women. Vanity is important to us."

"You're right. These rural women are beautiful, and we've seen them everywhere. It's part of the human performance, I guess. We seek a loving audience, even if it's an audience of one — a strangely dressed, young *gaijin* woman on a bicycle, who admires a ninety-year-old compatriot, lying in a field and pulling weeds. You have to wonder where the men have gone. Dead? Watching TV? It's the same thing, I guess. We're definitely the weaker sex, both in brain and longevity. But I fear the next generation of women will not have the same courage and direct contact with life. They'll be playing weed pulling computer games for octogenarians, instead of pulling weeds in real fields."

They talked a little more, and turned the overhead fixture down to the night light setting. The room was quiet. Lying on their futons, they could hear distant small-town sounds from vehicles and people. Signs of life. It was raining, and the wind increased. It was time to sleep or maybe just to dream — to listen to their breathing. He took her hand.

"I feel your heart, strong and slow. I can see the color of it. It works and lives. It keeps the pace — day and night in rhythms, strong and fast or slow and easy, but always yours and mine. My heart is your heart. I love you."

They found the pilgrims in the lobby at 6 am. Nobody seemed to mind their bicycle clothes. A monk led them through an indoor passage to the main temple, a richly decorated and yet spacious sanctuary that seemed more Chinese than Japanese. The ceremony started with a procession of six monks in impressive robes. It included chanting, bells, gongs, prayers and a sermon. The sermon seemed extemporaneous and informal, almost like a family event. They listened to the music of the language, rather than the words. Something communicated — something peaceful and human, with a note of prehistory, going back and redefining the fundamental questions. Who are we? Why are we here? Where are we going?

At the end of the ceremony, they were invited to descend into the tunnel called Kaidan Meguri. The printed instructions said to walk with the left hand touching the wall in a quest for self-purification. The point of the darkness was to reflect on "your human nature and rid yourself of your sins that you have made unconsciously. In short, Kaidan-Meguri is a place where you cultivate the mind."

Following the instructions, they chanted "*Namu daishi henjo kongo*," as they walked in complete blackness. They were alone in the 228-meter, circular tunnel, walking on sand brought from the 88 Temples. The walls were painted with Buddha images, invisible in the dark, showing the way to heaven through rebirth from darkness to light. Toward the end, they heard chanting and came into a dimly lit underground room with an altar and religious paintings on the walls. Hidden loud speakers quietly chanted mantras. They were underneath Kobo Daishi's birthplace.

Back in the light of day, they returned to the guesthouse for breakfast; then they visited other temple buildings, including a museum showing objects that had belonged to Kobo Daishi, also known as Kukai. He lived from 774 to 835, and he founded the Shingonshu Zentsuji branch of Buddhism, after studying in China. Zentsuji is Number 75 in the 88 Temple Pilgrimage. He built it at his birthplace, and the massive camphor tree is thought to date from his childhood. Kobo Daishi was also a scholar and builder of public works. He helped introduce Chinese culture to Japan, building a monastery at Mount Koya. He was a calligrapher, a poet, and he invented the kana Japanese alphabet.

They rode a few kilometers to visit two nearby pilgrimage temples on the flank of a trio of volcanic peaks rising from the plain. It was raining by the time they got there, so they ate their lunch under an overhanging roof, looking out over orange groves. The rain intensified during their temple visit, and they took refuge on a porch in the temple compound, watching the storm and listening to the rain. It cascaded down a chain of bronze cups, a downspout, accumulated in puddles on the ground, splashed off leaves and copper roofs. It was strong, cleansing and sustained — like Buddhism. His thoughts turned to the pilgrims.

"I wonder what it means to be a pilgrim. Are we pilgrims? Must we believe in a religion to be a pilgrim? Is cycling a religion?"

"Cycling is definitely a religion. Maybe pilgrimage is related to the seasonal migration of animals?"

"I agree. Our basic instinct is to migrate. We're an exploring and expanding species. Cycling can be a pilgrimage, without being religious, and here a religious pilgrimage can be a kind of tourism. We're pilgrims in the most basic sense, exploring new territory — physically and spiritually."

"I propose we migrate back to Zentsuji and explore an afternoon nap."

Which they did, and their nap on their futons with the rain outside was both spiritual and physical, discovering new territory in their journey to enlightenment through love.

"Before coming to Zentsuji, I was a bicycle gypsy. Now I'm a convert to love — to stay-with-one-man love. You've shown me the path. I know love for the first time. I believe in the power, the beauty and the eternity of love."

"Ours is a love pilgrimage, and I worship you."

They returned to the *shokudo* for dinner and the young chefs and waitresses were happy to see them back, greeting them with "*Irrashaimase!*" They found new and unexpected culinary surprises, including a stew served in a thick stone pot, heated on a gas flame. The sauce was red, with orange and yellow objects jumping through it.

Lying on their futons, they had their bedtime chat and talked more about love and religion.

"I've seen temples in India decorated with explicit statues of people making love."

"And I've read there are still shrines in Japan that display erotic images and objects. Before World War II, when Western culture came massively to Japan, mixed nudity was accepted in most public baths."

"And our Western concept of love is religious. We love god, and we draw lines to separate the kinds of love, but are they really different?"

"And we build walls to keep men and women from seeing each other's bodies."

"Now there's an explanation for the dismal Japanese birthrate: the public baths are segregated!"

The morning was bright and clear. Breakfast was Japanese at long tables with handwritten place names. They talked with the pilgrims around them, who were curious and friendly. Several were fluent in English. The pilgrimage was retirement tourism for the many who traveled by bus, unlike the pilgrims they had seen walking the roads, for whom it was also an endurance test.

They took time to admire the camphor tree, said to be at least 1000 years old. The multi-shaded spring foliage was mixed with dispersed autumnal leaves in dark orange and brown. Crushing a leaf released the intense scent of camphor. They sat on a bench and watched the world go by. Women, dressed much like the women working in the fields, were sweeping the grounds. Children walked to school. The birds were active, with the ubiquitous Japanese crows having raucous conversations on telephone wires. It was a lively spring morning. She felt mellow.

"This is the ultimate luxury: taking time to smell the camphor and soak up the sunshine. I'm puzzled by the rock tied up in black rope that was sitting in the middle of the courtyard in front of the first temple. It was just a normal rock, but it was so artfully tied, with loops for carrying it. The rope loops were like wings — like it wanted to fly."

"It seemed to have been placed there on purpose, like a rock in a dry garden, but there was no raked gravel — just the courtyard pavement."

"What could it symbolize?"

"Rocks in Zen gardens are sometimes mountains rising above water, which is represented by raked gravel, but this rock was far smaller, and neatly tied with doubled black rope. It was meant to be portable."

"It was left there for a reason. We can only guess what it was. It could have been purely aesthetic or just a forgotten doorstop. Maybe it was art? There are so many mysterious things in this country."

"What mysterious thing should we visit next?"

How about a seventeenth-century garden in Takamatsu? I would love to see another traditional garden before we leave Japan."

"Ouch, Sara! You're already talking about leaving Japan?"

"No. But we could think about leaving Shikoku. Takamatsu is the ferry departure point for islands in the Seto Sea that have art installations, and one of them, Shodoshima, has a mountain we could climb. I'm feeling like another big climb, now that we've caught up on our Buddhism."

They took the train to Takamatsu to avoid the urban build-up of the coastal plain. They checked into the youth hostel, a converted hotel with spacious rooms, and rode to Ritsurin Garden. As they entered, they were met by a Japanese man, who spoke excellent English. He gave them his card and explained that he worked for the park, hosting visitors and writing English language information pamphlets. He was officially retired, but he worked two days a week to maintain his English and enjoy the contacts with visitors. He invited them to park their bikes in front of his office, and gave them maps and information for their visit.

The garden was built by successive lords over 100 years, starting in the early seventeenth century. Mount Shiun served as a backdrop, providing a natural reference for the landscape art. They began their stroll along well-swept paths, finding their way to a hill with views over Hoko Lake, with islands — all planted in elegantly trimmed and trained pine trees. Across the pond was a vermillion Japanese arched bridge, and several traditional buildings nested in the landscape. Perhaps they were teahouses?

The next lake contained a swarm of extravagantly colored

nishikigoi carp that were being fed by visitors. They crossed arched bridges in natural wood, and used stepping-stones to cross the stream flowing through clumps of irises into the lake from Fukiage Spring, providing clear water throughout the garden. A canopy of freshly minted, yellow-green maple leaves descended over the dark water. From the top of Shozan mound they viewed Nanko Lake with islands, rocks in the water, pines with fresh spring yellow needles and the teahouse on the far shore. The pines were sculpted like bonsais, and they had produced tiny, light yellow, female cones. A grey heron stood immobile on a small island.

They came to the teahouse from the side away from the lake, facing another pond. Inside, they were served matcha tea and sweets, kneeling on the tatami mats. They stayed for a long while, soaking up the visual thrill of the lake, with its perfect islands and bridges and the many-colored foliages as a backdrop. He was thinking about how lucky they were to be there.

"For centuries this garden was the privilege of a few aristocrats. Here we are — two *gaijins*, basking in their exclusive pleasure."

"It's so artificial, and too real to be true. Nature revisited, tamed, remodeled and glorified. It's a tribute to the real thing."

"Nature is rendered with respect in Ritsurin, which is not always the case in our art world."

"I'm wondering why the feudal lords built this garden? Was it a need to possess nature?"

"It's human to capture beauty for exclusive use. I imagine a seventeenth-century strongman admiring the mountainside in the spring, with all of the colors and wild cherries, and finding it beautiful and moving — falling in love with it, and then buying it. We try to possess the beauty we love, Sara. But it wasn't really his. It belonged to nature, so he took it away from nature and made it his, putting his personal stamp on it. He printed his design on nature for his exclusive use."

"And now it's for everybody to enjoy. No single person possesses it."

They moved to the side views of the shore and the dry gardens, with rocks, stepping stones, raked gravel and bonsai sculpted pines. An interior room had a large window, framed with shoji screens that outlined a perfect forest scene. It was a living painting, seemingly hung on the wall.

After the teahouse, they continued their stroll along the pond at the steep base of Mount Shiun, where there was a small waterfall, which in feudal times functioned only when servants carried water up the mountain to a tank that was emptied on cue for the lord's viewing pleasure.

They returned to the youth hostel via a long shopping arcade; then continued until they found a restaurant. Sitting at the counter were two middle-aged men and a not-so-young woman wearing a kimono. She was made up, and wore her hair in the classical style. The men were drunk — one so drunk he could hardly stay on his stool. They were having quite a feast, and she kept their cups full of sake. She disappeared from time to time — perhaps to fill other sake cups in another room. The food was inventive, prepared before them by the chef, who kept the conversation flowing with the sake. Questions were put to them, and attempts to communicate were made in primitive language on both sides. It was fun, but the sake had done its job, and the other guests made their staggering exit after effusive goodbyes.

Back in their room, she started their late evening recap.

"It's our first city since Matsuyama, and I'm glad we saw the stunning garden. The hostess in the restaurant was something out of a movie. She was completely in control but submissive and gentle at the same time. Her featur' were stately — a beauty, and still a beauty. It's a strange profession — helping men get drunk."

"Helping them trash their illusions and remember nothing of it the next day."

"Is there no equivalent for women? A male gigolo drinking host?"

"Maybe that should be my next profession!"

As he fell asleep, a strange word sequence came back into his head:

The knight is not young; tomorrow is not just another day; tomorrow is today.

He tried to untangle the layers of meaning in these words, but the hostess from the restaurant kept filling his glass — until he almost passed out. He wanted to pay the bill, but he was too drunk to see straight. She took his wallet and extracted the required amount, plus a generous tip.

He awoke much later. Rain was hitting the window. He was just falling asleep again, when he found himself back at the restaurant, serving sake to a coed, who was wearing a dark sweater with a low neckline. All he could say was "*compai*" over and over, fading into silence. As the girl leaned forward to toast, her neckline swung open. He dared not look down. Instead, he took a mouthful of sake, and he ʌve her a hot sake kiss on her lips; then he buried his face in décolleté and let the warm sake flow into her cleavage.

was called into the dean's office and reprimanded for the girl's sweater. His punishment was to pay for ʌaning. The irate dean told him that if he wanted ʌe and become full professor of gigolology, he be more careful with expensive sweaters and

ʌ

The next morning they took a ferry to Naoshima, the first of the art islands. Landing in Miyanoura, they saw a large red object, shaped like a pumpkin and decorated with black polka dots.

"Oh! I know that artist! That's by the polka dot lady, Yayoi Kusama. She's obsessed with polka dots, and puts them everywhere. She's high fashion."

They inspected the hollow structure, watched school-children playing in the pumpkin, and looked at the map of the island. They decided to ride along the coast to visit the three major art installations: the Chichu Art Museum, the Benesse House and the art house project in Hanmura. The sun was warm and the hillsides were studded with pink azaleas. They came upon a sculpture of a trashcan about twenty times normal size. It contained perfectly sculpted trash. Next they visited the Chichu Museum, designed by Tadao Ando.

It was a large concrete structure, mostly buried in a hill-top, but with concrete-lined light shafts. The only view to the outside was from the cafeteria. They saw a room of Monet water lily paintings and installations by well-known living artists. They ate lunch in the museum cafeteria, look-ing out over the sea with Takamatsu in the distance.

"How do you feel, Sara?"

"Happy to be outside. Inside, I felt a clash of egos between the architect and the artists."

"And the Monet water lily paintings are not as communi-cative as those in the Orangerie in Paris, but if you've never seen his water lilies before, I'm sure these are worth the price of admission."

"But the architect draws attention away from the water lilies. It's like a vocal recital where the pianist is too loud. It's a relief to look out over the sea and the islands from the cafeteria. Ando is saying that his building is as art as Monet's paintings. Unfortunately, the serenity of the Japanese aesthetic is missing in the building, but it's strong in the water lilies. Monet collected Japanese woodblock prints. The architect replaced the Japanese aesthetic with the cold concrete of western culture. It's a tragic reversal."

From the museum, they tried to descend a small road to see the Benesse House, but they were stopped by a guard, so they took the main road down to the seaside. The Benesse House was also designed by Ando as a luxury hotel, restaurant and spa. The grassy area in front of it contained artworks that could be seen without paying the admission fee, including an optical illusion glass structure using two-way mirrors by Dan Graham, a bench by Niki de Saint Phalle and another pumpkin on a pier — yellow this time. They sat on the bench, and as they looked out to the mountains of Shikoku a young girl ran by, looking away from them at the sky/mountain/sea/grass interfaces.

"What a vision of beauty with a child running through it!"

"Can you possess it?"

"I do possess it — sort of — at least I took a picture of it."

"That's more than you could do in the Chichu Museum, which belongs to a benevolent corporation that doesn't allow photographs. They must be afraid their art property will be stolen by people taking pictures."

They rode to the third major art site, the village of nmura, passing a *minshuku* on the way, where they ʳed for the night. Honmura was a rusting fishing vilʳil the Benesse Corporation invested in the island ¹uced art to promote economic revival. Traditional ʰe village were transformed into installations. ʰe living there now, but their work could be

ᵏets at the central ticket center and saw

as many installations as possible before closing time. One was a dark barn where they became aware of dim light once they adapted to the darkness. Another was a traditional house that contained a shallow pool of water with numbers flashing on the black bottom. Another house had a garden with a small stone arch bridge over gravel. On the hill above the village, they visited the Go'o Shrine, redone by Hiroshi Sugimoto, paved with round white stones and glass blocks for stairs. A narrow, shiny-walled tunnel had been installed underneath, opening onto a view of the sea.

"Have you noticed, Sara, that this is the only installation that uses the natural landscape? Others are open to reflected light, but here art and nature are brought together, like in Ritsurin Ggarden."

"Yes, and I love the sensation of the tunnel, an echo of Zentsuji."

They returned to the *minshuku*, recently opened by a Japanese man who had lived in Italy. Before dinner, they went for a walk in the village. The wind had come up and salty air was blowing from the sea. The weather was changing.

"So today we saw an island art installation, and I stole quite a few pictures. I read that these art islands are packed in high season, with waiting lines at the museums and with lodging booked way in advance. It seems like a success."

"It's also a corporate success. It has a well-run feeling, but it's definitely museum art. The artists don't live here."

"Of course the corporation leaves its stamp, like the feudal lord, the city government, the gallery or the private collector — there is nearly always a go-between to filter and approve. On the other side is the mass of artists pleading for recognition. Isn't it strange, Sara, how some float to the surface and are recognized by the world of money, while others sink to never emerge or to be recognized after they die? At the end of his life, Vincent van Gogh wrote that he believed he would have a one-man exhibit in a café. *'Un jour ou un autre, je crois que j'aurai une exposition à moi dans un café.'* It seems arbitrary, but money defines quality in the world of art."

The *minshuku* owner made an Italian dinner for them. They shared the evening with a French documentary film-maker, speaking French all evening. Later lying on the *futons*,

"What is art?"
"Art thou art."
"We are art."
"We are love."
"We are life."

The next morning, rain was threatening, so they rode to the ferry terminal to discover that the ferries to Teshima were cancelled due to the approaching storm — but then they were told that, in spite of the weather, one and only one speedboat would depart immediately. So they got on, bikes and all, just before it churned out of the harbor and into the agitated sea. The ride was fast, with the windows of the boat constantly slammed with spray. When they arrived in Teshima, it was raining lightly, so they put on rain gear and headed off to the town of Karato to see the Teshima Art Museum, the "Archives du Coeur" and any other art (intended or not) that they could find. In the port they had learned there was no available lodging on Teshima, but that a single ferry was scheduled to leave late in the afternoon for Shodoshima.

The wind was strong, driving a light rain, but the sky was luminous in mottled grays and blacks. Climbing gently over headlands, they came upon a fishing boat sitting on a hilltop, seemingly abandoned by a tsunami and left to molder. Riding over a crest, the Teshima Art Museum appeared as two shallow, white domes nearly buried in the landscape. Their curves fit the natural curvature of the land, and the larger of the two had its top cut out. They looked like igloos. The larger dome turned out to be the museum, while the smaller one was the visitor center. The museum was the only artwork. They were given slippers to walk inside, where tiny fountains released water onto the slanted surface of the floor, mixing with leaves that had blown in with the storm. He was attracted by the aesthetic of this non-museum.

"This is very different from the angular designs of Ando. It's open and connected to nature, and the light is diffuse and gentle. It's Japanese."

"The brochure says it's the fruit of a collaboration between a female artist, Rei Naito, and a male architect, Ryue Nishizawa. It would be a different experience at different times of day or season."

The domed visitors' center was a welcome warm place. They had a simple lunch, sitting on the circular bench under the skylight. They conversed with a Dutch artist who was on an art pilgrimage to the islands. The dome felt like a cozy igloo. The shape and the light generated by the ceiling aperture made the space friendly, inviting and soothing.

"Teshima feels less corporate than Naoshima. The art angle is kinder and less exploitive, and there seems to be more real Japanese life here."

"The young woman artist brought femininity to these structures and the grey sky added diffuse light."

They descended into Hama, and riding through town they saw a curious array of anchors, nested together. There were at least a hundred of them, freshly covered with thick, black paint. In the center of town they found a stone jetty, made without mortar, but with large flat rocks, finely fitted together. He stopped, drawn to the jetty.

"Now look at that. The light makes the stone radiant and the vision of depth and perspective draws us away from the land and through the gap in the breakwaters protecting the harbor. The sky completes the symmetry, with patches of white running through the dark clouds. This is art without the pumpkin. It invites the viewer to see and to sea."

"Maybe you should buy it for your personal collection? You could charge admission. That would instantly convert it into art. There is money to be made in this business."

"I think I'll take a picture — capture this scene and hang it on the wall or maybe just hang it in my head for a few days. This image attracts me. It makes me want to go there, to jump off the end of the jetty and fly."

"Does it matter that the jetty was probably made by motorized equipment, driven by a construction worker, instead of an artist? How about the black anchors? Will they be transformed when you hang your photo? Maybe you have to sell the photos to make these objects into art? Maybe that's the difference…"

"Suppose I give the photo away, rather than sell it? Will that qualify?"

"Sure. I'll take two at that price…"

"And if the anchors are sold just as anchors?"

"Too heavy to carry on a bicycle. Definitely not my kind of souvenir."

They rode through town in search of the Les Archives du Coeur (by Christian Boltanski), continuing on an unpaved road. They passed an old van parked by a vegetable garden. It was used to store gardening tools and supplies. The wheels had sunk into the ground, and there was more rust than paint on the outside. Put in a museum, the van would definitely be an art object. He took a picture. The road ended at a secluded, sandy beach.

A low building facing the beach was marked "Les Archives du Coeur." The outside was sheathed in charred wooden planks. The inside was simple and newly minted. One could listen to the current heartbeat being played in a special chamber. It was also possible to record a heart or search a database and listen to another heart. They tried the listening chamber.

It was a long rectangular room with light-colored walls decorated with black squares. In the middle hung a single light bulb that pulsated with the heartbeat, with occasional green light coming from another source lower down. The heart sound was loud and booming, like the sound from a large Japanese drum. The first beat was regular and intense; the second was irregular in rhythm and content, punctuated by pauses and isolated, intense explosions of sound. A third beat was regular, but less intense than the others.

"The first and third are normal, but the second is bad news. It sounds like aortic stenosis."

"Did you encounter heart beats like that in the emergency room?"

"Most patients with acute symptoms were brought in by ambulance, with an ECG done in the ambulance and transmitted directly to the cardiac unit. I rarely saw those patients. When they came in by themselves, usually with less acute symptoms, I would listen to their hearts. A case like that went directly to the cardiac unit for a work-up. The hard part was turning off empathy. You need to console without getting emotionally involved — otherwise you don't make it through the week. It made me confront my own fragility."

"Should we record our heartbeats?"

"My heart is yours. You can listen to it whenever you like. Just put your ear on my chest."

"I would love to, Sara, but maybe we should go to some quiet, more private place and have a heart to heart mutual listening? Unfortunately there is no available lodging here, so we have to catch the only ferry, which is at 5:30 pm, if I remember correctly."

"Sounds good! That should leave enough time to visit a few more art sites on our way to the ferry, and we can have our heart concert on Shodoshima."

They found a narrow road that climbed the mountainside behind the village, and as it started to climb they stopped to visit the village cemetery, attracted by a pyramid composed of tombstones, which they learned later had been removed from the cemetery to make room for more recent graves. Kobo Daishi had a majestic perch at the top. The stones were weathered to varying degrees, and many of them were finely sculpted. A narrow slit without tombstones went up each of the four sides to the top, accenting the symmetry of lines leading upward. A short distance farther on they stopped at another cemetery, which was probably a family plot. The ground was strewn with pink petals from the surrounding plum trees. There were two main monuments plus stone lanterns, elegantly installed on a slightly raised platform. The whole was built into the hill, held back by a fitted stone retaining wall.

The climb was steep, taking them to Shima Kitchen, an old building reborn as a restaurant by the architect Ryo Abe. The feeling was of warmth: an open kitchen, a structure on three levels, flowing gently downward, with a large veranda covered by a shake roof. They sat at the bar and sampled cake; then they were offered an hors d'oeuvre made with fern shoots and other local plants. The ladies working in the restaurant were friendly and happy to be serving their only customers. The food was beautiful and delicious. But something was not right. The ladies in the kitchen were dismantling a dinner they had prepared for a large group, perhaps unable to come because of the cancelled ferries. They seemed sad to be undoing their work.

From Shima Kitchen, they explored cultivated terraces, recently restored by local residents, and they followed a paved path downward to get another view of the sea. A convex mirror, intended to make oncoming cars visible on blind corners, was perched on a pole against the sky. He caught his self-portrait as he rode by. They discovered a wooden shed, clad in weathered planks, showing vestiges of charring, probably to protect the wood from the salty air. Terraced rice paddies were flooded in preparation for planting.

Back on the main road and descending to the ferry terminal, they stopped to see an installation by Mariko Mori. They climbed on foot to a pond in which a white monolith sat on a pedestal near the center. The backdrop was a bamboo thicket. As the light changed, they admired the simplicity and beauty of the monument, rising from the dark water. A sign explained that it changed color when neutrinos were detected at a distant site, but they were unaware of any changes, except those due to the softening afternoon light. It rained lightly from time to time, obscuring the reflections on the pond. It was a place to wait and contemplate, but the ferry was leaving soon.

The large ferry took them to Shodoshima. It was nearly empty, and parked near the vehicle exit was a large handcart, covered by a tarp. It seemed incongruous in a world where most of the tools of trade are motorized. He wondered if it might be a sign of the return of muscle power.

Nearing the island, they saw a mountain, and surmised that it was Mount Hoshigajo, the one Sara had picked to climb. In Tonosho, they spotted what looked like a hotel just outside the city on a bluff overlooking the sea, so they climbed the road and asked for a room with a view. The staff invited them to park their steeds in the lobby. They took a large room with a terrace and a view over the sea. They sat on the terrace, drinking hot sake, while watching the last light fade away, leaving just ships floating through the darkness. Dinner was a buffet in the hotel, followed by baths outdoors, with sea views. They then had a heart to heart encounter on the futons. He began.

"I'm no doctor, but I hear your heart, young and strong, musical and deep. With the overtones of a fine cello, a Stradivarius. The bass is rich, and the top is pure joy."

"And yours... yours is golden... let me listen... yes, a field of golden wheat, the sun rising over the sea horizon, glancing over wet sand on a wave breeze — then a rush of solar light. A powerful, light-hearted Apollo."

They pressed their hearts together, and their music and light combined and recombined in a wave fountain, swirling and tumbling, to come to rest on an island. Then, as they slipped from shore into a tropical night, he said,

Plea

Carefully, architect of my intentions
Lovingly, mason of my desires
Faithfully, carpenter of our collaboration
Longingly, mistress, sister, spouse
Flowingly, passer of hours and days
Assuringly, keeper of souvenirs
Candidly, assessor of deeds done
Liftingly, moments of understanding
Sparingly, chef of seasonings
Laughingly, mirror of blank images

Creator of new mornings
And reaper of rich harvests
Generous solver of mysteries
Keep this life as a token of my
Respect and subjugation
Accept this sacrifice,
Heart to heart
Hand in hand
Terrible
Truth
Alive

They were up early and on the road on a beautiful day, riding in cool air and full sun. No wind: perfect conditions for a tour of the island, staying as close to the water as possible. Shodoshima has three long peninsulas running southward into the Seto Sea. The *Touring Mapple* showed small roads and a few towns, which were concentrated along the two long bays between these peninsulas and connected by a more traveled road running east to west. The rest of the island was served by a coastal road, linking the rare villages. The first peninsula was technically an island, since a narrow channel of seawater ran through the town of Tonosho, separating it from Shodoshima. They started by following the coast road around this pseudo island.

The ride was easy and fast on good pavement with little traffic and nearly constant views of the sea. The sky was cloudless with no wind. The beaches were sand or pebbles, and the occasional buildings unobtrusive. They had fine views of Teshima and islands beyond. They were soon back in Tonosho, where they stopped in a supermarket to pick up bentos for an early lunch.

It was a big supermarket, according to the USA model, but with Japanese contents, including bentos of all sorts, freshly prepared in the glassed-in kitchen. Armed with food, they rode the main coastal road east, mostly in sight of the sea. They had lunch on a ferry pier, overlooking a couple of small islands in the bay. As they ate their sashimi bentos, the outgoing tide uncovered a sand spit, leading out to the islands. After lunch they walked out to the first island. A sign said that this was Angel Rock, a special place for lovers.

Back on their bikes, they started down the second peninsula, riding on smaller and smaller roads as they went south, mostly within sight of the sea, often climbing over headlands. Vapor collected over the water, and the far away islands took on mysterious forms. They came upon a road washout repair zone, but luckily they were let through; otherwise it would have meant riding back around the peninsula. Beaches and headlands alternated, with few signs of civilization. From the high points they saw distant islands and wide expanses of sea, punctuated by passing ships and ferries.

The more populated area leading to the third peninsula was also an olive producing region, but they didn't stop until they were well down the third peninsula, where they found a soy sauce factory, proposing soy sauce-flavored ice cream, which was strangely delicious. Out of nowhere appeared a cemetery, like the one on Teshima with a pyramid of stones and Kobo Daishi on top. Many of the beaches were clean fine sand, with no sign of people, and the scenery got wilder as they rode south. When they rounded the tip of the peninsula, they stopped to admire a lighthouse; then they were stopped by another washout zone, but this time the road was completely destroyed over a long distance, so they backtracked a few kilometers and took a road crossing over the narrow peninsula to a point just north of the construction zone. As they climbed through a village, they saw a tall pole with fish kites strung from it. They were carp of all sizes and colors, with wide-open mouths, catching the breeze. It was boys' day, and fish flags were flying all over Japan.

They are in the climb over the mountainous peninsula. He is ahead, standing and feeling *genki*, full of energy and oxygen. The hill steepens, so he shifts down with the fingers of his right hand on the shift-brake lever. The grade abruptly increases again. In reaction, his right-hand fingers forcefully sweep the lever inward, but after the usual resistance… nothing happens. No shift. He tries again. Something is amiss. There is no resistance when he shifts. He reaches down and pulls on the exposed part of the rear gear cable. The derailleur shifts down. They stop, and Sara asks what's wrong.

"Something isn't working in the shifter. It looks like toolkit time."

He moves the shift-brake lever to its extreme position and peers intently into the mechanism. It's a complex assembly of clock-like parts. He slides the housing off the upper part of the cable, and tensioning the cable with one hand, he gently shifts the lever inward.

"I can see it's not catching on the downshift, but it's hard to say why. There are surely no bike shops on this end of the island, and it's a long way back to Tonosho. I suppose we could walk back to the main road and try to catch a taxi or a bus, but that would take a lot of hiking. I wish I knew how this thing works."

He plays with the shifter and the cable and realizes that a small lever inside isn't engaging a flange; instead it slips over it.

"I can see that something isn't catching. It's loose inside."

He takes the front light from his bag, and inspects the shifter from the other side.

"Ah-ha! There's a threaded hole where a screw should be.

That could be the whole problem. A screw fell out and the lever is loose, so it no longer engages the flange."

Sara has a look.

"I can see the threaded hole. It looks like you've found the problem."

"I'm afraid that's the easy part."

"Where were you when it failed to shift?"

"Well, I think it was near those yellow irises along the road. See them? About 100 meters on the right?"

They leave their bikes and walk down the road, hoping to see the screw against the black asphalt, but even searching well beyond the yellow irises turns up nothing but a bottle cap, a 100-yen coin and a hair clip.

"Well, there's certainly no hope of finding it in the gravel. Maybe it bounced off the road into the bushes. I can block the derailleur in an intermediate gear and get along like that until we find a garage or bike shop that can provide the screw."

"True, but it's going to be tough riding back to town in one gear."

"OK. I have no choice. I'll start working on blocking the derailleur."

"And I'll come along slowly. Just give me one last chance."

Sara walks down the road, well past the irises, without finding the screw. She sits down, and conjures up a mental picture of the screw, with its flanged head and shiny threads. She talks aloud to it.

"Dear screw, please believe that I love you and need you very much."

Back at his bike, he uses his knife to cut a green branch and whittle a short section that he inserts into the derailleur to block it in an intermediate gear. He is just finishing when she appears.

"Looks like you're ready to roll. I like your trick of the

piece of wood jammed into the derailleur. Very clever! You're my bike fixing genius. You could fix anything!"

"I've just proved you wrong about that. I need to carry a bigger range of screws in my repair kit."

"You shouldn't feel bad. It looks to me like it's functional. At least we won't be walking. Besides, you're my bike mechanic hero."

She puts her arms around his waist, looking at him fondly.

"Hero or not, I can't do much without a screw."

"But you're my hero mechanic, and you needn't worry about a little screw. It's the big screw I care about."

She leans toward him, touching her lips to his. He feels comforting warmth wash over him, and he realizes how frustrated he is at not fixing the shifter. He feels her tongue between his lips; it slips into his mouth, pulls out, and she presses her lips against his… he feels something hard, and a metallic taste hits him. She pulls back, her face in a radiant, mischievous grin. He takes the object between his thumb and forefinger, and the metallic taste is replaced by the taste of bicycle lubricant.

He inspects the hard, small object between his fingers. It's the missing screw. Her eyes are wide and laughing. He is stunned. They are laughing and hugging.

"I don't believe you did this! How did you find it?"

"Ah, that's a woman's secret. We have our ways…"

"But seriously, where did you find it?"

"In the gravel just this side of the irises."

"What? You actually picked it out of the gravel on the side of the road?"

"Well not exactly. You see, I started talking to it, telling it how much it was loved and needed. Then I walked up the road very quietly with my eyes almost closed. I stopped at the irises, closed my eyes completely and listened. That was when I heard a faint voice. I turned my head, moving slowly and following the voice as it got louder. I knelt at the edge of the road. When I opened my eyes, there was the little screw, gleaming between the stones."

"You're making this up!"

"I was afraid of dropping it, so I put it in my mouth, under my tongue. When I got to you, you looked dejected and frustrated. It seemed like you needed some cheering up! I figured you probably wouldn't swallow it."

The screw fit perfectly, and he was relieved to find that his 4 mm hex wrench fit the head. In a few minutes he had the shifter working perfectly, with the screw held tightly in place with a drop of thread lock.

"So now I owe you! You get a medal for finding it. Another for the mischievous way it was delivered, and another medal — no not a medal — a trophy this time for using your head and intuition. Only a woman could do that!"

"I don't want no medals. No trophies. All I want is pay in kind. A screw for a screw."

"You mean right here? In the middle of the road."

"Yeah, why not? Well… OK, I can wait… but not for long!"

Riding north, they came to a village and bought snacks. The day was getting on; they needed fuel. They ate in a park above the village with a view south, along the peninsula that almost disappeared in the hazy sea air. They rode by an abandoned and disintegrating fishing boat, left high on a headland — perhaps as a monument to a deceased fisherman. They were now on the east side of the island, on a wider road, with the mountainous interior on their left. They passed rock quarries and remembered reading that Shodoshima was the source of the granite used to build the Osaka Castle 400 years before. They stopped to admire a life-size sculpture of a forgotten warrior, holding a sword, lying near the road, almost covered by vegetation, and as they rode north they saw sculptures on pedestals, installed at viewpoints.

The road narrowed and, as fatigue set in, their minds focused on keeping the pace. The road climbed and dropped with no respite. They rounded the northeast tip of Shodoshima and rode the north shore to a town with a ferry terminal, where they stopped again for snacks. The road to the northwest corner of the island was flatter and along the water, with fine views of islands to the north. It was endorphin time, when the rider feels drugged by the effort and the rhythm of turning the pedals. The rolling was addictive, and they had to remind themselves to manage fatigue. Their mantra was, "Drink and eat. Spin and stand to take pressure off soft tissues. Be wary of chafing. Keep the hands moving to different positions. Settle in for the long haul."

They passed through few villages on this wild side of the island, and they stopped to take a picture of a woman who had harvested green onions and was loading them onto a handcart. She was another ancient beauty from the rural generation, elegantly dressed, wearing a straw hat.

They finally rounded the northwestern tip of Shodoshima and followed the coastal road south, with dreamy views of the sea, islands and horizon lightly decorated by a water vapor haze, increasingly backlit by the sun sinking slowly toward night.

They arrived at the hotel feeling tired and happy. They ordered beers and sat on their terrace watching the sun beginning to set, with ships coming and going and the sky glowing, while the landmasses darkened. They continued to watch from the outdoor baths; then they returned to the terrace in their *yukatas*, so enchanted by the spectacle that they forgot they were hungry. The glow intensified until the sun passed beneath the horizon, and the haze ignited vermillion. So began a magical denouement, with red and gold gathering in intensity to a climax, and then slowly diminishing in a long decrescendo. Passing ferries floated in the air, buoyed by their strings of lights into the sky, but what sky? Night had come and all was dark water.

Then the phone rang and everything changed. It was a man's voice, speaking American English.

"Greetings. Please excuse this intrusion, but I noticed your bicycles. I'm also a cyclist and the owner of the hotel. I was about to have a late dinner, and it occurred to me that you might like to join me. Do you like Japanese food? Yes? So please come down to the lobby. My name is Shiro, and I'll be pleased to meet you."

The timing was perfect. They were starving, and soon shaking hands with a Japanese gentleman waiting for them in the lobby, where there was a table decked out in delicacies.

"I see you're riding racing bikes, but with seat post racks and clipless touring pedals, so you must be touring, but you obviously appreciate riding fine racing bikes. That's most unusual and intriguing. Most of the cyclotourists we see here are on touring bikes. I suppose you came to watch the bicycle race the day after tomorrow.

"You don't know about it? Please let me tell you. Pardon my enthusiasm, and please again pardon my intrusion. I lived in the USA for much of my life, so I'm very happy to encounter Americans again. I'm one of the race organizers. This will be our fifth year. It's an unusual race. I encourage you to watch. The riders come from bicycle clubs all over Japan. Each club can send one rider. The race is from Tomosho to the top of Mount Hoshigajo. There are sections at 14 and 17%, so it's a steep uphill race, which is an enormous challenge, because speeds are reduced in a climb this steep, and the usual tactic of riding in teams and packs to combat wind resistance is less useful. There is only one downhill section, near the top and final climb. The finish line is at the top of the cable car."

"I'm interested! Thank you for telling us about it. What do you think, Sara?"

"Me too. I'm very interested. Could I ask a few questions about the race?"

"Please go ahead."

"Since you're the organizer, perhaps you could tell us if foreign racing clubs are allowed to send contestants."

"Now that question interests me. I would like to open our race to foreign clubs, and there is nothing in our rules that prohibits it. We have not sent out invitations to foreign clubs, but we plan to do so next year. I had not thought of the USA, but perhaps you know some clubs that might be interested?"

"We do. Is there anything in your rules that excludes women?"

"Women?"

"Yes, women."

"Women, bicycle racers? But we would have to organize two races!"

"Is there anything in your rules that says women can't race against men?"

There was that fast drawing in of breath, reminiscent of Japanese samurai movies; then there was silence.

"I race for the Metropolitan Cycle Association of New York. I'm traveling with my coach. How would you feel if I raced in your event?"

Shiro was leaning forward holding his head in his hands, covering his face. There was a long silence.

"I lived in the USA long enough to know something about gender equality — woman's liberation and all that

— but men are stronger than women. You couldn't possibly win. There are elite riders in this race. Could you even keep up? How would the other riders react?"

"I don't promise to win, but I can keep up with the peloton."

"I don't doubt you. You have the body of a climber. I sense your strength and determination. But I would have to convince the organizing committee, and this is very last minute. I wrote the rules myself, so I know there is no rule excluding women from the race, but we have to be careful here. You would need an official letter from your club, and you would have to sign a waiver, and so on… and we would need to do some work on your bicycle… Come to think of it, it would be a triumph for women all over Japan if you could race here. It might start a new trend. I'm beginning to like your idea! Are you sure you want to do this?"

"I'm positive, as long as my coach agrees."

"Well, I'm taken by surprise. We've been on a gentle tour of Shikoku, with only a few hard climbs, but you've been riding nearly every day for almost a month, so I think you're in good shape. I take your point, Shiro-san, about this being an unusual race. The clubs send only one rider, so the usual team warfare will be tamed, and your comment about the wind resistance factor is an important one. Speeds will be greatly reduced on such a steep climb. Sara is an excellent climber, and she's much lighter — with a good power to weight ratio. I can take the rack off and tune the bike, but her pedals are not racing pedals."

"Don't worry. I own the bike shop in Tomosho. We'll take care of everything. I just have to get an OK from the organizing committee, but that should not be a big problem. I'm the president, and I personally finance the race. If your club president can send me a letter by email, I think I can convince my committee. I will call you the mystery contestant, and they will be instructed to not tell anyone about you. I think I can enforce that."

"Wow. You're magic. I'll do my best in the race. I won't disappoint you."

"I trust you. Now let's put together a schedule, Japanese style. Here is my proposal. This is going to be fun."

He pulled out a notebook and pen, and wrote in English:

Tonight: finish dinner / get letter from bike club / get full night of sleep.

Tomorrow: hot bath at 6 am / full breakfast with rice, fish, tofu and vegetables / show video of last year's race / visit racecourse by car with bicycle to try certain sections / take bike to shop for revision / full lunch of your choice / R and R / test ride bike after tuning / dinner in your room / hot bath.

Day after tomorrow (race day): awaken 6 am / stretching / breakfast / prepare for race / warm up 30 minutes on your bike on trainer / transport by car to race start, arriving about 15 minutes before start.

"There are a couple of important matters you should be aware of. First, this race includes amateurs, but there will be elite professionals racing, and there will be prizes. Secondly, there will be journalists, and the whole race will be shown live on television. At the top there will be a podium, with distribution of medals. Lastly, you will have to give urine and blood samples just before starting and after arrival. If you're taking drugs, they will be detected, and you will be disqualified."

"The only drug I use is my own adrenaline. I understand and accept your conditions."

The letter from New York was received by email that evening, following a phone call to the club president, who was surprised to hear from them, but quite willing to partici-pate in the adventure. Over dinner they learned that Shiro-san's mother was a Japanese-American, who had married a Japanese businessman and moved to Shodoshima, where he grew up. He did an MBA in the US, and he owned and cooked in a restaurant in Washington DC, and then he branched out, owning several restaurants and hotels. He returned to his native Shodoshima, and continued his restaurant and hotel business, but on a small scale in order to devote himself to bicycle advocacy. He cycles nearly every day, and dreams of crossing the USA by bicycle.

Climbing the stairs to their room, he could see Sara was agitated. When they got inside, she threw her arms around him and started sobbing.

"Please forgive me! I don't know what got into me. I didn't even consult you. I just saw an opening and jumped in without thinking. I feel terrible. Please forgive me."

"You're forgiven for being young and strong-willed and the most beautiful and exciting woman on earth."

"But I feel like I've killed something. We were so happy being just the two of us, and now I've dragged us into this crazy bicycle race. It was a gut reaction. I lost control."

"Are you worried about the race?"

"The race? No. I'm worried about ending this trip with you. We're losing two days with this thing."

"But we have less than a week before our flight, and we have to return to New York… that is… unless you want to cancel our return and stay here forever."

There was a look of wonder on her face; then she said, "Ten years ago in Hiroshima I decided to make a go of it in the USA. It's tempting to reverse all of that, but it would still mean returning to New York now to unwind many matters. I'm for making no decisions at this point. Things will evolve naturally."

"Maybe this race is a good thing after all. It will put a cap on our Shikoku adventure, leaving us a few days in Osaka, and I want to show you something there."

"I also have a surprise for you in Osaka. So you're really OK with this bicycle race?"

"You're fearless, and I'm fearless with you. You'll be well prepared after seeing the video and visiting the racecourse, and you're in top shape. I've never seen a rider climb like you. I'm truly lost for an explanation. You're never out of breath! I'm honored to be your coach. Now you need to find the calm to sleep deeply. We had a long ride today. Would you like a massage?"

He started with her feet. Forty minutes later, as he was finishing her head and neck, he presented her with the finder's trophy for brainy intuition that had saved the day. The award ceremony was long and passionate. The trophy was a fitting reward for her extrasensory perception that had allowed him to fix his shifter. Finally, her eyes closed; her breathing slowed; and she was asleep. He pulled the comforter over her and stepped out onto the terrace. The air had thickened to fog. A ferry was passing with windows ablaze and a string of lights between the masts. He could smell the sea. It had been quite a day. A feeling of relief washed over him. She was ready to face returning to New York.

This race might help me understand at least one of the many mysteries about Sara. She seems so normal, but she's not normal. She translates energy into pedal power like no man or woman I've ever met. Competing with really strong riders will be revealing. I thought I was strong, but she's way beyond me. I can only imagine that she'll do well… but a young doe racing a pack of wolves?

They followed Shiro-san's schedule precisely. They were up for baths at 6 am, and the early morning light over the sea was magical from the outside *rotenburo* bath. Breakfast was served in their room: fish, vegetables and lots of rice. Sara was relaxed and happy. She had come to terms with the end game of their stay in Japan, and she realized that the race would be a fine way to say goodbye to the islands of the Seto Sea.

"I don't feel pressure to win, you realize. I would be happy to place in the middle somewhere. The point is they're letting me crash their exclusive, all male party."

"Did you say crash?"

"Oops."

"Now Sara, as your coach I must remind you to ride by the rules. No crash-provoking maneuvers, please."

"I promise, coach. I'll behave myself. I promise. Is it OK if I use some of my Col d'Aubisque tactics?"

"You mean lying low; then sneaking up from behind when they least expect it?"

"Yes, and getting my female pride worked up and shattering the male image of women as weak and dumb creatures only good for sex and housework."

There was a knock on the door, and Shiro-san appeared with two men carrying a large TV screen. They watched the video of last year's race, while Shiro-san made comments. It showed every moment, filmed from cameras by the side of the road. He left the recording for them to study at their leisure and indicated that the car was ready, and he would drive them up the mountain. She changed into biking clothes; her bike was already on the car.

The race would be starting in Tonosho; moving north and gently climbing up a river valley, dominated by a monumental statue, which Shiro explained is a fifty-meter high rendition of Kannon, the Buddhist goddess of mercy, completed in 1993, and it houses a temple. He said that Kannon transmits unconditional love and compassion — his personal philosophy and the philosophy of the race. She was their emblem and creed, watching over the race start and the entire island.

The race began at sea level, and the climb started at km 2.5, contoured up to 200 meters at km 4.8 and turned east at a road junction on the ridge crest. It contoured until km 6.3. Next it climbed steeply through two hairpin turns to 300 meters at km 7.6. Then it began a long traverse, climbing to 400 meters at km 8.4 and to 500 meters at km 9.3. It hit 600 meters at km 10 and 700 meters at km 11.3. It reached a top of 750 meters at km 11.7 and descended to 700 meters at km 12.6. It contoured and descended rapidly to 600 meters at km 14.2, going through tight turns and switchbacks. After that, it dropped through two more hairpins to a road junction at 560 meters. Finally, there was a climb to the top of the cable car (600 meters), where there was a restaurant and large parking area.

"All roads will be closed off the day before the race starts, and the spectators will start coming up at dawn on shuttle buses and by the cable car. If we have the predicted good weather, there should be people lining the entire race route. Of course as organizer, I can't give you detailed advice, but you should have the same information as the other riders, and many of them have ridden this race before or trained here. Here is the detailed altitude profile given out to all riders. The other riders know that last year's winner is racing again this year. He will be wearing Number 22."

"How about the descent after the race?"

"The roads will remain closed to cars all day. There will be many people riding or walking down, but since there are three descending roads, it should not be too crowded. People will be instructed to descend slowly and carefully. The cable car and shuttle buses will operate until late at night. We will of course provide a car to take you back to the hotel. I will be interviewed by journalists before and after the race, which will be broadcast live. Many people will come from the Kansai area. We see this race as an opportunity to show off our island and promote both recreational cycling and bicycle racing."

They descended by car slowly, stopping at the steepest parts so that Sara could try climbing them on the bike.

Something unusual happened below the restaurant at the bottom of the steep section, just under eight kilometers from the start. Sara had stayed on her bike, and was enjoying riding down the section of road that contoured under a steep mountainside, covered with dense trees and brush. Suddenly she stopped and jumped off.

"I saw something! Could it be an animal? It's a monkey! I've never seen a monkey in the wild before. I'm so happy!"

"I forgot to tell you that there are about 300 Japanese macaques living on this mountain, and they tend to congregate here because of the monkey zoo, just up the road, where visitors can watch trained monkeys in a show. The wild monkeys wander in and out of the monkey park, and they like to hang out in this part. They are good observers of people; they even watch the race from the trees. Visitors are discouraged from giving them food, so that they stay as wild as possible and don't become pests."

As he talked, there were noises in the trees and a troop of monkeys descended onto the road. Sara was excited.

"Oh, look at the mother with her baby! He's so cute! Look at the way he clings to her belly while she runs."

The monkeys were congregating by the side of the road, engaging in typical monkey grooming behaviors, with some lying on their backs, while being groomed by others.

"This is wonderful. They have beautiful red faces and expressive eyes. Do you see the mother nursing her baby? What an opportunity to be close to wild creatures. I'm so excited!"

She slowly approached the nursing mother, keeping low. She sat on the ground just a few meters from them and watched. Finally she moved back.

"Did you see the big monkey lurking around? He must be the alpha male."

Now there are monkeys everywhere, and they are clearly interested in Sara's bicycle, which is leaning against the guardrail. A young female sits on her rack trunk. Sara approaches and the monkey jumps off. As Sara reclaims her bike, there is a scream from the road behind her. The alpha male has the young female by the neck, and he's dragging her across the pavement. He has an obvious erection. She screams and fights back.

Sara grabs the pump off the rack bag and wades into the fray, swinging and narrowly missing the alpha male, who drops the female and pulls back. Sara and the male hiss at each other and show their teeth. She advances toward him, swinging the pump. He makes guttural sounds, and slowly retreats, watching Sara intently. Sara slowly backs away, never taking her eyes off him. She only turns when she is near the bicycle. The female is sitting on the rack trunk again. This time she doesn't jump off when Sara approaches and takes the handlebars. Sara walks down the road with the monkey riding on the bike, She seems happy to get a free ride for a few minutes, and then she scampers away into the foliage.

All this happened too fast for the men in the car to do anything, but when Sara came back and put her bike back on the rack, Shiro-san was clearly impressed.

"You could start a monkey rape prevention squad! I wouldn't want to meet you in a dark alley. You scared me!"

From the car, Sara noticed a warning sign depicting a monkey. It was a monkey crossing. Back at the hotel, Shiro-san took an insole from one of Sara's shoes for fitting racing shoes for her, and drove off with her bicycle.

Lunch was laid out for them on their terrace. The fog was gone and the day warm and breezy. The food was sumptuous Japanese. After lunch they reviewed the video, using the altitude information from their visit and the elevation profile. They both took naps; then Sara presented her strategy.

"I'm going to hold back for as long as possible. I don't want Number 22 to know I'm there. The down section will be OK, if there aren't too many riders, so I need to break away before the top. I assume that Number 22 will be riding near the front, but I'll stay in the background and try to catch him on the down. What do you think?"

"It all depends on how many riders are with you. They should disperse when the climbing gets steep, so there'll not be much of a peloton when you get to the top. Please minimize risk on the descent. Don't forget the tightness of the switchbacks. Try to remember it's only a race."

"I have the course memorized. I'll try to catch Number 22 at the bottom of the descent and pass him on the final climb. My idea is to surprise him. The descent will be critical, but don't worry. I'll be careful."

"Of course there could be many riders of 22's abilities, but in the video from last year he was already well ahead when he got to the descent, leaving him free sailing."

"I'll play a different game if there are more riders going into the descent. But at least this is my goal. I figure it all depends on what happens in the ultra-steep climb after the restaurant. That will separate the women from the men! I'll have to stay within my aerobic limits. If I go into oxygen deficit half way up, the race will be over for me."

"That will mean keeping your cool and saving your secret motivation weapon for the end. Do you want me to post a picture of your former boyfriend along the last sprint?"

"No. I just look forward to making it to the finish and seeing your smiling countenance."

The phone rang, and they were invited to the lobby to test the bike. It gleamed. The wheels were changed to new ones with tubular racing tires. Her leather touring saddle was replaced by a racing saddle with a new seat post. The chain and cassette had been changed. The handlebar tape was new, and there were racing shoes and pedals. They had changed the brake shoes and given her a new water bottle. They had even provided a woman's jersey, bib shorts, helmet, gloves and glasses.

"I don't believe this. You are too kind, Shiro-san!"

"It's just stuff that was lying around my bike shop."

She rode the bike for a few minutes and returned beaming.

"Excellent. Thank you, and please thank your mechanic."

They chose a Japanese mostly fish dinner with lots of liquids. It was served on their terrace. Sara seemed serene.

"Are you excited?"

"Yes, but looking at this view is calming. The moisture is back in the air, and the glow is returning."

They finished the evening with outdoor bathing, and he gave her a long massage. Sleep was coming to both of them.

"I feel like we've won the race already. We're the lone riders, nearing the finish. Race or no race — we are the winners — just you and me."

Sara was up at six, drinking water and doing warm-ups, stretches and yoga on the terrace, finishing with a meditation. Breakfast was at seven and chosen to be easy to digest and deliver a balance of carbohydrates, fats and protein. She was given energy gels to put in her jersey pockets. She decided to drink before the race and carry little water during it. The bike was on a trainer in their room. She rode it for a short time, and spent an hour studying the video, the profile and their notes. He talked to her as little as possible. She did another session of yoga, with a long meditation. The race start was 11:30. She gave her urine sample at 10:15 in the hotel, and she was on the bike warming up on the trainer at 10:20. She was picked up at 11:00 and driven to the race start with her bike on the car.

The streets in the center of town were closed off, and many people were gathered at the race start, including the fifty-one competitors wearing numbers. She spotted Number 22, and tried to stay as much as possible out of sight. Her number was 28. In the hotel, He had pinned one large number to her back and one to her chest, which conveniently concealed her feminine attributes. With sunglasses and her hair pulled up under her helmet, nobody would know that a woman was in the race. Lots of spectators were on bikes. There was going to be a second, all-comers race, taking place shortly after the official one, with an organized start and finish and medals for the winners.

He gave her a big hug, wishes for success, various admonitions about crashing, and he got into the car with Shiro, who was making one last inspection of the course. As her coach, he had been invited to watch the race from the arrival, where a big screen showed live video. Other screens showed the same images at two other points on the course, where spectators had congregated in large numbers. A fourth screen was placed at the bottom. Shiro explained that they wanted to avoid using helicopters and motorcycles to carry cameramen, so there were fifty video cameras, linked by cable along the road, with their output edited in real time. Each bike was fitted with a GPS locator beacon under the saddle to track and record the coordinates of each rider, allowing for real time display of speed and altitude parameters in the video stream. The course was lined with spectators who had come from long distances by train and ferry to enjoy the spring weather and watch the race. Spectators' phones and tablets were connected to the video network by antennas along the racecourse, which allowed them to watch the entire race as it unfolded.

Shiro was being interviewed, and an onscreen clock counted down to start time. The area around the start had been cleared and cordoned off. The race began precisely at 11:30 with a warm-up loop through town, with the riders going slowly in a disciplined peloton. A large crowd cheered them. They gathered speed on a straight and passed through the starting gate, clocked at 42.5 km/h. The cheering was intense.

Sara is in the middle of the pack, focused on the rear wheel of the bike in front of her and the shoulders of the riders on either side. They are nearly touching. The peloton is already riding and breathing in unison when they reach the end of the flat after 2.5 kilometers. The road suddenly climbs and everybody down shifts, but still in a tight peloton, spread across the width of the road. The statue of Kannon beckons from above.

They come to two steep turns and the peloton strings out, and then partially reforms. Sara is feeling good and riding well with regular, deep breathing and hands loose on the brake hoods. She is excited by the mass of bikes and riders around her and the cheering from the crowd along the road. The bike is perfect, and the tubular tires feel fast and solid. She watches the other riders carefully, and realizes that their Asian bodies are more suited to climbing than the usual American body types. She watches the breathing of the riders ahead of her as an indication of whether to pass or stay behind. She passes a few, careful not to put out too much effort as she goes around. She starts to heat up, so she unzips her jersey and feels cool air flowing over her chest.

Got to keep the motor cool. It's going to be tough. Watch the road. Watch the next rider's rear wheel. Don't overlap. Ten centimeters equals danger. Keep breathing free and deep, arms bent, chest open.

They are still in the approach climb and moving fast.

Keep a low profile and hang just behind, out of the wind, deep in the pack. Draft, draft and more draft.

As she nears the statue of Kannon, Sara nods in her direction, and receives the blessings of compassion and mercy carried by the wind onto all the racers. They arrive at the junction and take the right turn. The road suddenly gets steep. Everybody shifts down, and the peloton fragments. She passes two riders; she spots Number 22. She falls in six riders behind him and watches. He is cool, calm and in the background.

They are in the long traverse of the Shodoshima Skyline Road. They pass through the steel and concrete avalanche protection tunnel. The road steepens. Number 22 passes. She waits, and then passes as well. She takes stock.

Still in the aerobic zone? OK. Pulse? OK. Food, water? OK. Temperature? OK.

All lights are green, and she feels good, riding with the strong guys. It's going to be an endurance race and a strategy game. The lead riders are in single file at the front of the pack. They are saving for the super steep section after the restaurant. Giving too much now would be a bad move. She sees the map in her mind. They're coming to the two hairpins, visible ahead. The road above is obscured by shrubs, so she will be invisible in the turn to the riders above. Number

22 passes a rider. She stands and passes the one in front of her. Number 22 is third from the front. She is still the sixth behind him. They come to the hairpin, spread out with the riders single file on the outside of the turn. The distance is shorter, but it's steeper on the inside.

Stay outside. Stay cool. Play the non-aggressive.

But just before the turn, she does the unexpected, the rule breaker. She stands, cuts inside and takes three riders by surprise. She is breathing hard.

Recover, cool the motor, spin, weight on the saddle. Pump air. Bring the oxygen back to the quads. Get the pulse down.

There are now two riders between her and Number 22. He is strong, breathing regularly. He passes. So does she. The front rider peels off and drops behind Number 22. They seem to know each other.

They're riding together. It's a mini pace line.

The next hairpin comes into view, and the approach to it is steep, but she remembers that in the turn the road is wide and less steep, with space on the inside for passing. She is fourth and Number 22 is first. She listens to her breathing and pulse. She is fully aerobic. They shift down in the steep section before the turn, and she can see it in her mind. The cheering is already loud. They are on the left, before the right turn of the hairpin. The pace has slowed; the grade demands. The others don't shift down, knowing that the crest just before the turn is near. On her left is a view all the way to the sea; on her right is a huge crowd of cheering people. She shifts down, enters the turn and breaks away again, taking the shortcut on the inside. She quickly passes four riders, who are taken by surprise. So now she is first, and breathing hard. She knows the exit from the turn isn't steep, but the road suddenly gets steeper 100 meters after the turn. She has 100 meters to catch her breath.

She has thrown out the bait, and Number 22 swallows it. She feels him coming alongside her; she hears his breathing. He is standing up, going around her. Now they are in a steep grade for another 100 meters, and she makes the best of it. She accelerates just enough to keep him from passing. She can hear his lungs, sense his pulse. He is pushing, testing her. She is killing him. She sees him being wheeled into her emergency room. She listens to his heart. It's pounding at 95% max, pushed by the screaming spectators and his desire to win. He cranks up the burn. She holds her own. He tries to pull back, but she slows, pacing him. He makes another effort to pass, and she gently lets him go by as they hit a steeper section. Now she is on his tail, and they are climbing hard again. The road is lined with people, yelling and urging them on.

She takes stock, Number 22 has taken a hit, and now he has to recover in a steep grade. The third rider is on her tail, and behind them the peloton is exiting the hairpin, filling the road. The peloton watches and hopes the leaders' heroics will wear them out before they hit the ultra steep section, which is not far ahead. She is feeling the workout, but confident she can keep up.

Number 22 must be thinking the same thing, because the pace is slowing. They pass the warning sign with the image of a cute monkey beneath it. They come to the place they saw the monkeys; she sees nothing but people lining the sides of the road, and she hears them cheering. The road is in its long traverse. Number 22, riding first, has slowed some more. What's he thinking? She refuses to pass him and pulls back, baiting the third rider, who passes her, and Number 22 slows again, and lets him pass. They are definitely riding together. It's the buddy system. Number 22 is the favorite, and he's saving himself. He did take a hit. Maybe he needs a little heart massage?

Now the peloton has come up closer. She looks back to see the front riders break away. She is enjoying letting up, thinking she has sunk her teeth into Number 22, and now it's time to cool it. She pretends to be losing ground to the second breakaway behind her, but in fact she is fine. Now it's their turn to do battle. She will pace them, and try to tempt the whole peloton into riding too fast into the super climb.

She looks back. They're closing in. She looks forward. There is a vertical wall on the left, covered by metal mesh to keep rocks off the road. People stand several deep with their backs against it. On the right is a guardrail. People are lined up in front and behind it, and standing on it for a view, with the mountain cliff behind. Farther up on the right, in a narrow turnoff, is a TV truck with a camera on the roof. The peloton is on her tail, and the two leaders are about thirty meters ahead.

She sees a movement above the mesh wall, ahead on the left. A branch is shaking. It's a small monkey; she sees another, and the branch breaks. They are both on the pavement! They try to escape, but people line the road. The crowd freezes. They are young monkeys, and the two lead bikes are now on top of them. There is the sound of brakes and the bikes swerve, but just ahead she sees dozens of big monkeys dropping onto the road. The game is changing. It looks like a rescue. The two lead bikes just make it past the monkey squad before it closes ranks. Now it's her turn, but the monkeys have left no gaps, and they are two or three deep, running straight at her in tight formation — intent on saving their young. Now a monkey breaks away from the squad and comes at her lightning fast. Sara is on autopilot. Time slows and slows, and things happen beyond her control. She enters falling mode, ready for the crash, but not for an instant letting up the pressure on the pedals.

Pedal at all cost, whatever, whenever it happens...

Then the fast monkey whips around and runs up the road just a meter in front of Sara. The rescue squad parts and they shoot through. The road is clear of monkeys, except for the one just in front of her: the monkey who led her through. And that one drops behind. Sara is free, saved by a monkey and a miracle.

Now the wild card is played. The most unexpected happens. Sara feels something hit her back. Her savior monkey has landed on her back — feet on her hips, hands on her shoulders — and she is screaming. Sara screams with her, and she feels a surge of power flow into her legs. The front riders look back, and they are terrified. The crowd is in shock.

He is glued to the big screen at the top. The crowd around him has quit breathing. He sees Sara with a monkey on her back; then the image switches to the peloton, and it's chaos. Riders and monkeys everywhere, panicked spectators. All the riders in the peloton are off their bikes. The monkeys have found their young, and they are heading back up the road, but it's lined with terrified spectators, who have no place to run. The only way out is the video truck, which is quickly engulfed with monkeys, and the image goes black — then white. The camera is pointed at the sky.

The image comes back just as the savior monkey jumps

off Sara's back. Sara turns and blows the monkey a kiss. The crowd from the bottom to the top of the mountain goes wild, because they have seen everything on their phones. The mountain rings with their cheers. He sees the peloton getting back together and the race starting again.

Sara is giggling, now laughing, now calming.

> *You can't laugh and ride. Got to concentrate. You saved me, sister. We're primates. We're together. You're a doll. I love you.*

And that is the thought she carries into the super steep section just ahead. They are arriving at the restaurant, with the big screen and thousands of people cheering their lungs out.

It goes directly into 17%. Sara downshifts and tries to relax.

> *Spin, spin. Got to keep it down, let them go ahead.*

The front riders seem to have forgotten they are buddies. They are side by side. Sara is being conservative. They have 3.6 km to the crest, and it climbs between 14 and 17%. She stays on the saddle. They seem to be going into a macho battle for the top.

But they are good riders, and they know the course, so it's come down to a game of chicken. They dare each other to go too fast, to redline and blow their oxygen. They have to stay aerobic as long as possible. Only near the top can they risk a sprint. In the meantime, they use every trick in the book to goad each other. It's a standoff, and Sara watches from well behind.

They pass the first sand trap for runaway vehicles, and then they are in another 17% section, and it hurts. Sara can feel the lactic acid accumulating in her thighs, so she lets off the pressure, listening to her lungs and heart.

Hold on, it's going to be hard, but stay calm, let them go.

And it's an epic battle, the locking of samurai swords. The crowd cheers them on, and they are moving into the danger zone. They have passed the second runaway vehicle sand escape, and the two leaders accelerate, standing on their pedals. Finally, Number 22 slowly pulls ahead, and the fight is over. Sara is closing on the second rider, letting Number 22, now leading, continue to sprint for the top, alone, as if it were the end of the race. He has let up slightly, but he is standing, raising his fist in the air. Sara goes around the second rider, and she feels the primal joy of conquest she felt on the Col d'Aubisque. She has dumped him. One more to go.

When she hits the crest, Number 22 is just rounding the first corner of the descent. He has forgotten all about her. Sara accelerates and continues to accelerate through the down corner, pedaling madly, hands down on the drops, back flat. The crowd is behind barriers, terrified, holding their breath when she comes to the second turn, a tight hairpin with a vertical cliff on the outside and a view all the way to the sea. She brakes hard, enters from the uphill side and shoots through, passing a few centimeters from the guardrail on the downhill side. She is taking all risks — going for broke. There is a left turn; then another switchback. She hears the crowd cheering Number 22 just below her in the switch back. She hits the hairpin braking as hard as she can, hugging the uphill side; now she slams across with all her weight on the outside pedal, hands tight on the drops, arms squeezing the bar, leaning to the extreme. She barely clears the outside barrier; then she stands on the pedals and shifts up, sprinting hard. This is her moment to mix gravity and energy and set the burn to full throttle. Her acceleration explodes with wild pedaling.

She hits terminal velocity, and it's time to let gravity finish the job and to recoup for the final sprint. She drops like a rolling bolder. She stops pedaling and flattens down, pushing herself back on the saddle, chin almost on the bar, with her legs moving just to keep the inside pedal up on the corners with her full weight hard on the outside. She shaves into the centimeters between her and disaster on each corner, but she is in her speed element, and the wind hits hard, blowing into her jersey, across her chest, slamming into her open mouth and filling her lungs with precious oxygen with each inhale. She sees nothing but the lines on the road. It's a dizzying video game, and she is in control, leaning extremely hard on the corners and braking only when absolutely necessary. She is still accelerating when she comes to the last two turns; then she sees the overhead sign for the road turning left, down to the north side of the island, and the road up to the cable car. She hits the pedals with all her force, and feels the monkey power rush back into her legs. Number 22 is just coming to the sign. She flies under it, back horizontal and pedaling wildly in top gear. Number 22 is just ahead, flying as well, but slowing as the road starts the final climb.

He is pushing hard when she goes around him so fast that he has no idea what has happened. He feels wind and sees movement. Now her back comes into focus, and he sees her flying, standing and accelerating. He hears thousands of people screaming, and he stands and gives it everything he can… and more.

She is alone and going for the top, way above the red line — then going farther into afterburner land. No pain. No air — just riding on desperate, blind, insane love and more love for 400 meters. And up it is. Steep. She doesn't look back. She gives all, and she hears nothing, sees nothing — feels only the runaway drum roll of her heart and the distant pain in her legs.

Now she imagines him cheering her on and new power surges from her legs. She is standing, "*en danseuses*," a ballerina defying gravity, flying into the sky — into the air — pure white light forever.

She sees the right turn into the parking lot, and people everywhere, screaming crowds, barriers, a finish line under banners, cameramen, a large flat arrival area surrounded by people behind barriers, screaming and waving. She crosses the line alone at full speed, brakes hard and starts a slow turn around the arrival area. She comes to a stop, dismounts and gently lowers her bike to the ground. Number 22 is crossing the finish line. She is breathing desperately, but he is in terminal agony. He drops his bike and falls to his knees, collapsed, head on the pavement. He finally stands and bows deeply, with his face almost touching his knees. When the third rider arrives, she and Number 22 are standing in the center of the arrival area — their arms around each other's shoulders. The third rider drops his bike and staggers over to them, desperate for air. They face the crowd, arms linked, bowing deeply.

The peloton is nearing the bottom of the descent, with a breakaway just starting up the 400-meter uphill sprint to the finish. Race officials run into the arrival area to remove the three bikes. Sara takes off her helmet and glasses, and the mystery rider, as the announcer has been calling her, has removed her mask. Her hair flows down her back. She is a woman, and she has won a man's race. On the big screen, the camera zooms onto her smiling face.

The three winners walk to the podium as the breakaway and the peloton riders cross the finish and fill the arrival area. The informal racers will be arriving for the next two hours. The loudspeakers play music and the cameras are focused on the podium. Sara is drinking water and eating ice cream.

On the podium, Shiro-san gives her the winner's medal and hands her an envelope, and they somehow manage to play "The Star Spangled Banner" (probably downloaded when the race organizers saw that she was likely to place in the top three). She is led into a small room behind the restaurant. The door closes, and they are alone.

"Well coach, are you happy? You look happy, but why the tears?"

"I'm speechless — probably speechless for life. Let me look at you. You're alive. That's all I care about. I've never been so terrified. You're out of your mind."

"Are you proud of me?"

"Proud! Much more than proud. I'm blown off the Earth proud, right up to heaven. I never imagined I would live to see someone I love in such total triumph. Yes, I'm proud and honored to know you, and I'm even more madly in love with you."

"Now that's the reward I wanted! Dry your tears, coach, they're waiting for us."

There is a knock at the door, and Shiro enters, excited, hugging both of them.

"I don't believe this! Nobody will ever believe this. This is crazy. I had no idea you could win. I thought we might make a polite statement about women's rights, but this is something entirely different and so unexpected, and the adventure with the monkeys… I'll never forget this day! You won the bicycle race and the monkey war, guided by your monkey friend. Amazing! You smashed the course record. You were going 88.5 km per hour at the end of the descent, and you never stopped accelerating in the final sprint. I don't believe it. You're crazy, out of your mind! How did you do this?"

When they walk outside, the photographers are in a feeding frenzy, fighting for a picture with their flashes going off continuously. The three of them brave the photographers together in the walk to the race headquarters, where Shiro is to be interviewed. It is calm and dignified inside headquarters. The interviewer is a woman journalist. Finally, she turns to Sara and says in accented English, "How do you feel? You are the first woman in the history of cycling to win a major race in direct competition with men."

"This was a special race, a steep climb where endurance and weight were critical. It was a perfect course for a woman. We're lightweight, and we can endure pain. We can go beyond our limits. It just takes training, a good coach and knowing yourself. I'm grateful to the Metropolitan Cycle Club of New York and to the race organizers for letting me compete."

She turns directly to the camera, "I'm in love with Japan, with the Japanese people and with this beautiful island."

She wanted to ride down, and Shiro-san explained how they could get back to the hotel with a minimum of interference. They descended the steep and windy north road, dropping 600 meters to the sea; then they retraced their ride from the day before, but instead of staying close to the water, they cut inland and contoured on a small road at about 200 meters, until they came to another leading through a gap in the mountains. They thus arrived at the hotel just before dinnertime.

Everything had changed. There was a video truck, and a large crowd had formed. They were escorted inside by hotel staff, who were waiting for them. Their room had been changed to a rooftop suite with a 360-degree view and a private outdoor bath. A bottle of champagne was waiting in an ice bucket.

The phone rang, and Shiro-san asked if he could disturb them for a few minutes before they bathed and had dinner.

"I'm very sorry to bother you, but there are three urgent matters to attend to. In fact you have had two important phone calls. The first is from the president of your cycling club, who urgently wants you to call him back. The second is from a Japanese woman who claims to be Sara's adopted Japanese mother. I didn't believe her at first, but she convinced me. I thought you should know."

"It's Mama-san! How could she possibly know about this?"

"The entire race was broadcast live on national television, and parts of it, including the encounter with the monkeys and your statement about loving Japan have been repeated ever since. I assume you want to call her back?"

They heard an emotional Mama-san on the phone. She was beside herself.

"Sara! Dear, beautiful Sara! Television. Saw you! So worried! Scared! Sara, talk to me!"

"Mama-san. Please forgive me. I didn't know you would be watching."

"No excuse. Very proud. Love you, my wild, wonderful Sara."

The next call was to Patrick. He too was excited.

"It's 5 am, and the phone is ringing off the hook here. CNN and The *New York Times* are desperate for a bio. The American ambassador to Japan has called from Tokyo. Help! What am I supposed to do? By the way, congratulations, Sara. I understand you had a good race. I'll try to find out more about it, that is, if the phone ever stops ringing. Anyway, seems you've done us proud!"

The third urgent matter was to decide how to proceed with

the journalists. Shiro-san showed them a stack of their professional name cards. He proposed that Sara make a short appearance in front of the hotel with her bicycle — just to calm the photographers. They could then bathe and eat dinner, and if necessary meet and talk later in the evening.

They did as he suggested.

After Sara's short press conference, they changed into *yukatas* and went to their outdoor, private *rotenburo*. They had a view of the mountains behind, the sea and distant islands with ships passing. The golden air was slowly thickening; all was serene and quiet. The water was hot. The air was cooling, and slowly their naked bodies melted, defied gravity and flowed upward, forming a living link between the sky and water worlds. The light faded on cue, leaving them suspended, weightless and warm in the black pool of the night.

Dinner was waiting when they returned to the room, with water, fruit juices and sake as the beverages. It was high-end Japanese food at its best. After dinner they watched the ferries and their colorful lights gliding through the black ink below. She fell asleep on his shoulder, and he carried her to her futon. He went downstairs to talk to Shiro-san.

Shiro-san offered to have their bikes, including the new clothes and equipment for Sara's bike, boxed and sent to Kansai airport in time for their departure. He also suggested they leave early in the morning to avoid the photographers, who were likely to return for a last chance at a picture of Sara. He promised a wakeup call at 5:30 am, and suggested that they notify the desk when ready for breakfast. He had purchased ferry and train tickets to Osaka. He wanted to reserve lodging there for them. He also explained that their hotel and food expenses on Shodoshima were paid for already, and that the race was also paying for their expenses in Osaka.

"Shiro-san, you might find this strange, but I've already reserved in the youth hostel near the Shinkansen station. We're very fond of youth hostels in Japan, and staying there will help us get back into normal life."

They talked about Sara, and Shiro-san was not surprised that she was an emergency room doctor. He called her a genius with extra-human physical and mental powers. He said that he had never before witnessed anything like the explosion of raw power in Sara's final sprint. He talked about her courage, generosity and personal beauty — both interior and exterior. They talked about cycling and the place of women in sports. Shiro-san brought up the repression of women in Japanese society. He said the future of the country depended on giving women an equal status with men, because in the present system the female half of the talent pool was largely wasted, and it was not due to a lack of education. Women were excluded from leadership roles. He said the present male leaders in both politics and industry were weak, and Japan needed new ideas and energy. Sara had shown that women can win in the male game. He intended to promote women in competitive cycling and everything else, using Sara as a model.

It was an intimate encounter between friends. They felt a bond that would connect them in the future. They agreed that the true story behind the monkey encounter would remain a secret, known only to the three of them, to be divulged only when Sara wanted it to be known.

"Shiro-san, there's one thing you can help me with. I'll need access to a computer for a few hours tonight."

"I'll provide you with an American laptop in my office, which will remain unlocked all night. WiFi is connected. Be my guest."

He has returned to their penthouse room. Sara is sound asleep. The rooftop garden is dark, but there is light from the night sky. He tours the penthouse terrace, inspecting the large pots and planters with their shrubs, flowers and bonsais. From his jacket pocket, he removes the third and last of the sealed plastic pouches with the white powder inside. He cuts it open with his pocketknife, and dusts the soil in each pot and planter with the powder. Finished, he taps the pouch with his forefinger to release the last residue of powder onto his tongue, and he feels the astringent sensation for the last time. He sits for a long time on the bench by their private bath, until he hears his wife's voice calling his name. Another voice echoes the sound. He recognizes his mother and then another weaker voice, his grandmother, and then faintly another voice, and yet another echoes his name, infinitely.

He sleeps for a few hours, lies awake, and finally gets up and makes his way to Shiro-san's office. It takes just a few minutes to find the first link to Sara's great secret. An hour later he is exhausted from sifting through details — trying to see a grand forest through dense trees. He takes a scrap of paper from the wastebasket and writes CLUH on it.

"Now I have one, and I don't know what to do with it. My intuitions were right. She has seemingly endless metabolic and oxygen assimilation capacity, which she was hiding, even from me. Today, she fully revealed all — astonishing everybody. I don't dare let on that I know. Maybe snooping on internet wasn't such a good idea, but now it's too late to put the genie back in the bottle. Be patient. It will have to come from her. I must conceal my knowledge."

The morning went as planned, and they soon found themselves watching the port of Tonosho getting smaller, with their hotel on the hill above the sea and Mount Hoshigajo behind it all, like something out of a dream, unreal, but more real than real.

"Any regrets?"

"I miss my bicycle, I can't stand the thought of this trip ending, and I regret losing two days of being just with you. I don't want to be a bicycle racer. I want to lead a normal life."

"We have two days in Osaka to look forward to. Shiro-san promised to tell no one where we are, and we agreed that the real story behind the monkey encounter will remain a secret, until you decide to reveal it."

They had an hour in Okayama before their train, so they wandered into a nearby department store and bought street clothes. It seemed strange to not be cyclists, but a relief to know Sara would probably not be recognized. In the train station, they bought bentos for lunch, and they were soon flying through the countryside on the Shinkansin.

"What was in the envelope you were given on the podium?"

"I don't know. I haven't looked at it. It's in my rack trunk."

The envelope contained a letter in English and Japanese, certifying she had placed first, drug free, giving her winning time and thanking her for her participation. It was signed by Shiro-san, with his personal stamp. There was also a 64 GB memory card, containing the race video and GPS data, and there was a check from a New York bank for $300,000.

The youth hostel was high up in a modern building, with views over Osaka. They had their own room. The staff was helpful and polite.

"There's something I want to show you tomorrow morning, Sara. It's a very special place for me."

"And I promised you, dear coach, a surprise for tomorrow evening."

They spent the rest of the afternoon visiting the castle of Osaka, which rises above a sakura park. They admired the stone foundations from the quarries of Shodoshima. They had a simple dinner in the youth hostel, and enjoyed the Japanese bathing facilities. Back in their comfortable and serene room, Sara was asleep as soon as the lights were out.

She had given everything to please him, and she would take a couple of days to recover. He felt serene and patient; "coach" was his role now. The butterfly would soon be flying again. Maybe needing him. Maybe not. Time would tell all. They had to build on the foundation they had constructed over the last weeks. He would have to be wise, generous and patient. He would have to resist protecting her. He would have to put her needs before his, and watch the time pass carefully. But he needed her. He could not live without her. A compromise between his needs and hers was possible. New York was far away, but coming closer by the minute. He needed time.

They arose early, and had a quiet talk over tea, discussing details about the race, how the bike felt — Sara had never ridden on tubular tires before, and she liked them — wonderment at the monkey business, details about passing on the climbing hairpins and the dangerous descent. It was all coming out, in scattered pieces, but it needed to be said.

"I was sure I was going to crash and take a lot of monkeys with me, but I didn't slow. I was in basic instinct mode, ready to die, but not willing to give up an inch of the race. Everything was in slow motion. Suddenly there was my monkey in front of me. Then she breached the monkey wall, and I sailed through behind her. A second later, I felt something on my back, and I knew what had happened: she had made a perfect four-point landing. I could hardly feel her weight, but she was pressing my hips with her feet, and her hands were squeezing my shoulders. She was riding the bicycle, screaming and spurring me on, like a jockey on a horse. She wanted to win! I felt a surge of power coming from her, through me and into the bike. It carried me through the tough, steep section, long after she jumped off."

"The descent was wild. My eyes were watering, even behind the glasses. I was desperate to catch Number 22, and I knew where he was and the risks I had to take. I had to close the gap, and I had to go around him while I still had momentum from the descent. Yes, I took chances, but you don't think about that. You trust your instincts and the bike, and my monkey was still with me in spirit. She wanted us to win. It was a point of honor for us. When I passed him, I felt a surge of hot desire to accelerate forever, and I felt total power over him. Such a basic triumphant instinct! I was a black widow spider. The human and non-human females of the world were with me, proving that we can do it.

"In the final uphill sprint, I thought only of you, and how we would be reunited when I crossed the finish line. I could see your face before me and hear your encouragements. I had recovered my oxygen on the downhill, but my pain receptors were numb, so I kept pouring on fuel, ignoring accumulating anoxia, lactic acid and the stinging sweat rolling into my eyes. My metabolism kicked into a new space — it was like the Aubisque, but much more. The more I pushed, the better it felt. I was going for broke, drunk, and my body did its part. At the finish, I was swept away by a tsunami of joy. I wanted to be with you instantly. I wanted to hug you and cry on your shoulder. I desperately wanted your love. I did it for your love. That was my sole motivation and the only reward I want."

They took public transportation to the port of Osaka, and walked along the river until they came to schoolchildren having picnics in small groups, sitting on *hanami* table cloths. They were dressed to perfection, but the real perfection was in the bento lunch boxes, assembled by their mothers with unlimited attention, artistry and love. They sat in the sun and watched the children; then he said, "Now for your surprise. Please come with me," and he led her from the river, up steps to the front of the large building, the Osaka Aquarium.

"I came here years ago, and I've always dreamed of returning. This is where the underwater world comes to life."

The aquarium was vertically organized, with a land to water transition at the top, and a deep-sea environment at the bottom. A sloped path descended in a spiral, allowing visitors to observe animals as diverse as penguins, seals and sea otters at the top, and spider crabs and jellyfish at the bottom. There were many tanks, large and small, around the outside of the spiral, and on the inside was a nine-meter-high tank made of acrylic glass, ten centimeters thick. The first tank was traversed by a transparent tube that visitors walk through as if under water, surrounded by fish, including a shark. The large tank contained (among others) a manta ray, a whale shark and school of sardines. They spent nearly three hours in the aquarium, trying to assimilate the diversity and beauty of the life forms that live in and around the water.

"Now it's my turn for a surprise, but first we should have some dinner. I suggest a *gyoza* bar I heard about from the woman at the desk in the hostel. You know, Chinese raviolis, but in the Japanese style."

She took him to a tiny restaurant run by a young man and his mother. There was room at a counter for about ten people, and all the cooking took place in front of them. *Gyoza* were the starting point for most of the dishes, and there were many others as well. Everything they saw or tasted was original. But it was not just the food; there were smiles everywhere, *gyoza* smiles, and they were treated like old friends.

"Now for my big surprise! Please come with me, coach. It's not far from here."

As they descended steps, he noticed a polished glass plaque, engraved with the word, "Bécaud." Once inside they found an intimate cabaret with seats around tables, a bar and a stage with a grand piano. They ordered sake, and soon a pianist appeared with a woman holding a microphone. She spoke in Japanese for several minutes. The pianist began the intro to... yes it was: "Mon Légionnaire." The singer began, singing the Edith Piaf standard in Japanese, with a dramatic delivery. It was startling at first, but then it seemed old-fashioned and charming. There was a second singer, a break, and the first singer returned and spoke in Japanese, introducing the third singer.

Mama-san entered, dressed to the nines...

He was completely surprised and unable to reconcile this image of Mama-san with the conservatively dressed woman he had met in Kyoto. She was wearing a strapless sequined gown, a glittery black bracelet, matching earrings and a large gold and opal ring. She was lavishly made up. She sang "La Vie En Rose" in a low, sultry voice, and followed with "Les Amants de Saint Jean." It was all in Japanese and well sung, with an intense, dramatic delivery.

Mama-san spoke for a few moments, looking at the audience. Suddenly she stopped, shading her eyes with her hand. She had finally spotted Sara. She put her hand over her heart, became serious, and said something in Japanese. People in the audience were looking around; Mama-san beckoned to Sara, saying her name, and called her to the stage. There was an enormous embrace. Applause. Mama-san whispered in Sara's ear, said something to the pianist, and stepped aside, leaving the stage to Sara to sing "Autumn Leaves" in French, with a second verse in English. Mama-san returned, and they sang the refrain in Japanese. After the applause had died down, Sara left the stage, and Mama-San finished with "Non, Je Ne Regrette Rien."

Mama-san sat with them during the break. They ordered champagne to celebrate their reunion and connect the beginning and the end of their trip. Mama-san had no idea they would attend her performance. Sara had found out about it in Kyoto, and had noted the date, since it was the night before their departure. Mama-san's teacher was the first singer, and the owner of the club. Mama-san didn't mention the bicycle race, and they parted with tears and promises to reunite.

After leaving Mama-san, they walked in the entertainment district of Osaka.

"Your surprise was a total delight. I couldn't believe what I was seeing. Now I know you get talent from both your French-Canadian and Japanese mothers. Hearing those songs in Japanese, I realize how universal they are. She really didn't know you were coming?"

"I don't think she had a clue."

As they walked he was thinking about their imminent return to their former lives.

"So Sara, where do we go from here, you and I?"

"I don't know about you, but I've had the most intensely fulfilling time of my life. I'm alive like never before. This is love, and I want more. I want nothing but this love."

"I'm with you. I was an emotional zombie, and you rescued me…"

"And I was a basket case!"

"How can we stay on this level?"

"We can, and we will. For the moment, we have to pick up the pieces of our former lives. I submitted a book proposal before we left. I haven't given it a thought since we've been in Japan, but if the publisher is interested, I want to give it a try. I should have their response in my mail."

"And I was trying to find a compromise with my past. I will have to confront all of that when I'm home. I can't imagine how I'll do it."

There was a pause, and she said in a soft voice, "I hope sometime, if you feel like it, to hear the story of how you met your wife and the life you shared. I would like to get to know her through you, and to learn how your relationship was built… but only if you feel like it."

"I'm willing. I'll tell you the story of our meeting when we're back in the youth hostel."

They never slept that night.

"Her name was Anna. — Anna for Annabelle. If only she could see me now, drinking tea and in love with a ravishing young woman in a youth hostel in Osaka. She would be so amused. I can hear her giggling. She had an infectious girlish giggle right up to the end."

"Maybe she's listening?"

"If she is, I better get my facts right. She was a stickler for facts. She kept everything organized — even me."

"How did you meet?"

"I heard the giggle in the breakfast room of a youth hostel in Madrid. I was 21 and she was 22. I turned around, and there she was, talking to some people at the next table. She saw me and smiled, and that was it: a classic coup de foudre. I felt like I couldn't breathe. I started feeling euphoric and my pulse was racing. I'm not kidding. It was pretty funny, thinking back on it, but I just fell in love with her in the first instant. It was a textbook case of being lovestruck, the classic, but that was just before an extraordinary event that cemented our relationship. Something terrifying and unexpected happened."

"I'm all ears."

"Ok. You're not going to believe this. I walk over and introduce myself and ask if I can join them, and she and the others say 'sure' and tell me their names. Somebody says that the coffee is being served in the lounge, so we go in there, take seats and drink our coffee. A guy is carrying on... he didn't seem quite right. He's giving a disjointed political discourse, dominating the room. He's a northern European, judging from his accent. People are trying to carry on other conversations, but he seems to want to take the stage.

"Suddenly he talks about Jews and how they conspire to take over the world. All other conversations stop. Nobody reacts until Anna asks him to give examples, and he brings up the music world — how he is a musician and how the Jewish conductors only hire Jews. Anna asks him to be specific. He goes into orchestra conductors, but Anna seems to know many of these people, and she gives counterexamples, including names, showing that they work with musicians of all origins.

"The guy gets worked up. He's clearly got problems. He stands and looks violent. I see the man at the reception desk reaching for a telephone, and then Anna stands and walks slowly toward this guy. I stand, thinking I'm going to help, but she waves me back, without taking her eyes off him. He yells at her, and she gets very close to him and says something I don't hear — then she suddenly steps back — just as he swings at her. He misses. I didn't see it coming, but she did. I'm rushing forward, as are a couple of other guys, but she waves us off. The people at the desk are on the phone. Anna never takes her eyes off this guy. It's a standoff. Finally, he lunges at her, trying to grab her throat. All hell breaks loose, but only for about three long seconds. The next thing we know the guy is face down on the floor, with

Anna on top of him. She has him in some kind of wrestling grip, pulling his head back by his hair, with one of his arms locked behind his back. I grab his legs. Anna doesn't seem particularly perturbed, but the people in the room are terrified. She talks into his ear, gently. I can't hear what she's saying. Finally, he starts to calm down; then I see him closing his eyes. When the police arrive, she is still holding him, firmly, but not hurting him. They handcuff him. She talks to the police in Spanish, but I don't understand a word. The police escort him out, and she exits with them. I follow, and offer to be a witness. Other police stay to collect information from the youth hostel staff, from Anna and from me. Anna tells the police she will not press charges. When it's all over, Anna says something about changing her clothes, and I say I'll wait for her in the lobby. She appears about five minutes later in a sundress. She is drop dead gorgeous. I'm in heaven. We head out to see the Prado."

"Sounds like a scene from a James Bond movie."

"It was. I walk out of there feeling exhausted from the adrenaline in my blood. Anna is calm. We take a streetcar to the Prado, and I try to pretend this is a perfectly normal morning in Madrid. We engage in get-acquainted small talk. I feel electricity. After the museum, I invite her to lunch. She says she would be delighted, just so she can invite me to dinner. I'm happy; she's happy. We have a wonderful first day together, in spite of the fireworks at the beginning. Later that evening, I get her to tell me what was going on and what she said to the guy. It turns out that she had worked in a psychiatric ward with violent patients. I learned much later she held a brown belt in karate. The morning's event was sort of business as usual at the psychiatric ward."

"What did she say to him?"

"She said, 'I'm a Jew. Please don't hate me.'"

"Wow. Tough woman."

"You may have noticed I'm attracted to tough women."

"Not many men are. We're so lucky!"

"We were together for forty-one years. Very together, but no children. Maybe we waited too long. Who knows?"

"So what happened after the Prado?"

"We stayed in Madrid two more nights in the youth hostel; then we hitchhiked to Barcelona together and took a hotel in the port and ate seafood for dinner. We made love that night, and it was a revelation. It was my first time. I learned everything from her."

"I'm honored to be the beneficiary of her teaching. What else did you learn from her?"

"I learned how to love in all of its dimensions, how to savor time, to get things done, to believe any problem can be solved with thought and patience. Anna was not normal, and at the same time she was completely normal. It's hard to describe. She was abnormally talented, but she didn't like to show it. Her talents were private. She was French, from a Jewish family from Odessa. They had moved to Paris at the end of the nineteenth century. They were doctors and bankers. They were wealthy until WWII. Her parents loved the mountains. They escaped the Nazis by climbing the Mont Blanc in the dark, arriving on the summit for the sunrise. Anna was born in Switzerland. They moved back to Paris when she was three years old, but their old life there had been stolen by the Nazis, including their house, their possessions and the members of her family who had refused to leave. Her parents rebuilt as best they could, but most of the things that they had cherished were never returned to them, including art works, their wealth and worst of all, the people who had been murdered. Her parents turned to Anna. She was their future.

"After Barcelona, we hitched to Paris. Anna had called them to say she was arriving with me. There was a room waiting for us with a double bed. They were that kind of people. They trusted their daughter, and they were thrilled she was in love with an American guy — with an American goy. Their acceptance of me was the most generous gift anyone could give to a young man in love. I've always cherished it. It's a model for the way I live.

"We spent six months together, living with her parents, while I took the Civilisation Française course at the Sorbonne, and she continued her economics studies at the École Normale Supérieur. At the same time she was a full time student at the École des Beaux Arts, but it took me a while to realize this.

"I had admired the beautiful contemporary oil paintings in her parents' apartment for weeks. One afternoon when we were alone in the apartment, I asked her about them. She didn't answer at first, but then she asked me what I liked and didn't like. I was so naïve — I never imagined they were hers. We did a tour of the apartment, and I commented on each painting, saying that they were obviously by the same artist — clearly a mature contemporary artist — but one with deep respect for the history of painting. I tried to find the references, and commented on the bold use of color and form, with an underlying connection to our world as we see it. She was pleased, and she took me by the hand, down the hallway to a door I had never noticed. She opened it, and I saw narrow, steep stairs. We climbed into a luminous room. It was an artist's studio with a glass roof. There was an easel, and paintings were everywhere. I was speechless. She was the artist.

"She led me to the easel, and saying nothing, she sat me down on a wooden stool. She opened several tubes of paint, and handed me a palette and a brush. She put a fresh canvas on the easel; she walked slowly to a sofa, and began taking off her clothes — very slowly, with her back to me. I watched. She turned to me, naked, and she smiled the ageless smile of a woman in love. She was Manet's Olympia, Goya's Maja and Titian's Venus all rolled into one. I was hot — very hot to make love. She stretched out on the divan, and she said only one word: 'paint.' I painted and panted for over an hour of ecstatic joy. I was so high that no drug could have touched me. When we finally made love, it was for the first time all over again, but much more. Like the Iya Onsen for you and me: there was no going back.

"I returned to the USA, and we were finally reunited in New York after six long months of separation. Her parents came for the wedding, which took place in a synagogue. I had converted, and everybody seemed to be surprised, saying it wasn't necessary, but I wanted it, so I did it.

"Anna had graduated by then, and I had only a year to go. She had no problem finding a job with an investment bank, while I finished my bachelor's degree. She took a leave from the bank, and we both did doctorates at Columbia. I had switched from Chemistry to French. After getting her Ph.D., she got her bank job back, and I took the university job I've just left. At first, we lived in a tiny apartment in a rotten neighborhood near Columbia, but we felt at home there, and we loved the people around us. Everybody respected her. She was tough, but never showed it, except when all else failed; then she turned into a tiger. I never saw her use her martial arts after our meeting in Madrid. But those skills were always there. People sensed it in the way she moved, the way she stood and the look in her eyes.

"We moved to Brooklyn, on a subway line that took her directly to her work. We found a building with apartments looking out on Prospect Park. It should have been perfect; except that it was the 1970's and the neighborhood was so dangerous that even the police avoided it. The building next door had been gutted by fire, and the one on the other side was a dealer den. We knocked on their door to say we were the new neighbors. They were heavily armed, which turned out to be a good thing, because once they got to know us, we had protection.

"Anna got a loan through her employer. We borrowed from our parents, and we bought the whole building for what it was worth, which was nothing, compared to today's prices, but even nothing was a stretch for us. We had no money to make it livable. We slept in a camping tent nailed to the floor. It took a month to get water and four months to get electricity, and we didn't have heat for two years. At first we cooked on a camping stove. We spent most of our spare time trying to make our apartment livable, ignoring the rest of the building. It took five years to get everything working so we could rent the other apartments. Anna never complained. We were happy. We both liked our jobs. The building was a shared passion, and there were three other parts of us that we managed to keep alive: Anna never stopped painting; both of us cycled in the park; and we took vacations in France, mostly on bicycles.

"Time passed extremely fast. We were in our late thirties when we decided to have a child, and it didn't work. We tried everything, so we finally concluded that our life together was as perfect as life can be, and that we could happily keep it for ourselves."

"Where is Anna's art?"

"It's dispersed around the world. She sold about 1500 paintings through the Parisian gallery that took her on when she was a student at the Beaux Arts. She refused solo shows. She never had a vernissage, but they sold everything as fast as it arrived in Paris. The gallery keeps track of each work and its journey through the art world."

"Do you have any paintings?"

"She kept some paintings, and when she was diagnosed with brain cancer, she quit selling, but continued to paint.

She said she wanted to concentrate on me and be my muse for as long as she could. She joked that she wanted to delay becoming my museum.

"There are about 150 paintings stored in our apartment that the gallery doesn't know about, and there are maybe fifty more in Paris. I want to photograph them and send a catalogue to the gallery. I intend to organize a show with some of these unknown paintings, and I hope to get a retrospective at a major French museum."

"Why do you think she shunned attention?"

"Anna was not a recluse, and she was well integrated into the art worlds of New York and Paris. She was simply being efficient and focused on her art and her economics. She didn't need publicity, and she was afraid that it would interfere with her life. She was a pure economist. She didn't care about making money. She never asked the bank for a raise, but they regularly raised her salary out fear she would leave them. She worked mostly from her office in our apartment in New York or later in Paris. Early on, she relied on the Brooklyn Library, and then computers changed her life. She became even more efficient. In theory, she went to her real office in Manhattan once a week for a meeting, but she often replaced it with a conference call. She made many, many billions for that bank. She resigned when she realized she was ill. She had always limited her bank work to three days a week. The rest of her working time was devoted to painting or scholarly research. Her bank job allowed her to test her economic theories, aided by computer models she devised. She was a math whiz. Her office and studio are intact. I've entered neither one since she died just over a year ago."

"How can I help?"

"You've already saved my life and my soul. Now I need to face her death and confront the remains of our years together. I want to take her through the final transition: from muse to museum, as she put it. She fought it bravely for five years. Now she's dead, and I have to come to terms with it. I hope there will be exhibits of her work. You saved me by becoming my new muse. You gave me a new life."

"I'm moved and honored. We can start organizing and cataloguing as soon as we get to New York."

At Kansai airport, their bikes and luggage were waiting at the baggage service. The fourteen-hour flight to New York was spent sleeping and feeling cramped and stressed. They arrived at JFK dizzy and disoriented. They picked up their boxed bikes and the suitcase containing their new clothes from Kyoto, and they walked through the double doors into the arrivals hall. They were surprised to see Patrick smiling and waving.

"Pat! So good to see you! Thank you for this surprise."

"No problem. Do you think we could have a cup of coffee before I drive you into town? Maybe in the restaurant over there?"

"Sure. Sounds good. I can see you're tired. So are we."

They ordered tea, and Patrick ordered coffee.

"So what's new in New York, Pat?"

"Not much. I haven't been sleeping. That's all."

"What's the problem?"

"The fucking phone has been ringing off the frigging hook day and night. People are camped out on my lawn, and my wife has moved in with her parents."

"I assume you're joking, Pat."

"No joke. I suppose you don't have a clue why? Where have you been for the past three days?"

"We were being tourists in Osaka."

"Have you completely forgotten about a bike race?"

"No, but what's that have to do with anything?

He looked at Sara. She had gone white.

"Well. It seems our sweet Sara here won an obscure little amateur race on an island somewhere in Japan. I suppose you're aware of that?"

"Sure. What's going on?"

Patrick pulls a *New York Times* from his jacket pocket and holds the front page up to them. There is a picture of Sara, and below it is an article with the headline, "New York Woman Cyclist Shatters Last Bastion of Male Supremacy." The picture shows Sara, hands on the brake hoods. Her mouth is open, showing her teeth in a snarl. Beside and above her head is another, smaller head, wearing the same expression. It's the monkey.

"Oh shit! How did they get this, Pat?"

"Sara, you innocent creature, I suppose you haven't seen a newspaper or looked at the internet since the race. You don't realize what you've done. You've blown competitive sports off the map. Women are demanding an end to gender segregation in all sports. They want to compete directly with men, even in American football! Can you imagine a football team composed of equal numbers of men and women? Women are demonstrating outside the offices of the Olympic Committee. They want to desegregate all olympic sports. You can't buy a racing bike in New York City. That was no little race you won. The guy you beat is Japan's star racer. Thirty thousand people were on that mountain. The whole thing was broadcast live all over Japan. It's viral all over the net. There are TV crews camped in front of your apartment building. *Vogue* and *Time* are desperate to do cover stories. You have proposals for book contracts with six figure advances… and then there's this business with the monkeys. People are going nuts about the monkey story. I'm exhausted. I'm turning you over to professional management."

He takes his phone out of his pocket, "Jim, I think they're ready for you."

Turning to them, he says, "OK guys. Remember a tall guy from the club named Jim Anderson? Well, he manages celebrities, and he has agreed to advise you. He'll be here in a few seconds. One last thing: the only reason this arrival hall isn't full of photographers is I told them you'd arrive on this same flight, but twenty-four hours from now. It's going to be a zoo here tomorrow. You're lucky. I hope you stay that way."

They recognize Jim from the club. He had been waiting in the wings for Pat's call.

"Hi guys! Have a good trip? Don't answer. Here's the scoop. My job is to manage celebrities. I don't make them famous. Instead, I'm paid to keep them that way. I don't charge for the first consultation, so this is on the house. As Pat explained, you have some decisions to make. Sara, you've pulled off a major publicity coup — potentially the most lucrative publicity coup of the decade. Managed right, you could be sitting on millions in a few days, with much more down the road. This could be bigger than Harry Potter and the presidential election combined. I'm not kidding. You have hit a nerve, a very big and sensitive nerve, and it's a triple hit: a sensational race, women's rights and something to do with monkeys, but nobody knows what the monkey story is really about. It's a mystery. There's no doubt it happened, but how? Why? Disney, News Corp, Time Warner, CBS — they would give many millions tomorrow to know why that monkey was taking care of your interests in the race. The videos of the monkey landing on your back are awesome. Some people think you already knew each other. Others think it was incredible luck."

"Is this a joke? Some kind of set-up by the guys in the club? You photoshopped that picture into a fake *Times*, right?"

"*The New York Times* article isn't a joke, Sara, and that's just one picture in one newspaper. If you don't believe me, just walk over to the newsstand over there and pick up any paper.

"Let me briefly explain how our management works. We hire experts in key areas to work for you and with you. We'll move you to a high security building, and you'll have an escort, who will also be your driver. You'll have a professional publicist and a scriptwriter. They will help you compose what you say in print interviews and in TV broadcasts. You'll have a personal accountant and a lawyer, and your investments will be handled by professionals. Your clothes, hair and makeup will be designed by pros in keeping with your chosen image. I'll coordinate, presiding over a weekly video conference meeting, but you will remain the boss in all of this. My team will be there to protect, assist and guide you.

"You are viral, Sara. You had the good sense to completely disappear after the race, signing away nothing, and that has only increased the hype. The journalists of the world are trying to find you. Whatever you do, don't try to return to your apartment without bodyguards. This is serious stuff."

"Is it reversible?"

"What do you mean? You want to give your race prize back?"

"Yes. I want to lead a normal life. I don't want to be rich, and certainly not famous."

"Are you sure? You realize you're making a major decision here. If you want to make the most of this, now is the time. If you want to go back to your former life, that's going to be difficult — at least in the short term, but it's possible to cool this thing off, if that's really what you want to do. The attention span of the world is short — on the order of a month or two. If you play your cards right, you can be pretty safe in a couple of months, but the big potential will be gone. That doesn't mean you can't have another chance at it later, but the returns will probably be diminished."

"You have lots of experience with celebrities. What would you do in my place?"

"I don't know. Nobody ever asked me that question… but come to think of it, I would probably get the hell out of there."

"That's what I want to do."

"And the monkey?"

"I might tell that story to my grandchildren."

She signed a two-month contract with Jim to advise her and handle queries from journalists. He was normally paid a retainer plus a percentage of earnings, but he agreed to just the retainer, since there should be no earnings, and he gave her a steep cyclist's discount on that. Pat drove them to Brooklyn.

"Fortunately, nobody has picked up the 'coach' angle. I'll keep the bikes at the club, and deliver them in a few days. You can just walk into the building like normal people. Good luck. I'm going to turn off my phone, after I convince my wife to come home."

They were riding up in the elevator. "Any regrets or second thoughts?"

"I just want to have more of the happiness I've felt being with you. I truly have no desire to be a celebrity, and I have no idea what I would do with a lot of money. Also, if what they say is true about women demanding that competitive sports be desegregated, that's good news for women, but it will happen without my help. There are plenty of brilliant woman lawyers out there to wage that battle. What would you do?"

"For me, freedom is more important than money. I wouldn't want to be a slave to success. I admire your decision."

It was Sara's first visit to the apartment. The elevator opened directly into the living room, and before them appeared a long expanse of glass, with the park beyond. On the left was a large living room, and on the right was a homey and well-equipped kitchen, with the same view over the park. The living room had a second series of large windows on a lateral wall. On either side of the elevator were two doors. One led down to the floor beneath, where there were bedrooms, offices and a room for storing paintings. (A bicycle room and a wine cellar were in the basement.) The other door led to the roof.

"Let's start with the hard part — Anna's studio."

He opened the door to the stairs going up; then a second door at the top. They were on the roof of the building in a garden, with a view of the park on one side and Flatbush in the other direction. There was a small house at the far end of the garden."

"That was her studio. Please come. I've not gone in there since she died."

Inside, it smelled of oil paint. There was a skylight and large windows overlooking the garden. Stocks of art supplies were neatly arranged on shelves, and a painting sat on the easel. Her palette was thick with dried paint.

"She painted until she couldn't hold a brush. She died on the sofa over there. I was hugging her with my ear against her chest. I heard her heart stop."

"How would she feel about me being here?"

"I think she would be delighted and very proud."

"You're not afraid of ghosts?"

"Yes, terrified, but it's time to face them. I feel surprisingly serene, being here with you. I could not have done it alone. Would you like a cup of Japanese tea?"

And that is how Sara moved into the apartment. It felt right, and she had no other place to hide. She sifted through her emails to find the response from the publisher, which was negative. They said they liked the proposal, but they were obliged to downscale, concentrating on their core activity of publishing scientific journals. They recommended another publisher.

They often cooked Japanese food, and the apartment was big enough so they could be together or apart, depending on their activities. Their bikes were on indoor trainers, and they rode them daily and walked or ran in the park. Sara was completely rewriting the book's sample chapter, and he had started a novel. The weather was warming, and they had many good talks, sitting in the roof garden or walking in the park.

"How's the novel going? Can you tell me what it's about?"

"It's the story of our bicycle trip through Shikoku, but you're my age, and we're riding folding touring bikes, like the one we saw at the flower center on the first day of the ride. There will be no bicycle race, but I'll keep the monkeys. Tell me about your sample chapter."

"It's about the importance of sleep and the role of exercise and other environmental factors in getting the benefits of sleep. It also borrows from our experiences on Shikoku."

Jim called once a week to explain what he had done to defuse the hype. He said he knew many of the journalists making queries, and that they were decent people who understood her decision. Others were more insistent, but he had ways of convincing them that his cooperation might be useful in the future, for instance if she were to change her mind…

They looked at some of the internet blogs, forums, YouTube comments and print articles. There was intense speculation about the monkey business — particularly whether Sara had set up the whole episode using trained animals. Technical cycling discussion focused mostly on the descent, where over and over she had come irrationally close to the guardrail. Commentators discussed her ability to repress fear, with some saying she was crazy and others saying it was calculated risk, necessary to win the race. Other comments, blogs and print articles concerned the climb and pushing physiological and psychological limits. Sports psychologists were saying her personal motivations were the key, and if she would divulge the source of her mental drive, other human endeavors could benefit. There were estimations of her weight and calculations of her power output during the climb. Her estimated power to weight ratio was off the charts. Several commentators called her "superhuman."

The data, collected by the GPS locator beacon under her saddle, were available on a server as graphs, synchronized to the video, so the curves developed as the race took place in the video. Data were also provided on the memory card in Sara's envelope and compiled as a table with time, position in meters from the start, altitude and ambient temperature in the first four columns. From these data, the succeeding columns calculated power in watts and climbing rate in meters per minute. They studied the graphs and tables together, and Sara did further analysis, including adding a column giving power to weight ratio, since she had weighed herself the morning of the race. She also added annotations giving events and her perceived state of mind and body. The two power surges she had felt from the monkey were obvious. They had put her into a new performance level, but the most impressive performance increase was during the final sprint, when she was riding, as she put it, "for love."

"I'm trying to understand how the brain controls performance. The monkey power boost changed the race for me, and it stayed with me after she jumped off. I felt it in my legs and lungs. According to the GPS data, the monkey gave me a 46% power surge. I therefore entered the descent with metabolic and mental reserves, so I built maximum acceleration by pedaling during the descent, letting me overtake Number 22 at the start of the final climb. He had used his reserves in his battle with his buddy on the ultra steep part after the restaurant. He thought he had won the race, so he didn't take enough risks on the descent. The GPS data from the final sprint show a maximum power increase of 68%, and that was your contribution. The love boost trumped the monkey boost. Love was my secret drug. I can do anything when I'm high on love for you. You're a genius coach!"

"And I have the most fun coaching job on earth. Don't worry. I'm not going to write a book about it. Even if I wanted to, nobody would believe me, and I wouldn't have a clue where to begin."

"But you do. How do you spell, clue?"

He stared at her. She knew he knew.

"I wondered what had become of that piece of paper."

"I found it in the *Mapple* book of road maps of Shikoku."

"I'm ashamed. I opened Pandora's box. It was childish curiosity. After the race and all of those wonderful climbs with you… there had to be an explanation for your abilities, but once I realized — there was no going back. The genie was out of the bottle."

"I think we should talk about it."

"You're right. I'm relieved. Thank you. So you really identified the CLUH gene variant associated with enhanced performance? Congratulations. Your paper has been cited over 2000 times."

"I was just the student they were kind enough to put on as first author. It was teamwork. It started during an optional research rotation when I entered med school. I stumbled onto something interesting, and I went with it. I worked on the project for four years, and I defended my Ph.D. thesis at the same time I graduated from med school. Basically all my spare time and vacations were spent on it. We were able to partially explain why some people are elite athletes. We were lucky. Subject 1080 was discovered just after I joined the project; until then a ton of work had been done, without finding an outlier. But 1080 was the dream outlier — really off the charts. The challenge for me was to find out how 1080 did it."

"So you did the molecular biology?"

"I did part of it, but I also worked with 1080 and other subjects during stress tests and training. I was involved in the physiology, as well as the molecular biology."

"How was 1080 discovered?"

"Through a screening program, using volunteers, who were paid to take a bicycle stress test, while we recorded various parameters, such as ECG, blood oxygen, VO_2 max, blood chemistry and mitochondrial markers. Promising subjects were invited back for more tests. I learned a lot about exercise physiology and also about psychology. So 1080 was off the charts from the start, even before training, but things got really interesting with training, particularly with the physiology and molecular biology we did in parallel. We also did brain scans."

"Did you get to know 1080 personally?"

"No. I never saw or talked to 1080. All tests were performed in another room. We communicated via text, so we didn't even know if 1080 was a man or a woman until the DNA work was done. So 1080 remains anonymous for reasons of privacy and security."

"Security?"

"Yes, the uniqueness of a subject like 1080 could attract the wrong type of attention. You can imagine the breeding applications — even cloning. So nobody knows the identity of 1080, not even the scientists. It was a true double-blind study, and all of the records, including 1080's DNA sequence, were encrypted."

"So what was the final conclusion?"

"Our study confirmed that performance correlates with mitochondrial capacity. More mitochondria produce more energy (ATP), so basically, you get a bigger motor. The CLUH gene was important, but there were other genes involved. Obviously, it doesn't help to have a bigger engine, if you can't get raw materials like glucose, water and oxygen in and waste like carbon dioxide and nitrogenous compounds out."

"Were you able to identify the key factors and underlying genes?"

"Some of them. An unknown number of traits interact. A subject like 1080 must be extremely rare. We don't know how rare, but we know that most of the genes we identified are unlinked, so conventional breeding with 1080 would be difficult, due to segregation, unless a complementary mate is used, one lacking just a few of the necessary genetic elements. So you would have to find another 1080 variant to do breeding, helped by 1080's genomic sequence. Also, we were afraid an existing genome could be engineered to partially mimic 1080, using editing techniques like CRISPR CAS-9 and transgenesis. That's why we stopped the research and encrypted the records before enough was known to create a new 1080 or find a similar subject."

"How did 1080 feel about this?"

"Well, 1080 didn't know about being 1080. We did parallel studies on other subjects who were called back after the initial screen. The subjects were not given their results. 1080 isn't even the real subject number. It's just used for public consumption. And 1080 isn't even an athlete. Plus 1080 has an unfortunate disability I won't go into. We've been told that attempts have been made to find another 1080, but we think the probability of success is very low. There might be less than 100 individuals like 1080 in the human population. We were lucky, 1080 was a surprise — not even the original object of the study."

"Did you apply what you learned to cycling?"

Sara seems surprised. She hesitates, considering her answer carefully.

"Well, that's sort of my little secret, but I'll give you the gist of it. I've known since I was a child that I could easily win running races with my friends. I also learned to pretend being tired and to avoid winning too often. Nobody likes constant winners. I wanted to be like my friends. Even so, in junior high school the gym teacher noticed something and wanted me to be on the track team. I said no thanks, but I was always curious about my physical abilities. My lung capacity was good, but there was something else. That's how I eventually got interested in the research project. I wanted to understand how different people respond to challenges.

"I identified the first of the relevant genes in 1080 by applying my intuitions about myself to what was known about the genetics of energy production in muscle cells. I was doing PCR and sequencing on DNA samples from 1080 and other subjects. PCR is a simple way to amplify a defined segment of DNA. I had a hunch about a gene, and when I looked at 1080's DNA, I found a variant of that gene, called CLUH. CLU stands for clustered; H for homologue. This new CLU variant turned out to correlate with faster mitochondrial division, because CLU produces a regulatory RNA that promotes the translation of nuclear-encoded, mitochondrial proteins in the cytoplasm, in proximity to mitochondria, resulting in the transport of these proteins into mitochondria. 1080's mitochondria divide faster; their numbers build up — and so does the potential to make ATP, assuming, as I said, that other things like glucose, gas exchange, and free radicals aren't limiting. Mitochondrial buildup happens during training, particularly during interval training. So we now better understand how interval training, with short anaerobic sprints interspersed with slower aerobic periods, sets off a regulatory cascade that turns on CLUH and other genes involved in adaptation to a physical challenge, encoding functions like O_2 transport, glycogen turnover, muscle contraction — we've only mapped a small part of this gene regulation system. Research continues using laboratory rats and human cells in tissue culture, since the ethics of doing more in humans are debatable."

Again, Sara hesitates, seemingly lost in thought. He stays silent, intent on understanding her story. She looks at him searchingly, and then she starts again, slowly.

"Now the secret garden part. I was curious about myself, so I tested the same primers on my own DNA, and I found a genetic explanation for my physical characteristics, for my phenotype, as we say in the jargon."

"OK, I understand you were an invisible subject in the paper I found. You're positive for CLUH, the variant carried by 1080. How does that help you climb the way you did on Shodoshima?"

"It told me a little bit about what I had. We didn't publish everything we knew about 1080, because we were afraid somebody would use the information to create a superhuman, even a super species. I used it to help me understand my gift, both its strengths and weaknesses. I did this with the consent of the PI, the principal investigator, but the other team members didn't know about it. It's off the record, and it pushes the ethics, I admit, but it gave me a way to satisfy some of my curiosity and to train to get maximum benefit from my genes. I never used any of the information until the Aubisque, and I didn't really get interested in extreme exercise until this trip. Thanks for encouraging me to ride ahead and repeat the climbs. It was ideal interval training: intense sprints alternating with relatively low activity periods. It got me thinking again, and I worked up some new ideas, which I was eager to try.

"For instance, is sleep analogous to the rests between sprints in interval training? How about seasons? What happens during rest? How does an alternation of stress and repair improve performance and general health? One thing I'm sure of: being with you has allowed me to sleep again — like a child, deeply and happily — restorative sleep I had not known since my parents died. Part of my performance in the race came from having you next to me each night, holding my hand as I fell asleep. Thanks to you, I've rediscovered the benefits of untroubled sleep.

"I probably never should have entered that race, but I really wanted to know if my new ideas were correct. It's kind of like finding the screw from your shifter — you start by listening to your intuition; then you search for questions and answers, but not just on an experimental level. Chance and intuition can be useful, when managed with rational approaches. When I volunteered for the race, I honestly thought I would just stay in the peloton, but you and the monkey carried me away — into an unexpected metabolic state. That was the exciting part for me. We know that psychological parameters are important in physical performance, but it was exciting to experience it for myself, and I came away with my initial hypothesis reinforced, but it was an experiment with no control and a sample size of one. Maybe with the research shifted to a rat model, more of the biochemistry will become clear? The ethics are another problem.

"So now you know another reason why I don't want to be

a famous athlete, and why the details of our results, particularly those that concern me, are hidden. I don't want spies from some rogue state getting their hands on my DNA."

"I see your point. I never thought about stealing DNA, and I can just imagine the Tour de France after DNA doping catches on. Is DNA doping possible?"

"Right this minute, it's probably not possible, but in a few years — sure, using viral-based vectors, but who knows? Biotech will make the current electronics revolution seem insignificant and benign."

"Sounds scary. Could you elaborate on your super species comment?"

"There are many scenarios for engineering a new race or species. Some of them go back to the rediscovery of Mendelian genetics at the beginning of the twentieth century."

"Unfortunately, Sara, such eugenic schemes were favorites of Hitler and Stalin."

"Right, and now it's possible to bypass the slow traditional breeding constraints, using transgenic techniques, gene editing and breeding assisted by DNA sequence information. Just to give one example, it should be possible to make humans who are stronger, faster, smarter — and also include resistance to a viral pathogen for which there is no cure. Put the improved genome into as many key backgrounds as possible to ensure diversity; then spread the virus — everybody dies except the engineered race."

"I got it. I'm remembering the physicists, who started molecular biology after WWII, because they feared the atomic bomb they had created. Some of them were friends of my parents. Now I see that the molecular biology they invented has produced another atomic bomb, but in genetics. Why didn't you continue in research after your doctorate? Were you afraid of contributing to a future gene war?"

"I was tempted to continue full time, and the ethical questions bothered me, but the real reason was that I had set my sights on climbing the medical mountain. I guess I never told you my father was a surgeon. I wanted to honor his life's work, but being a surgeon was too confining for me, so I opted for the emergency room.

"Research meant lonely hours pipetting a few microliters of various reagents into plastic centrifuge tubes in an ice bucket. I wanted to interact with people. But I stay in contact with my research colleagues, and I'm still an official member of the team. I'm still asking questions. I'm trying to understand more about intervals. For instance, as I mentioned, what's their relation to the circadian rhythm entrained by light/dark cycles. Can we learn something about sleep by studying interval training — maybe using the molecular biological and biochemistry I was working on? How about seasons? Maybe on/off alternations are built into all life living in temperate zones?

"The PI had lots of questions to ask me about the bicycle race, particularly the performance peaks caused by the monkey and by you. I didn't reveal the whole story about the monkey, and I didn't say anything about being in love with you, but I did say there was an emotional basis for my performance during the sprint. We agreed to be discreet, but the lab has already had to answer queries about possible connections between the bicycle racer and the first author on the paper. The names are the same, although I've never used my middle name. I also asked that the close-up video from the race be removed from internet, and I've removed photos of me, the doctor, from internet… but it's not too hard to guess we're the same person. The important thing is that nobody knows I was a subject of the research, except for you, the PI and me. My DNA sequence is encrypted. Only I have the key, and only the PI has access to 1080's sequence.

"My potential liability is that the sequence of CLUH, which is essential to the performance phenotype, was published for 1080. I carry that variant, so anybody with access to a sample of my DNA could easily nail me. We've done mass, random screenings by PCR, and we have so far not seen another one. I need to keep my DNA to myself."

"So what are you going to do with your new knowledge about performance? It sounds to me that you're another 1080."

"No, I'm not another 1080. I also had a physical workup, like the other subjects. Unlike the other subjects, I know where I sit in the curve. I'm way off the mean, but not a total outlier like 1080. I want to enjoy a productive life without indulging in extreme behaviors. I hope to apply what I know about my genes to other endeavors. I'm a climber, so when I get to the top, I need to come down fast and look for the next climb. Now I want to descend less and make the next climb a higher one."

"Maybe in music, Sara. Maybe music is your next mountain…"

They tried to stay as normal as possible, but the subject of eugenics came up often, and the genetic undercurrent was carrying them away from normality. His thoughts often turned to the significance of his new knowledge.

I know only a little about genetics, and my molecular biology is rusty, but I can follow her story. The mountains she wants to climb are hung with avalanches about to fall. She was anonymous until the race. Now she's not just a doctor and scientist — she's also an athletic superstar. No hiding the connection. Just a search with face recognition software, and you've found her. Nothing directly says she was a subject in the study, but the curious observer will imagine that her race performance comes not just from knowledge of metabolism — but also from her genes. Somebody might even imagine that she's the famous 1080! How else to explain what happened in Japan? So she's the ultimate breeding stock. Screen her eggs for the CLUH variant, inseminate (artificially?) with selected sperm and implant in surrogate mothers: you're starting a super race. Her DNA sequence is a gold mine by itself, and she knows how to access it and use it. So it's not just to maintain her privacy that she shuns publicity. She had no way of predicting the effects of entering the race, but now the gene's out of the bag. A rogue state? But many people would go rogue, once they've understood the potential gains. She's the ultimate love object in the most basic biological sense. I'm getting carried away. Don't panic. Am I a rogue lover? Did I sense all of this in her way back at my retirement party? But our love must stay immune to eugenics! Now I'm a guardian of her secret. It's the price to pay for the privilege of being with her. So what's next? She's cooking up a whole menu of ideas about motivation in physical performance, about interval training, seasons… and other kinds of performance? I wonder what she's figured out about sleep? Is it just for recovery? As usual, she's way ahead of me. But one thing is certain. She needs a name change.

The "gender equality in sports" movement had received voluminous attention in print articles, blogs, forums and in the social media. Discrimination suits were being prepared against hundreds of sports organizations, covering team sports from baseball to ice hockey and individual sports from skiing to swimming. Funding and pro bono services were pouring in from both women and men.

Many sports enthusiasts had initially rejected the idea

that teams should be composed of equal numbers of men and women, but some were intrigued by the possibility of changing the basic logistics of games like football or basketball. The new mantra was that men and women should be equal partners in all aspects of life, including sports, because Sara had proved that the presumption of weakness in women was false. Individual sports, such as gymnastics, would also have to rewrite their rulebooks, letting men and women compete for the same medals. Some women were opposed to competing directly with men, particularly in sports like wrestling, but with each objection, imaginative solutions were proposed to put the two sexes on more equal footing, even for brute force sports like weightlifting. One idea was to compete in some sports for the power to weight ratio. Gyms and sports equipment retailers were flying high, pouring money into expansion and advertising directed at women in recreational and competitive sports. Women were training to break the taboos and directly compete with men, even in martial arts. The wrestlers and boxers complained that women would kill their sport, but the proponents of gender equality claimed that in equal weight categories, properly trained women could compete and win, and that's why the men wanted to keep them out.

Parts of the sports industry were preparing to battle these changes, but many commentators said it was time for shake-up and renewal. The world of competitive sports was in an intense uproar because of Sara, and it looked like the cause for gender equality would be carried through the courts with a good chance of winning. Many organizations were already working in the background to prepare for gender equality.

Sara was amazed, but unperturbed and determined to stay out of the fray. She continued to call Mama-san once a week. Their singing in Osaka had been a success, and

Mama-san wanted to bring her back to the club. Sara worked on her voice every day by herself and frequently with a voice teacher, polishing her vocal technique and repertoire. They often ate breakfast in the roof garden. One morning, sitting down to breakfast, she found a paper on her plate.

One Short Moment

When the growing curve and the aging curve
Cross their inverse paths and lie entangled
For one short moment,
Before rising and falling, out of phase
In their respective functions,

Then, my child, will we
For one short moment,
See each other as equals, as true friends
As siblings, as mirror images of
Our parents and future children.
Then, for one short moment,
Will we know who and why we are.

So don't resist, waver or slow. Let nature
Set the course and choose the time
Of inevitable and irreparable impact.
Let us spur and cry, as jousters
Seek the fury of the closing speed.
For the harder we embrace, the harder we will fall,
And the longer we will lie, entangled, and know each other
And our line, before and after
This one short moment of true and equal love.

Two months thus passed, slowly at first. As they established a routine, time flowed easily through, over and around them. They became closer, and in new ways. They worked on the painting catalogue together, spending time in the studio, and Sara started to feel she had known Anna. The paintings became friends, but one had a familiar and primitive resonance, without the sophistication of the others.

"I'm curious about the painting in the hallway. A child could have painted it, but there is something adult and direct behind the abstraction. It is unlike the others. Is it yours of Anna from the sitting in Paris?"

"Very perceptive of you. She always said it was her favorite, because it captured a momentous event: the no-turning-back-point, when we became inseparable.

"Sara, how do you feel about Anna? Many women would be threatened. You've never shown that emotion, and I'm grateful."

"You're right to ask; I value your honesty. You're deeply in love with her, and I want that to continue. I want to share you. I want to know her better through her art and through you. My love for my father was put on hold by his death. Until you, I couldn't build a competing relationship with another man. I guess I was in love with a ghost. Now that's changed. I'll always love my parents, but now I feel free to love you even more.

"So keep Anna as close as you can for as long as possible. I don't want to compete. How could I? My bicycle antics were nothing compared to her accomplishments. Look at these! These are great works of art. No gimmicks. Pure emotion in light, in color, in form. She's alive in these paintings. I want to know her. I want to share her with you."

"I'm relieved and grateful, Sara, but don't think of yourself as lesser. Your bicycle exploits are pure pleasure and pride to me, and you've changed competitive sports forever.

On the artistic side, you more than carry your own. You showed in Kyoto that you can deeply move an audience with your music. That's pure art, and it's priceless."

Sara's vocal work was paying off. She decided to concentrate on two Puccini roles: Mimi in *La Bohème* and Cio-Cio-san in *Madama Butterfly*. Mimi is close to Sara's culture, but Cio-Cio-san is a teenage geisha in love with an American visitor. The trip to Japan helped her with Cio-Cio-san, in whom she found crosscurrents, vortexes and conflicts of love, devotion and suicide — forces she knew in herself, but they were intensified through Puccini's music.

Jim had his final meeting with them, and suggested they break the quarantine by trying a Manhattan restaurant. But that above all, they should not appear in public on bicycles. The sports lib movement was gaining momentum; the initial furor had calmed somewhat, and it had matured into organized negotiations with the sports industry.

Sara began to substitute in an emergency room, and she worked hard on her book about sleep. She was coming slowly out of her isolation, but still enjoying her retreat.

> *I've never been happy like this before. I have love and company, and I can concentrate on my work without outside distractions. I've found my core family. I feel released from the past, and the present is cozy and exciting, leaving me free to be me — and us.*

Shiro-san called from Shodoshima to give them a glowing report. Lodging on the island was booked for months ahead. The race road was closed to motorized vehicles on weekends, in response to the flood of visitors on bicycles and on foot. Many people were coming up on the cable car with bikes and riding down; bicycle rental was an overnight big business. Shiro-san was fighting to keep new mass tourism hotels from being built. He had obtained a moratorium on all new construction, so many existing structures were being renovated as restaurants and hotels.

Much attention focused on the spot where the monkeys had done their show, with people on bikes trying to re-enact the event in the hopes that the monkeys would perform again. The monkeys were not cooperating, but they were often present, hanging out along the road or in the trees, observing human behavior. The island had found a new identity as a bicycle paradise, and dedicated bicycle paths were under construction. There was talk of closing the whole island to internal combustion vehicles, as an example to the world. Next year's race was being planned, and it would welcome riders of all sexes from around the world. The tight turns on the descent would be protected by pads and netting. He said that the number of ferries linking the island with Honshu had doubled, and there would soon be direct ferries from Kobe and Osaka. He also said that a sect in Tokyo had decided Sara was a kami, a Shinto deity. They called her a kamikase, goddess (kami) of the wind (kase), for her daring descent. He had read that a journalist in Delhi had described her as Hanuwoman, a play on the name Hanuman, the Indian monkey god. Shiro-san seemed amused by all of this, and proud to remain one of the three insiders who knew the whole story.

They had trouble assimilating this news. At first it didn't seem possible, but with the internet and something to spark people's fantasies, it was just conceivable that one bicycle race could have such an effect. Sara hoped that with time her role would become a minor point in the history of an improvement in women's rights. In any case, she was determined to remain an interested observer — keen to keep her distance.

They were dining on the rooftop terrace by candlelight on a sultry night in July. The sky was dark, with an afterglow in the west. They were having clams as a first course, to be followed by a salad of avocados, heart-shaped poached eggs and duck breast. They had made a French vinaigrette for the salad, and they were drinking a Sancerre with the main course. Sara was feeling happy and fulfilled.

"This is so perfect! I can't imagine how it could be better. Is there anything you would change?"

"Just time. I would change time."

"How would you change time?"

"I would make it elastic."

"It's already elastic. It stretches and contracts. Now it's stretched."

"You're right, Sara. Now it's stretched and slow, like this wine that lingers in its sensations. I guess I want time to slow even more, so we can prolong this part of our lives, this crossing."

"The crossing of generations in your poem?"

"Yes, this time when we're together mentally and physically."

"Are you worried?"

"Worried? Yes, a little. I'm thinking about my role in your present and future life."

"Serious stuff. What do you want to say?"

He took her hands.

"Sara, at some point, not now, but farther down the road, I should… I should find another role. You will need a younger lover, a husband, and I see you having children. I don't mean now, but in the future there should be a way for me to gently graduate into a more senior fan of yours."

"But I'm happy the way things are. I never imagined such happiness, and you're the ultimate lover and companion. I couldn't give you up."

"I'm not asking you to do it now. I'm just opening the door slightly so if the time comes, you'll know that I'll be ready to let somebody take my place."

"But who but you would put up with me?"

"Somebody who is strong enough to not feel challenged by your strength. Somebody generous, who shares your interests. You'll know when he appears in your life. Trust in your luck and keep your heart open."

"And you? What will become of you?"

"I'll be there, closer than ever — always with you, always in love with you. I promise."

The sun and summer were in full force, with no clouds in sight, and the air temperature was perfect. But they were caught in the currents of time, and its deep pools, rapids and eddies could not be ignored. They had acknowledged the need to build a future. A first step was taken, so their conversation retreated to safer subjects.

"How did you and Anna keep your marriage fresh?"

"We shared adventures. Renovating our apartment and restoring our building was a passion and physical labor we shared, and it was rewarding to see the neighborhood around us being fixed up, without losing its charm. (But we did miss our dealer friends next door after they left.) We often got dressed up and went to the opera or had romantic evenings at home with just us and good food and wine. We broke routines whenever possible, and we made love in exotic and surprising places and at unusual times. We were passionate lovers, and we never stopped learning about love from each other. Anna was French in her respect for the separation of family and work, so we took many travel vacations together — often on bicycles."

"Please tell me more."

"Anna believed in having a French vacation, meaning a full month completely away from work. We often went to

France to spend a week with her parents; then we would head out on our bicycles, loaded with camping gear. We put our bikes on the train, visiting different parts of France each year. We stayed in hotels only when the weather was terrible, or we saw a hotel we found irresistible. These shared experiences kept us and our love affair young and surprising. After Anna's parents were gone, we lived half the year in their Paris apartment, since I was able to group my teaching into one semester, and Anna could work any place there was a computer, a telephone and an easel."

"Sounds divine. When do we leave?"

"The Paris apartment is waiting for us, and the bikes should be in good shape. Say we leave here in a month? That would give us a deadline and put us in France in mid-August, which is a good quiet time for me to show you my Paris. We could use Paris as a base for a while, branch out and go to the Vosges and Jura mountains and maybe to the Alps. Or perhaps we should cycle the Loire Valley?"

"Yes, yes and more yes. I want more — more adventures, more love and more you. You've convinced me that love thrives on shared experiences, and I want our love to grow, so let's go to France. Leaving in the middle of August would give me time to resubmit my book project. I can't wait to discover France with you. In Japan I loved feeling that you were the only person who spoke my language, so we can continue to speak English together in France. But this trip will be different, because we know the local language, and we can also feel French. Just the idea of French bread, wine and cheese makes me salivate. Will there be monkeys?"

"Maybe I can arrange some, if not, I know where to rent a monkey suit…"

Their peace and quiet was interrupted by a phone call from Jim, who was looking out for Sara's interests, even though he was off retainer. An article had appeared in a tabloid claiming that Sara was in New York. A credit card under her name had been used in a grocery store in Brooklyn. He said that for a people journalist, this was the time to revive the story, because the interest was still there, but subdued. It could be reignited by a small spark, and journalists were keen to catch this second bounce and run with it. She would have to be careful about exposing her identity. They told him about their plans for a bike trip in France, and he said he had no competence in France, but that if Sara showed up at a hotel on a bicycle with her passport, she was likely to be recognized anywhere in the world.

The whole near-disaster of becoming an overnight celebrity was back. Their beautiful world of freedom and light had darkened. It felt like starting again from zero.

"I guess I could have a sex change and get a job as a female impersonator."

"You do that, and I'll become an ageing gigolo who specializes in young women in love with their fathers."

"I'll write an excellent endorsement for you, based on personal experience. You can quote me on your website."

"Thank you. What other identity-changing ideas do you have?"

"I'll let you pick. You're my coach. You can think of something."

"To tell the truth, I've been preparing this for a long time. I'll be right back."

He went to his office and came back with a file folder.

"I wish I could back pedal and join you in your time. I've tried hard, but a ratchet disengages me, so I spin to no effect. These are adoption papers that would make me your legal father. I would prefer to be your husband. I wanted to propose marriage to you during our lunch in Grand Central Terminal. I wanted to sweep you off your feet and carry you all the way down to City Hall, but I knew I couldn't get away with it, and I'm glad I didn't try after seeing you in action against that alpha male monkey."

He paused, and then continued watching her reactions intently.

"Marriage would be bliss for some years, and then our paths would uncross, and my decline would become your tragedy. Adoption gives you a badly needed name change, and it gives me an heir. My only family is a couple of childless cousins, whom I never see. Anna's estate deserves better. You're the daughter we never had. She was a passionate worker. The fruit of her efforts should not be dispersed too quickly. Adoption would solve two problems at once: a name change for you and an heir for Anna and me."

"And create a third: incest."

"Right, but incest can be fun."

"You're terrible. I really am going to get a sex change and become a female impersonator."

They had a good laugh.

He dropped to his knees in front of her.

"Sara, dear Sara. I love you madly and passionately. Will you become my legal daughter?"

She dropped to her knees and took his hands in hers.

"Sure. I'm game. Just so I can keep loving you and being with you."

"Shall we consummate this adoption?"

He led her from the garden into the studio, where they sat on the sofa, holding hands — silent for a time worthy of the intermission in a passionate Verdi opera, waiting for the sets to change and the singers to rest and drink their herbal tea in their dressing rooms. Then the orchestra started to play, and the curtain rose on another act, full of crossings and entanglements, twists of plot and soaring music.

Daylight found them lying on the carpet, rolled up together in a comforter, like a giant maki sushi.

"*Ohayou gozaimasu!* Did you sleep well?"

"Yes, and it was deliciously cozy being all wrapped up with you. How about you?"

"I slept well, but I had a curious dream just now."

"Do tell!"

"OK, but I warn you, it's a bit odd. We're staying in an *onsen* in Japan, and I get up early to take a bath, leaving you a note to say where I'm going. I go down to the baths half asleep in my *yukata*, with my little towel, and I do all the usual stuff. I'm all by myself because it's so early. I fold my towel on my head, and I'm enjoying the hot water. Then I hear female voices; the voices get louder and louder; and I realize they're in the dressing room, behind the frosted glass door. It seems that in my sleepy state I confused the kanji characters for men and women. I'm in the wrong bath, naked, and they're about to come into the room.

"I'm thinking fast. There's only one exit, which is through the dressing room. I'm trapped. I quickly get out of the water and into another bath with a stone pillar, where water is falling down in a cascade. I do my best to hide behind the pillar, covering my head with the towel, but my legs are sticking out and my male ID is clearly visible through the shallow water. But I remember reading that female impersonators hide their genitals by tucking them behind them, between their legs. So I try this, and it's a bit uncomfortable, but it works. I have an instant sex change. The first women are just arriving. I can't see much because of the towel over my head. I figure I should just wait there until the bathers finish, and I can make an escape through the dressing room.

"The women are carrying on like birds on a wire. I manage to sneak a few peeks out of curiosity. They're congregated at the far end of the pool I'm in, and there's a little boy with them, who's running around and splashing in the water. I think everything is under control… then they fall silent. I'm afraid they've spotted me, so I sneak another peek. They're paying no attention to me. Instead, they're looking at a woman who has just entered the pool area. Her hair is wet from showering and she is totally naked. She has a perfect body — really stunning — with curves galore, but in ideal measure and harmony. She's a living marble statue from ancient Greece. As she walks toward the bath, I can see her flesh is firm and strong. She has muscles behind her harmonious curves. I'm getting excited, which is causing some difficulties with my female impersonation."

"I can't imagine your pain. Who's the babe?"

"I'll tell you in a minute. As I said, I'm having problems with my female impersonation, so I pull the towel back over my eyes and lie back in the water and do arithmetic problems in my head, trying to forget her. I finally calm down, but then I hear the kid screaming and splashing and coming closer. I steal another look, and the babe is standing in the pool, not far from me. I can see her back and butt above the water. She's perfect. Her curves and straights are in ideal harmony. Her waist is slim, and her back is strong. I'm getting excited again, but I can't take my eyes off her. She turns around and starts walking my way. I see a beautiful face and a dancer's body, but her breasts are full, beautifully shaped and they swing gently as she walks. I can't stand the pain in my male ID anymore, and I pull the towel back over my eyes, and try hard to get this image of Venus out of my head."

"So how did it end?"

"I hear the kid coming closer, splashing water everywhere, and then there is silence. I don't dare look, but I can hear the kid coming over to me, wading through the water.

I'm scared, because this little boy is curious about me, and I've got serious anatomical problems from attempting to do a female impersonation while watching a perfect, naked, sex goddess walking toward me through shallow water. I can see the legs of the kid in the water, right by mine. Suddenly: wham! He pulls the towel off my head. He laughs and points at me, and everybody looks at me and screams. The women at the other end get out of the water. Everybody but the beautiful babe runs into the dressing room. Miss Venus de Milo is coming toward me, and I'm getting so excited, I can't do the impersonation any more. I lose control of the situation; my body floats to the surface; and my male ID comes popping out of the water. I wake up. Now how's that for a crazy dream?"

"Pretty interesting. I agree, but who was the beautiful babe?"

"Oh! I forgot to tell you. The beautiful babe was you of course!"

"How exciting and flattering. I wish you hadn't awakened. I would like to know what happened next. I can't wait for the next episode!"

Over breakfast, he suggested transforming their bicycle trip into a kayak descent of the Loire River in central France, with free camping on islands and only occasional use of official campgrounds, hotels and restaurants. They would do most of their own cooking, using supplies bought in the villages and towns along the way. They would take an inflatable two-person kayak by train into the foothills of the Massif Central Mountains and paddle the Loire — perhaps to the seacoast. He had done part of this trip with Anna many years ago, but most of it would be new to him. They studied the maps. He ordered a paddler's guidebook in French about the Loire, which is considered to be the last free flowing river in Europe, with only a few small dams and lots of wildlife, historic towns, renaissance castles and wine country. It was decided. They bought tickets for a departure in three weeks. That, plus the six weeks in France, was hopefully the time needed for the adoption to go through.

The remaining time in New York was spent winding down their work and preparing for the kayak trip. He felt peace and relief in knowing that Sara was willing to go along with his adoption idea. It changed nothing for the moment, but left him a graceful exit when the inevitable time came.

Sara submitted her revised book project to the new publisher. She worked on her singing and continued her weekly phone conversations with Mama-san. She was surprised to get a call with Mama-san using a translator. It seemed that something important was happening. Mama-san had received a letter from the jazz pianist from the wedding in Kyoto. He was coming to New York, and he wanted to contact Sara. Sara agreed that Mama-san could give him her phone number. He called a few days later and invited Sara to jam with him and his trio. They would be rehearsing in a loft in Brooklyn before their gig at the Jazz Standard. Sara was delighted.

She found the trio ready for a break after a couple hours of rehearsal. She was introduced to the American bassist and the French woman drummer. They talked, and it was a good hang. She felt comfortable with them and their diverse nationalities. The pianist asked her if she would sing with them, and she said she would be thrilled. It was bliss for everybody. They worked for about an hour on standards and a couple of original compositions by the pianist and the drummer that had never been performed. When the session was over, the pianist invited her to sit in — part way through their second set at the Jazz Standard. She would be a surprise guest artist, called up from the audience.

"Are you really sure you want me?"

They all agreed that they did, and they made a short list of songs she might sing, including one in French, written by the drummer, and one by the pianist in Japanese. They wanted to know how to introduce her. They didn't know her last name. Without hesitation, she said Sara Kami was her stage name.

The gig would be the night before they left for France, and it seemed like a fitting goodbye to New York. She had the time she needed before the concert to learn a new song in French and another in Japanese. She worked hard on the new music, while he gathered information and acquired the inflatable kayak, which could be easily transported on baggage wheels.

All was ready the day before departure. Sara had a final rehearsal with the trio, and she was deciding what to wear at the gig.

"What do you think?"

"I was stunned by the Japanese designer clothes you wore in Kyoto."

She tried them on in his presence, and they picked the flowing gown she had worn at the wedding reception. A fashion photographer friend recommended a hair and makeup stylist. Sara's inner glow was magnified, and there was no obvious artifice. She was as stunning as they get, gorgeous to the hilt.

They went into Manhattan by taxi, arriving at the Jazz Standard at the beginning of the second set. A table was waiting in a booth for two in the back, raised above the main floor. The Jazz Standard is a classy club, where food is served, but quietly, since people go there to listen to music. It was nearly full. The first number was a medley of standards, interwoven in intricate and original ways, sometimes with two happening at the same time. Next was a bouncy composition by the pianist. It constructed and deconstructed, taking off and freeing itself; then coming back to Earth with a soft landing. They continued with a composition by the bass player, starting with his solo intro, leading to a ballad that finished with another poignant bass solo, played with the bow.

The pianist took the microphone and introduced the trio. He credited the first three numbers, and then he said that he had a story to tell. He told of playing for a singer at a wedding in Kyoto, totally unrehearsed. He said it was a revelation, but he had not been able to get her name afterward, because he had left to play another gig. When he finally located her, it turned out she would be in New York when they would be playing at the Jazz Standard.

"As a special treat, I've invited her to sit in with us tonight, so please welcome…"

He calls Sara to the stage, using her new stage name. The house lights dim and a follow spot finds her as she moves or rather glides through the audience to the stage. It's much like Kyoto. They're playing before she gets to them, and she is on the stage just in time to come in with "My Funny Valentine."

At the table in front of him, he sees a man take a woman's hand in his. She reaches for a handkerchief in her purse, and is drying her eyes. As Sara sings, he sees other couples holding hands, and he wants to do the same, as if Anna were beside him. The breathing in the room unites with the singer and the music. She has them transfixed and transported, and there is not a sound anywhere, but on the stage. The waiters are immobilized. The barman is frozen in place. She sings it straight and pure, and then comes back with more, but in a different world — the world of improvisation, where melody and rhythm are unchained and anything can happen, and it does, with the melody cleverly disguised in the background. The song ends on a plaintive decrescendo, fading ever so lovingly to a blackout. There is total silence and darkness, and a woman in the audience says, "Oh my God!" Applause starts timidly, and as the light comes up, it roars. The band looks stunned. Sara is natural and unperturbed, smiling and beaming at people, looking down at the first row, turning to smile at everyone in the room.

The band is into the second song, and she faces upstage in a soft glow of rose-colored light. The follow spot catches her as she turns toward the audience. She lightly sings the intro — a recitative, but in French, perfect French — and the music seems French and 1950s, but new, alive and vibrant. The drummer is using brushes, watching every movement of her lips and breath. It's an original French classic that nobody has ever heard before — about lovers being separated and reunited after traumas and adventures. She sets the story up in the intro, and the verse takes off in waltz time. It swings. The band is with her. She repeats the verse in English. The band members take short solos, and she comes back with the second verse in French, followed by a repeat in English. Then she starts to scat. The piece ends on a daring and exuberant improvisation with Sara turning to each of the players — singing, dancing and going wild with joy. On the last note she turns upstage and throws her arms into the air, as the light switches from mauve to bright red. Blackout.

The audience is on its feet. Somebody shouts "Sara," and they start chanting "Sara" and clapping. She lets it go, and as people start to sit down again, she credits the drummer with the song and thanks her for sharing it.

"And now for another original — Japanese style."

Sara bows deeply to the pianist. He begins a ballad, gently sketching in a melody. It's strong and melancholic, with simple rhythms and chords, like a folk song played by a child. The light has gone blue, and when Sara starts to sing, she is in gold. She sings in Japanese. The word Hiroshima filters through. It feels like the world is ending, but there is no way to know what she is saying.

He hears sobbing coming from the middle of the room, and he sees two Japanese women. One is overtly crying, while trying to hide her face with her hands, and the other is gently sobbing into a handkerchief... and Sara sings directly to them, softly and simply; then she fades into a musical interlude, humming with the trio. It is quiet and intense. With the Japanese women sobbing in the background, Sara speaks to the audience softly in English, staying in the music. She tells the story of the song, which is a true story from the aftermath of the bombing of Hiroshima. A young man traveled from afar to look for his uncle in the destroyed city. He found his house, a charred wreck, with part of the house still burning. The young man never found his uncle, but he carried the flame home, and kept it going for the rest of his life. When he died, a monument was constructed, where the flame is still burning. The flame of grief and hope.

She repeats the song in Japanese, and more people are crying. The song ends with Sara humming the tune and the piano gently fading out with her in dimming red light. There is no applause. More handkerchiefs come out, and tears flood the room and wash away the people in it and its contents. There is darkness and a man in the audience says, "Never again. Never again!" There is no applause, and the room stays black as people rebuild their composure. When the light comes back, Sara is standing, holding hands with the pianist and bowing low. The applause is like rain on a tin roof, coming slowly, sadly — gentle and sustained.

The last song is "All The Things You Are." She begins

with the trio, giving the intro almost speaking. When the chorus starts and she sings, "You are..." the music swells and takes flight. It is pure love. She sings directly to him, and the intensity builds and builds, finally breaking into double time — an up and joyous improvisation that goes wild and crazy with solos and scats. Sara grabs notes from the air and sends them sailing into the audience. She sings a phrase into the mike, and then echoes it unamplified. The trio is unleashed. The audience dances wildly to the last note. There is an explosion of light. Blackout.

Now the audience is crazy, clapping and stamping their feet. The light comes up on the musicians at the front of the stage, taking their final bows.

He looks around. The waiters are gathered around the bar, and the kitchen staff is with them. The barman is jumping up and down and pounding his fists on the bar. The audience works itself into a frenzy. The performers leave the stage and the audience continues to clap and cry in unison, "Sara! Sara!" The pianist finally returns to the stage, alone. He takes the microphone. The audience sits down. He says that he wishes they could play all night, but he has to catch a plane in a few hours. He has a wedding to play in Kyoto. The light goes down, and the stage is empty when the light comes back up.

The man in the booth next to him wants Sara's name. He gives it to him, spelling out Sara Kami. Now other people ask him questions. They want to buy a CD. He answers politely, backing slowly toward the kitchen, and then backwards through the double doors, waving as the doors close, leaving him alone in the empty kitchen. He finds another door leading to a hallway; then to some stairs, and after descending more stairs, he finds dressing rooms in the basement. The band is there with Sara. She gives him a big hug, and introduces him as her spiritual bodyguard. They exit the stage door onto the street and walk until they find a cab.

"As I was fighting my way out of there, I heard a man say in a loud voice, 'This is history. I own this club, and I've never seen anything like this. This is history.' We're lucky to have a flight to Paris in a few hours, otherwise we would have to hire Jim for another round of celebrity control. Looks like you've done it again, Sara. Congratulations. I cried my eyes out. You're the music and the food of love. Anna was beside me, proudly listening to you."

At home, they opened a bottle of champagne, sitting on the bench in the roof garden, still dressed up. They talked about the show and what it meant to perform and move people.

"You're a magical, entrancing performer. You have a golden voice that speaks directly to the emotions. It's a silk scarf, a samurai sword and an eagle in flight. You're beautiful beyond measure, a feast for the eyes. But there is much more than all of that. You are you, and that's your unique gift. You're honest and true to the words, to the music, to yourself and to your audience. You go beyond the craft of notes, rhythms and words. It's like the final sprint on Shodoshima. You go beyond all expectations, and we accept your magic as true and natural. I wish I could explain it. I need to assimilate what happened tonight. I need time to understand you and the miracle you performed this evening."

"Thank you for your generous words. Everything was right for me. It was a great trio, and the new songs were dynamite. What an audience! I felt them with me from the beginning. It worked. I'm so lucky and so happy. I connected at a new level. You're right, it was like the final sprint in the Shodoshima race — like taking off and flying into the sky. I sang my love to you, and you were my only audience. You're all I want."

They took a while to come down. Finally it was time for rest, but not before one last ballad. It was a long and melodic song, perfectly in tune, with simple and unabashed lyrics, a gently swinging rhythm and a soothing build to a deep — ever so deep — and loving crescendo.

The plane took off. Nobody was next to them, so they could talk, but there was not much to say, except the obvious. He asked her about the lighting. She explained that when she had agreed to perform, the pianist had called the lighting technician from the Kyoto wedding, who had recommended a colleague in New York.

They discussed possible celebrity problems, and concluded that with the separation of the bicycle and jazz worlds, the celebrity angle would work itself out.

"Jazz is a tiny piece of the music market. I'm not worried. Besides I have a stage name and soon new identity papers. Now, please forgive me, but I'm a little short on sleep. Let's talk more after my nap."

He let his mind wander into the labyrinth of perceptions and emotions still vibrant from the Jazz Standard. It was not simply a repeat performance of Kyoto. This time she had attained a new level of communication. She had evoked an irrational, even religious, emotional response from the audience. He thought about the great religious leaders and their myths.

They were performers who could tap into people's love, as Sara did last night. Religious believers talk about loving God. Is it another of the love emotions or is it entirely different?

He tried to relate his own love for Sara to the euphoria she had inspired.

But the people in that audience can't possibly be where I

am. Sara and I have been through life-changing experiences together.

Then he realized that music was the catalyst in the explosive mix that ignited the Jazz Standard. Music and storytelling — a song and a prayer.

Could she have evoked, in a few short songs, experiences of the intensity of their meeting in New York, the wedding in Kyoto and the ride through Shikoku? The bridge without guardrails, Iya Onsen and the climb that followed? The race on Shodoshima? How could a mere song communicate the intensity and depth of our shared adventures? But why not? It's art. It's magic. Those people at the Jazz Standard are as crazy about her as I am, so I'm just another one of her fans!

Then he was relieved to recall she had sung "All The Things You Are" directly to him and she had called him her only audience.

Calm yourself. Don't be jealous and possessive. She's sitting beside me now, and those people last night have returned to their lives. Or have they? Anyway, at the moment she's mine, but I'll have to learn to share her, because I see more of this coming down the road.

He tried to think of other things, but the religious fervor of the reaction to her music kept coming back. He was reminded of pilgrims in the temples in India, and fragments of Bach's B minor Mass slipped into his consciousness. Was his love as intense as the Indian pilgrims' love for their gods? Was it as profound as Bach's masterpiece? He knew the answer to those questions:

No lover can compete with religion or music.

He told himself this was different. She was also in love with him, so their love belonged to them alone. It was two-way, but then he realized the truth.

I'm all wrong. She was totally in love with those people last night. That's why it worked! She offered them genuine, unabashed love — the love believers get from their gods. No mortal can compete with that. It was in her music and words and the way she looked and moved. It was Anna on the sofa. The reaction she evoked was pure joy — the joy of being in love. It was the bridge without guardrails. So I'm right to feel jealous. But it's upsetting to see myself in the classical trap of love and jealousy. I should be above all of this! I could take a lesson from Sara: she shows no sign of being jealous of Anna. I have to tame these emotions that roil up in me. I have a lot to learn about being in love with a reluctant star. I'm just getting to know her, once again…

His thoughts returned to her transformations. He looked for a pattern in her string of successes. It was too close, but he still tried to understand.

She said that the performance at the Jazz Standard was like the final sprint on Shodoshima. So it was a continuation of the pattern started on the Col d'Aubisque. She seeks a challenge, like medical school, and as if that weren't enough, she takes on a Ph.D. at the same time. She thrives on surpassing herself with new, unlocked powers, entering into a new existence — keeping her persona and changing her name. It's classical metamorphosis: pure Ovid. So performance is performance — on a bike or on a stage. She simply redirects her powers. Sara Kami is a magician who needs no illusions.

He tried to comprehend his role in these events.

Maybe our time in Japan helped her bury her tragic past? Maybe her power to evoke the euphoria of love was unleashed by our coming together? Maybe during her ten years of mourning she accumulated love with no outlet, and now it's pouring out? Maybe I helped? Now there's an antidote to my jealousy. We shared so many intense experiences... She called me coach and spiritual bodyguard. Now maybe she can call me father. But we're lovers: passionate, down-to-earth and eternal. It's so complicated, yet so simple, so natural, so right. Somehow, I've got to stay in this crazy play — even if I'm double cast. I can do it — at least for now. I'm lucky to be here, basking in her light. Yes, light is the answer. I go back to this universal metaphor. It's everywhere. It permeates our language. It's a deep current in the human psyche. It appears throughout our art, and it fits her perfectly. She radiates photon energy. I wish I understood the physics of it.

He had picked up a couple of newspapers as they boarded the plane. First he read *Le Monde*, and then he read *The New York Times*. All went well until he got to the culture section, where he found a review entitled, "Over the Top at the Jazz Standard." The reviewer praised the trio. Then he said that the surprise of the evening, the surprise of the whole season and even the surprise of the reviewer's whole life of listening to music — was the singing of an unknown young woman invited to sit in during the second set. He gave Sara's new name, and went on to describe her "luminous, god-like beauty" and the intense emotional reaction she evoked. Her singing was "divine," with a voice and musical imagination unequaled in his experience. Most of all, he said she was not a diva. There was nothing artificial about her. She was true to herself and the music.

He described the Hiroshima song as a "life-changing experience." He said the audience was so worked up after the final "All The Things You Are," they refused to leave, drinking and dancing for hours to the recorded house music. The reviewer concluded by saying he had tried to contact the singer via the pianist, and was told he could not give out her telephone number. Finally, he said he hoped Sara Kami would read the article and call him at *The New York Times*. The review ended with "I am smitten. I love you deeply, Sara!"

He tried to assimilate all of this, but he gave up and ordered a glass of wine from the passing drink cart. He tore out the review and slipped it into Sara's jacket pocket. He felt agitated and destabilized. He tried to imagine Jim's reaction…

Would he realize? Probably not. Fortunately, there was no picture of Sara with the review. He couldn't know about her singing, but then again, if he checked YouTube, he would see right away who it was. The club was using professional video equipment, and people in the audience were recording on their phones. Jim and plenty of other people were likely to figure it out.

But they had escaped, at least for the moment, and after six weeks in France, maybe this new excitement over Sara would taper off. He was thankful there were no monkeys involved — just jazz lovers. It seemed like it should be more civilized and easier to control this time.

Sara awoke two hours later, refreshed and wanting to talk. He said he was curious to know the origins of her new name.

"I guess I never told you... I'm using real names. Sara is my legal first name, and Kami is my real middle name, chosen by my parents to honor my great grandfather, a Japanese immigrant at the beginning of the twentieth century. Sorry, I didn't tell you about my Japanese ancestry. He married my American great grandmother, taking her family name, giving up his Japanese name, which was Morikami."

"Now I see. The pieces are finally coming together. First there was the dream I had in Kyoto about being seduced by a light-emitting Shinto kami, and then the Japanese sect called you kamikase, after your wild descent on Shodoshima. Now I learn you're part Japanese, and your middle name really is Kami. So you really are a kami! I'm just getting to know you, and now I understand everything! You must be Amaterasu, the Shinto Sun Goddess! So my Kyoto dream was true. You brought me the light of dawn and a new life, and you gave me the luminous sky at the top of the climb. You're the light of the universe, and I'm your devoted priest and disciple."

She looked at him as if he had gone crazy.

"You don't believe me? The proof is in your jacket pocket. Have a look. I dare you!"

- Checez mon ouganite dukeops.

- Blood results
- Lists Pau Tena froh
- Payez cc caudte.
- Tel Sush-n Marsh
- Alex.

Hello.
Nordau
Joe tchaos.
Mells

Yaux / lunettes
Rhume des Foins
Crème à rase
Savons.
Journal

9 781913 136093